Investigating Missing Children Cases

A Guide for First Responders and Investigators

Investigating Missing Children Cases

A Guide for First Responders and Investigators

Donald F. Sprague

CRC Press
Taylor & Francis Group
Boca Raton London New York

CRC Press is an imprint of the
Taylor & Francis Group, an **informa** business

CRC Press
Taylor & Francis Group
6000 Broken Sound Parkway NW, Suite 300
Boca Raton, FL 33487-2742

© 2013 by Taylor & Francis Group, LLC
CRC Press is an imprint of Taylor & Francis Group, an Informa business

Printed in the United States of America on acid-free paper
Version Date: 20120803

International Standard Book Number: 978-1-4398-6063-2 (Paperback)

Visit the Taylor & Francis Web site at
http://www.taylorandfrancis.com

and the CRC Press Web site at
http://www.crcpress.com

Dedication

To every first responder and investigator who may respond to or investigate a missing child case.

To my wife, Mary Anne, who stood behind me to complete this book and for her assistance in authoring it.

To every missing child, every parent or family of a missing child, and any community that has experienced a missing child situation.

To every missing child who has not been recovered, and to those parents who suffer the anguish that only a few know.

To every private or public organization that educates children and parents in the prevention of child abduction or exploitation.

Contents

Disclaimer

It is the intent of this book to establish a reference guide, to educate officers, and to assist those law enforcement personnel and agencies that have the responsibility of investigating missing and runaway children. The contents of this book are written based on personal knowledge, experience, and with the assistance of many different private and public entities that have performed studies, research, and compiled statistics or data through private or public grants or monies. Many of these studies will be used and referred to in this book. Every effort has been made to give recognition and credit to the appropriate entities. Anyone who does not receive appropriate recognition should contact the author.

To assist in any missing child case, the author and publisher gives consent to any first responder/investigator in his or her response or investigation in any missing child case to reproduce or copy in part or in full any checklist within this book. To download these files, please go to http://www.crcpress.com/product/isbn9781439860632.

Preface

This book is written to assist those law enforcement agencies and their personnel who are the first responders or investigators during cases involving missing and runaway children and those agencies that are responsible for the investigation of missing and runaway children. The main objective of this book is to aid in the recovery of missing and runaway children through an immediate and appropriate response by law enforcement agencies, their officers, and investigators.

As an officer or investigator, what you know and the decisions you make during the *first thirty minutes* of the investigation of a missing child may determine the life or death of that child.

Responding officers and investigators must understand and recognize that *when* parents first look around and realize they don't know exactly where their child is can be critical and can have an adverse impact on the investigation that will follow. How long did they look for the child? How quickly did they call authorities? Where did they search? What evidence may have been destroyed? The answers to these questions can be agonizing and frustrating to the first responder or investigator, and in some cases can be a life-or-death situation for a missing child.

This point was driven home when, during the early stages of developing the concept and outline for this book, an acquaintance had a bit of a scare. His son, then four years old, was enrolled in swim lessons for the summer. One day, when it was time to get ready for swimming lessons, the boy was not to be found, and his parents found themselves in the early stages of fear over where their son might be. They suspected that the boy was hiding somewhere in the house to avoid the day's dreaded swim lesson, but what parent has not briefly had a twinge of panic upon knowing that their child was "just here a minute ago," and then realizing that they are not entirely sure where the kid went since they last laid eyes on him?

In this case, fortunately, everything turned out fine. A thorough search of the home took the better part of an hour and led to the boy being found, safe and hiding in the laundry room, much to his parents' relief (and his disappointment, since there was still time to get to the swim lesson on time). This parent went over the events in his mind and reviewed what he was thinking as they began to realize their son was missing. It became clear in just this single incident inside their home what a stressful event losing a child can be, and the kind of emotions and uncertainty a parent experiences in the process.

He and his wife felt confident that their son was in the house and was, in fact, hiding to avoid his swim lesson. Nevertheless, there was a small, nagging doubt in their minds about whether that was indeed the case, what they should be doing, and what if, indeed, the boy had wandered out into the neighborhood and someone passing by had taken him?

If this had been a worst-case scenario, the critical three-hour window of time that maximizes an abducted child's chance of being found unscathed had been whittled down to just over two hours by the time the family was reunited in the laundry room. How much longer might they have looked without finding the boy before calling authorities?

That's anyone's guess, but many parents of missing or abducted children take an average of two hours or more before contacting authorities[*] and significantly diminish the critical time that law enforcement has to get an investigation and search up and running. They may be in denial over whether their child is really missing; they may feel, like the author's acquaintance, that their child is hiding for some reason; or they may be truly unaware that their child has wandered off or has been abducted. They may simply not want to trouble authorities because they just lost track of their child, and they are sure it is just a matter of time before he or she turns up.

All of these factors, in a worst-case scenario, create delays in the critical timeline, wasting valuable time that may affect the outcome of the investigation. That is why it is incredibly important that responding law enforcement officers and their agencies have solid training in missing children investigative techniques, enabling quick, decisive action when a missing child report is first called in and the response and investigation begins.

Most officers receive very little training in police academies or in-service training relating to missing or runaway children. The critical areas of law enforcement training such as domestic violence, first aid, firearms qualification, legal updates, and pursuit driving are the most traditional disciplines that receive in-service training for veteran officers. In regard to police academies across the nation, missing and runaway children are very likely not even in the curriculum.

It was the intent to collect the most accurate and current information available in hopes of filling the gap, and, in some cases, the void or the lack of training pertaining to missing and runaway children. This book has been written for the first responder/investigator and those charged with the

[*] Kenneth A. Hanfland, Robert D. Keppel, and Joseph G. Weis, *Case Management for Missing Children Homicide Investigation* (Rob McKenna, Attorney General of Washington, and US Department of Justice Office of Juvenile Justice and Delinquency Prevention, May 2006).

responsibility of investigating missing and runaway children to use as a tool and guide when they respond to that missing child report. Using this book, the first responder/investigator will be able to respond confidently and will have a plan of action. When he/she knocks on the door of parents who have reported their child missing, the officer will have the knowledge and ability to put the parents at ease and assure them that all the resources available to them will be used to recover their child.

Follow-up investigators will have a guide and a reference to assist them in their investigation, prosecution, and/or recovery of a missing child.

About the Author

Donald F. Sprague is a twenty-four-year veteran of law enforcement. He retired in June 1996 as a lieutenant from the Saginaw (Michigan) Police Department. He has been a Michigan state certified police instructor in many police disciplines including police patrol techniques, police emergency vehicle operation, and domestic violence. He has served on the International Association of Directors of Law Enforcement Standards and Training (IADLEST) task force that produced the Law Enforcement Driver Training Reference Guide 2000 and the Michigan State Domestic Violence task force that  produced Domestic Violence Police Response as either a contributor or curriculum writer. He is a Project ALERT member for the National Center for Missing and Exploited Children (NCMEC) who volunteers his time to review cold cases of missing children and has lectured for NCMEC on child safety and its resources. He and his wife, Mary, founded Servants & Watchmen Ministry, to educate places of worship on church security and Michigan Child Safety Advocates, to educate parents and children on child safety and missing and exploited children.

Introduction and Background

1

Former United States Attorney General Ashcroft probably said it best when he stated that *"few things grip law enforcement with more urgency than finding a missing kid."* There is something within law enforcement officers that, upon hearing this type of call, drives them to a particularly rapid response. Such cases make use of all available resources to recover a child who has been abducted or who has gone missing. That's important because *time is of the essence*, and *time is the worst enemy* of any child who has been abducted or is missing.

This book is intended to give you and your agency the best and most current information available to guide you through a missing or runaway child dispatch. It is designed to help you respond quickly, expeditiously evaluate the situation, conduct an endangerment risk assessment (ERA) of the child, and conduct a thorough, organized investigation, starting from the moment your involvement begins. The guidelines and methodologies presented in this book are based on combinations of personal police experience and statistical evidence from research and studies involving thousands of runaway and missing children cases. Details on those studies and their findings are provided in Appendix U.

Missing Children Cases: The Seen and the Unseen

Experts estimate that there are as many as 1.3 million missing child cases each year in the United States. Of these, 70–140 are *stereotypical stranger abductions*. These stranger abductions are situations where a stranger takes an unrelated child who was previously unknown to them. It is no surprise that 100 percent of these cases are reported to police. Of course, these are the types of cases we (i.e., parents, family members, police, community, etc.) all hear about—cases like Adam Walsh, Amber Hagerman, Elizabeth Smart, Carlie Brucia, and Jessica Lunsford—and they are the cases we most fear.

However, you may be surprised to find that overall, missing and runaway children cases are underreported. This fact has been well documented, in

National Incidence Studies of Missing, Abducted, Runaway, and Thrownaway Children (NISMART-2), which estimated:*

- Approximately 70% of the estimated 1,682,900 children classified as *runaways* or *thrownaways* are not reported to the police.
- Approximately 40% of the estimated 350,000 children abducted by a family member are not reported to the police.
- Approximately 52% of the estimated 58,200 children abducted by a nonfamily perpetrator are not reported to the police.

These unreported statistics should be staggering. You may be asking yourself, "Why the contrast? Why the difference?" One of the many reasons is that America's reporting and monitoring systems relating to missing children have flaws and have become antiquated, for example:†

- Confusion about kidnapping has been exacerbated by the absence of reliable statistics about the crime. Kidnapping is not one of the crimes included in the Federal Bureau of Investigation's (FBI's) national Uniform Crime Reporting (UCR) system, and individual states or other jurisdictions have rarely made any independent tally of kidnapping statistics. As a result, a national picture of, or even a large data set about this crime from the law enforcement perspective has been unavailable. In the past, several attempts were made to collect abduction data, but they were limited in scope or time. For example, the Officer of Juvenile Justice Delinquency Prevention (OJJDP) 1988 National Incidence Studies of Missing, Abducted, Runaway, and Thrownaway Children (NISMART) estimated the number of family and nonfamily abductions for a single year, but contained no police data on family abductions (Finkelhor, Hotaling, and Sedlak, 1990, 1991).
- The Washington State Attorney General's Office has compiled data on abduction homicides known to police, and the FBI has a database on the very serious kidnapping cases that have been reported to it (Hanfland, Keppel, and Weis, 1997; Boudreaux, Lord, and Dutra, 1999). However, despite these various data sources, a broad picture covering the full spectrum of kidnapping offenses reported to and investigated by law enforcement has not been available.

* Heather Hammer, David Finkelhor, and Andrea J. Sedlak. National Incidence Studies of Missing, Abducted,Runaway and Thrownaway Children series, Runaway/Thrownaway Children: National Estimates and Characteristics. US Department of Justice, Office of Justice Programs, Office of Juvenile Justice and Delinquency Prevention, October 2002.
† David Finkelhor and Richard Ormond, "Kidnapping of Juveniles: Patterns from NIBRS," p. 5, US Department of Justice, Office of Justice Programs, Office of Juvenile Justice and Delinquency Prevention, p. 5, *Juvenile Justice Bulletin*, June 2000.

Underreporting is not related only to missing children; underreporting involves all crimes against children due to poor reporting criteria or refusal to report crimes committed against children for various reasons. Consider these examples:

- 90% of Internet crimes against children are not reported[*]
- 60% of rapes are not reported[†]
- Missing children *are not* properly entered into the National Communications Information Center (NCIC) by law enforcement agencies[‡]

A quick review of the present reporting system for missing children shows why missing children are underreported:

- **National Uniform Crime Report (UCR)**
  - Established 1929
  - Method of reporting crimes has remained unchanged
  - Monitors only a limited number of crimes:
    - Murder
    - Forcible rape
    - Robbery
    - Aggravated assault
    - Assaults on law enforcement officers
    - Burglary
    - Larceny (theft)
    - Motor vehicle theft
  - Recovered property
  - Clearances
  - UCR does not monitor:
    - Crimes against children under 12, except for homicides
    - Kidnapping
- **National Victims Crime Survey (NVCS)**
  - Ongoing since 1973 and is the nation's primary source of information on criminal victimization
  - Surveys households through questionnaires and phone surveys
  - Does not survey children under 12

---

[*] David Finkelhor, Kimberly J. Mitchell, and Janis Wolak, "Online Victimization: A Report on the Nation's Youth" National Center for Missing and Exploited Children, June 2000.
[†] Rape, Abuse & Incest National Network (RAINN), "Reporting Rates," June 2011, http://www.rainn.org/get-information/statistics/reporting-rates
[‡] The Scripps Howard News Service study of computer files at the National Center for Missing and Exploited Children.

There is hope on the horizon. The federal government has realized that the UCR and NVCS are outdated and that methods for reporting crimes against children and adults must be brought into the twenty-first century. A new system that is being implemented, which will replace the UCR, is the National Incident-Based Reporting System (NIBRS). NIBRS is in its infancy. As of the writing of this book, only a small number of law enforcement agencies are contributing to NIBRS. NIBRS has the potential to assist law enforcement in the fight against crime and provide a better understanding of missing children. NIBRS was established in 1998 to replace the UCR and will allow more comprehensive reporting of crimes, victims, offenders, and circumstances that will far exceed the present-day UCR and NVCS.

NIBRS is an incident-based reporting system for crimes known to the police. For each crime incident that comes to the attention of law enforcement, a variety of data is collected. The data include the nature and types of specific offenses in the incident, characteristics of the victim(s) and offender(s), types and value of property stolen and recovered, and characteristics of persons arrested in connection with the incident.

Incident-based data provide an extremely large amount of information about crime. The information is also organized in complex ways, reflecting the many different aspects of a crime incident.*

Law Enforcement Attitude and Missing Children

Is it fair to state that law enforcement treats all missing children reports the same?

Statistics and experience show us that law enforcement *does not* treat runaways and other missing children as seriously as they do nonfamily stranger abductions. Cases of family abductions; runaways; thrownaways; lost, injured, or otherwise missing children; and benign episodes are looked upon differently by law enforcement. These missing children are seen as civil custodial incidents, or viewed as "just another runaway status crime," a situation where "the kid deserved to be kicked out of the home," or where the kid was "out just doing something with friends and didn't tell his/her parents."

Case studies, along with past and present practices of law enforcement, categorize these types of missing children as low priority. Complacency may set in by the first responder/investigator or calls are backed up and those missing children who are not seen as possibly being abducted are put on the back burner and are given a low priority status. But what is totally misunder-

---

* "National Incident-Based Reporting System Resource Guide," http://www.icpsr.umich. edu/icpsrweb/NACJD/NIBRS/

stood by responding departments is that case studies have well documented that "abducted kids" start out as a runaway or otherwise missing child.

It does not seem that former Attorney General Ashcroft's statement that "few things grip law enforcement with more urgency than finding a missing kid," solely referred to nonfamily stranger abductions. Law enforcement, in general, responds to missing children adequately, but attitudes that view a missing child report as "just another runaway" or is "otherwise missing" must change. As stated earlier, a high percentage of missing and abducted children begin with the first responder or investigator's initial opinion or classification as a runaway report (e.g., Carlie Brucia was abducted, sexually molested, and murdered).

Why should law enforcement be very skeptical about having a "runaway classification fits all missing children" as their initial response? And why is time is of the essence? The "Case Management for Missing Children Homicide Investigation" study* concluded that 74% of the children who are abducted by a stranger are murdered within three hours of their abduction; this study further concluded that it takes an average of two hours for a parent to report that a child is missing. Further research indicates that law enforcement, on average, takes five hours or more to enter a missing child into NCIC and National Law Enforcement Telecommunications System (NLETS),† a violation of the National Child Search Act, which mandates that this be done within two hours.

Given those three substantiated facts, you as the first responder/investigator, can imagine how much time is wasted and what the chances are of recovering that child alive and unharmed. Now let us throw in the ingredient that the responding police agency gives missing children a low priority—just another runaway call—and has a general practice of classifying missing children as runaways with very little or no investigation. Combine all of these ingredients, and you have a missing child case that spells disaster.

When it comes to any missing child, regardless of how they are perceived, they all deserve the same type of response, priority, classification, and investigation from law enforcement agencies and individual officers or investigators. It should be the practice and attitude of any agency and its officers and investigators, that any report of a missing child should be treated as any other crime or abduction until proven otherwise.

---

* "Case Management for Missing Children Homicide Investigation," Christine O. Gregoire, Attorney General of Washington, and US Department of Justice Office of Juvenile Justice and Delinquency Prevention, 1997.
† Marlene L Dalley, PhD and Jenna Ruscoe, "The Abduction of Children by Strangers in Canada: Nature and Scope," 2003, Royal Canadian Mounted Police, http://www.rcmp-grc.gc.ca/pubs/omc-ned/abd-rapt-eng.htm

Society, Social Problems, Missing Children, and Law Enforcement

American society is the most successful melting pot in the world. It has broad global influence, and US culture and trends are often adopted abroad. Within our own borders and throughout our history, certain social problems have been addressed that brought about either world attention or changes within the United States, including the changes in police policy and practices of law enforcement.

For example, American society addressed Prohibition in the 1920s. A myriad of laws were passed to prohibit the consumption of alcohol in the United States and direct how law enforcement would respond to Prohibition. Though eventually repealed, Prohibition was a major issue of the times and had a tremendous impact on law enforcement, its policies, procedures, and practices.

During the industrial decades of this country, numerous child labor laws were passed to protect the health and safety of children. In the 1960s, America dealt with civil rights. During the 1970s, America's society focused on drunk driving. A variety of laws and law enforcement policies and procedures were created to change how law enforcement responded to these issues.

The 1980s and 1990s brought about a call for the elimination of domestic violence. Laws were established to prohibit violence in households. Law enforcement, forced by society, had to respond to this new trend, which changed their policies and procedures to reflect what society expected of them to adequately respond and investigate domestic violence between spouses and those who lived in the same household, including children.

At about the same time, law enforcement underwent a national change in policies and procedures concerning police pursuits. Increased deaths of innocent citizens, public awareness, and media attention demanded a change in how and when police pursuits should be conducted. This awareness and public pressure set into motion revisions of police policy, procedures, and practices that changed how and when police would get involved in a pursuit. Society's needs were met.

What about society's attention to missing children? Increased public and media attention to the plight of exploited children, along with missing and runaway children, has also received increasing public attention over the last two decades. Society has responded by establishing laws like the National Child Search Assistance Act of 1990, the Amber Alert Protection Act of 2002, National Sex Offenders Registration Laws, and continuous revisions of those and other laws pertaining to the response, investigation, and registration of sex offenders.

Society, through laws, is sending a strong message to law enforcement that it will not settle for anything less than a rapid response to missing and runaway children. Society is also forewarning law enforcement that the first responder/investigator and the agency they represent shall use any and all laws and resources that are readily available to them to successfully recover any missing or runaway child.

How Will This Book Assist You?

So, what will this book do for you and the department you represent? How can the research used in this book assist you in the response and investigation of missing children?

As a first responder/investigator, as with any call you may handle, you always ask yourself on the way to the call:

- What type of call will I really be handling?
- What do I do on arrival?
- What type of crime will I have?
- Who is the victim?
- Who is the suspect?
- Is anyone endangered?
- If a child is missing, what type of missing child episode do I have?
- What department policy and procedure applies to this call?
- What laws will apply?

And the list goes on and on.

Without adequate training or policies and procedures to guide you through a missing child response, what will you have on which to rely? You most likely received no training in missing children in the police academy or any in-service training as a veteran officer. This book is designed to assist the first officer and the investigator in their response and investigation of missing children.

Caution Regarding Liability and Policy*

We must recognize and take note that reports of missing persons, especially children, are one of the most difficult, challenging, and emotionally charged cases that we face in law enforcement today. These cases are increasingly subject to litigation for our actions or inaction. In today's litigious society, it's not *if* you become involved in a matter of a civil lawsuit, it's *when*. The national

---

* Courtesy of Raymond Beach, Michigan Law Enforcement Training Council Director, (Retired).

attention that is directed almost on a daily basis to the too numerous reports of missing or abducted children has law enforcement's response under close examination. Therefore, we must, as a profession, take note of our liability exposure. We must also review the present duties we perform, in light of Federal/State directives, emerging protocol, and practices that can lead to an effective Planned Strategic Response and Recovery of Missing Persons/Children.

It must be understood that the fact remains a law enforcement agency can be liable when there is evidence that an officer acted neglectfully, carelessly, or unskillfully. Also, upon a search of various litigations across the country, liability is found not only for negligent acts of police officers in the course of their performance of duties, but also for negligence in training, or retaining an in-service officer unfit for duty. When a law enforcement agency is held liable for negligence in connection with police activities, the negligence must be shown to have been the proximate cause of the danger upon which the action or complaint is based.

The doctrine of Governmental Immunity has provided some exceptions to the general Rule of Tort Liability for police officers. However, police officers generally have a qualified immunity in the performance of a governmental duty, but may be liable if they misperform a ministerial act as opposed to a discretionary act. In terms of performance of missing persons/children activities, ministerial refers to a duty which is to be performed in a prescribed manner without the exercise of judgment or discretion (i.e. those acts directed by law or established protocols).

A Call to Action—Proactive versus Reactive Response

As a beginning, we must focus our attention as individual officers and law enforcement agencies to the critical emerging area of missing persons/children and take the time to analyze what currently exists as to the practices we employ. The following three precedent cases provided direction in that analysis.

> *Monel v. Department of Social Services of the City of New York*, 436 U.S. 658 (1978) established that a municipality is considered to be a person within the meaning of the constitution and can be sued, based on 42 USC Section 1983:
>
> Acknowledge missing persons/children is an area where officers interact with members of the public regularly.
>
> Look at existing policies/actions to ensure no directive calls for action that may be considered a constitutional violation.
>
> Check for areas where potential exists for civil rights violation to occur.

Tennessee v. Garner, 471 U.S. 1 (1985) determined that matters of policy are subject to review at any time.

> Continually review your activities involving the response to missing persons/children to evaluate how they affect the populous they are designed to protect.

> Evaluate how changing social standards, new equipment and new technologies effect the operational aspects of existing standards and procedures.

Canton v. Harris, 489 U.S. 378 (1989) established that liability can be attached when a failure to train amounts to deliberate indifference to the rights of people with whom officers come in contact.

> Since responding to missing persons/children is a duty, officers are expected to carry out, make sure proper training exists especially with a commitment to regular updates/in-service.

As we look to protect law enforcement agencies and individual officers from liability several factors provide guidance.

What precedent has been established in the same or similar situations?
What court ruling directs their conduct?
What legal opinion will justify their actions?
What law gives them directives and the authority to act?
What policy or procedure has been written to guide them?
What local practices have they been asked to follow?
What officer experience tells them to do?

Of critical concern is that our policies and planned strategies show our operational understanding of the many laws that have been enacted to protect missing children. The National Child Search Assistance Act of 1990 directs how and when an agency receives a report of a missing child and how it will be handled. In April 2003, President George W. Bush signed into law "The Protect Act of 2003." This law set in motion a nationwide system to coordinate AMBER Alerts. The same bill enhanced law enforcement's ability to investigate and prosecute crimes against children, and set bond restrictions on sex offenders who exploit children.

The Adam Walsh Child Protection and Safety Act of 2006 (in part) mandated that:

"missing child reports are entered into the FBI's National Crime Information Center (NCIC) within two hours"

"Prohibits the removal of a missing child reports from NCIC when the child turns 18 before being recovered"

One law in particular, the National Child Search Assistance Act of 1990 warrants careful review, because it directs and establishes procedure for law enforcement to locate and recover abducted children; to assist with appropriate search and investigative procedures; and to maintain a close liaison with the National Center for Missing and Exploited Children (NCMEC). Actions taken by law enforcement officers pursuant to this statute should serve to limit the threat of liability in missing and runaway children cases.

When analyzing existing or establishing new policy, the author highly recommends using the model Missing Person Policy (with emphasis on missing children) published by the NCMEC as a benchmark for change. (A copy of NCMEC's policy can be acquired by contacting NCMEC's website www.ncmec.org or calling 1-800-843-5678 or 1-800-the-lost.)

No one will disagree that a law enforcement agency must provide its officers with the tools that will enable them to act decisively. Without a doubt, one of the most important tools is well developed policy that becomes the everyday reality that officers will use to guide their performance of the discretionary and ministerial act they employ. Again, as we learned in the *Canton v. Harris* Supreme Court decision, a policy must be accompanied by initial and ongoing training to ensure officers understand its full intent. Coupled with the training, is the need for active supervision and a commitment to post-incident reviews to maintain the best up to date policy direction possible.

Summary Check for Risk Management

In summary, the risk management steps discussed to minimize liability exposure in the area of missing persons/children are as follows:

Understand the issues of liability that exist
Know the law (State and Federal)
Establish and maintain reality based policy and procedures
Pre-incident planning
Resource Development (community/technology)
Make sure officers are trained and are subject to regular updates
Require detailed incident reports (document, document, document)
Active supervision of established policy
Maintain a close liaison with the National Center for Missing and Exploited Children

The Problem

When we think of a missing child we think of incidents like Adam Walsh, Jacob Wetterling, Elizabeth Smart, and Jessica Lunsford. However, the problem of missing children is a far more complex issue than we can imagine. America does not know how many children are missing in the United States per year. A missing child could be a runaway, family abduction, nonfamily abduction, or a child who miscommunicated his or her whereabouts to his or her parent or caregiver. Each of these missing children classifications has its own complexity and unique characteristics.

Whenever statistical data are presented regarding missing children, we are only guessing how many children go missing every year in the United States. No one really knows. Research into missing children conducted by the National Incidence Studies of Missing, Abducted, Runaway, and Thrownaway Children (NISMART-2) is considered the most reliable data to date. NISMART-2 estimates that per year in the United States there are:

- 1,682,900 runaways
- 127,100 thrownaways
- 374,700 benign episodes
- 204,500 lost, injured, or otherwise missing
- 203,900 family abductions
- 58,200 nonfamily abductions
- 114,000 Nonfamily attempted abductions
- 70–140 stereotypical (stranger) abduction murders
- 100,000 international kidnappings[*]

Is It Perception or Is It Misperception?

Observation and *perception*—these two terms in police work are what the heart is to the human body. It would be a disaster for law enforcement to lose

---

[*] US Department of Justice, *A Family Resource Guide on International Parental Kidnapping* (Washington, DC: Office of Juvenile Justice and Delinquent Prevention, February 2002) and US Department of Justice, *A Law Enforcement Guide on International Parental Kidnapping* (Washington, DC: Office of Juvenile Justice and Delinquents Prevention, October 2002).

the ability to observe things and perceive them for what they are. Everything an officer does is through observation and perception.

So what does this have to do with missing and runaway children? Research, studies, and personal experience have shown that law enforcement, in the past and present, observes and perceives missing and runaway children as *status crimes* (status crimes/offenses are offenses that only apply to children, such as skipping school, running away, breaking curfew, and possession or use of alcohol) or as "just a runaway," until that perception becomes a high-profile case or a child is abducted, sexually molested, or murdered.

Missing and runaway children are a problem in this country. Historically, law enforcement and society generally have not addressed the magnitude of the problem. Yes, there are organizations such as the National Center for Missing and Exploited Children (NCMEC) and the Polly Klaas Foundation that have made law enforcement and society aware of the problem, but to this day, many departments and officers do not know about such organizations. They still have the opinion that missing and runway children are a low-priority crime or incident.

As stated earlier, society either progresses or regresses in trends. American society has gone through societal changes and trends that changed how law enforcement conducts its business. Examples of these trends are civil rights, drunk driving, and domestic violence.

Missing and runaway children cases are no different. American society will get on the bandwagon and establish laws that will change police policy, procedure, and attitudes about how to respond to missing and runaway children cases. As American society demanded changes in the way police respond to domestic violence and drunk drivers, in the future, they will demand changes in how police respond, investigate, and recover missing children, and how the justice system prosecutes child molesters and abductors.

When law enforcement responds to a missing or runaway child, they should perceive that a parent is calling on them for assistance and that parents are taking for granted that the first responder/investigator will do everything possible in their power to recover the child, whether they are reported as missing or as a runway. Parents also take for granted that the first responder/investigator does not have a preconceived opinion or attitude that all missing and runaway children are low priority or just status crimes.

Yes, there is a difference between perception and misperception in police work. The first responder or investigator that arrives at a home on missing or runaway child report has two choices—they perceive a missing or runway child as a *high priority* and do everything in their power to locate the child, or they misperceive a missing or runaway child as a *low priority* and do nothing. What will be your choice?

Criticisms of Law Enforcement's Actions

When a child is reported missing, the police are scrutinized and criticized in several areas in the processing and investigating a missing child case. These areas and their shortcomings are quite evident:

- **Response:**
  - The responding department does not respond in accordance with the National Child Search Assistance Act.
  - The responding department has no policy for responding to missing children.
- **Classification:**
  - The responding department has no endangerment risk assessment (ERA) that will guide them to an immediate evaluation of the type of missing child case they are investigating and help them determine if the child is in immediate endanger.
  - The responding department has predetermined that the missing child is a runaway or any other missing child classification without a thorough investigation and without information or evidence to prove or disprove otherwise.
- **AMBER Alert Activation (AAA):**
  - The responding department does not have well-established policy or procedure for AAA.
  - The responding department or its officers do not know the criteria for a national, state, or local AAA .
  - The responding department has initially classified the missing child incorrectly or incorrectly perceived the endangerment of the missing child, which may delay a valid AAA.
- **Investigation:**
  - The responding department does not have a well-established policy or procedure for investigating missing children.
  - The responding department does not use any and all credible private or public organizations and their resources that are immediately and readily available for missing children.
  - The responding department does not have an open-door policy for immediate readily available assistance from any credible private or public organization.
  - The responding department does not have an open-door policy for other agencies to assist.

- **Insufficient Training:**
  - Department's failure to train officers in the response and investigation of missing children
  - *City of Canton, Ohio v. Harris*[*]
    - Deliberate indifference theory of what the department wants their officers to respond to and how they train them to respond. In this case, the U.S. Supreme Court was asked to determine if a municipality can ever be liable for constitutional violations resulting from its failure to train municipal employees. The U.S. Supreme Court held that, under certain circumstances, such liability is permitted by the statute.
- **Reunification:**
  - No training or lack of training in reunifying the family and locating the missing child.
  - No policy or procedure for officers and investigators to follow.
  - No other agencies outside of the department involved, for example:
    - Social Services or
    - crime victim advocates, prosecutor, and so on.
  - Placing a located, missing child back into a dangerous environment, such as:
    - a domestic violence environment or
    - a child abuse or child neglect environment.

Training

Every state has minimum police standards that are taught in police academies. Yet there are few to none that contribute any significant hours in academies dedicated to runaway, missing, and exploited children. So what does that mean? As stated earlier, understanding missing children is a complex issue. In general, entry-level police officers do not receive any type of training in this area, even though data and statistics tell us that they will be called upon numerous times during their career, to handle runaway or missing children. Without proper training, how is the officer supposed to handle a call involving a runaway or missing child?

This bears repeating. Law enforcement has had this lack of training dilemma in the past. All one has to look at is driving under the influence (DUI) of alcohol and domestic violence. During the 1970s, DUI was known to law enforcement, but the enforcement of DUI was not a priority. Law

---

[*] U.S. Supreme Court. *City of Canton, Ohio v. Harris*, 489 U.S. 378 (1989), *City of Canton, Ohio v. Harris*, No. 86-1088, Argued November 8, 1988, Decided February 28, 1989, 489 U.S. 378.

enforcement responded and adjusted to this deficiency by creating minimum curricula for training in police academies of entry-level officers and created in-service training for veteran officers who were already out on the street.

The same thing happened with domestic violence. Prior to the 1980s, officers experienced the same lack of training and the lack of good department policy and procedure to guide and assist them in domestic violence calls. Law enforcement responded to this crisis and made adjustments by creating curricula and standards that were included in police academies nationwide for the training of entry-level officers and created in-service training for veteran officers. With those initiatives, law enforcement's responses in domestic violence have improved drastically, lives have been saved, and the number of offenders who are prosecuted has increased.

So what about runaway and missing children? Law enforcement has a long way to go (as it did in the previous examples) to respond adequately and efficiently to runaway and missing children. Law enforcement has to develop national standards to train entry-level officers in the dynamics and characteristics of runaways and missing children. But such training has to be given to the veteran officer, too. You can only imagine, if every responding officer and investigator of a missing child was on the same page, what a difference that would make.

When an officer receives a call of a missing child, and unless there are extenuating circumstances to show the missing child has been abducted, that officer and the department they represent will most likely classify that missing child as a runaway. Right or wrong, this will most likely be the way a missing child will be classified and how the investigation will proceed.

A child is missing and it should be treated that way. The misconception that missing children are just children who do not get along with their parents and decide to run away has to be eliminated from the officer's mind. From the time that officer receives the radio call and until that child is located, every reasonable effort and resource should be used to investigate and recover any missing or runaway child.

The United States Supreme Court states (in part) in its ruling in *City of Canton, Ohio v. Harris*, 489 U.S. 378 (1989):[*]

> 2(a) A municipality may, in certain circumstances, be held liable under § 1983 for constitutional violations resulting from its failure to train its employees.

---

[*] U.S. Supreme Court. *City of Canton, Ohio v. Harris*, 489 U.S. 378 (1989), *City of Canton, Ohio v. Harris*, No. 86-1088, Argued November 8, 1988, Decided February 28, 1989, 489 U.S. 378.

2(b) The inadequacy of police training may serve as the basis for § 1983
     liability only where the failure to train in a relevant respect amounts
     to deliberate indifference to the constitutional rights of persons with
     whom the police come into contact.

Training the first responder/investigator in the response or investigation
of a missing child is critical to the life and death of that missing child. Time
is of the essence, and through proper training that is not indifferent to what
is expected of the first responder/investigator on their arrival there should be
no deliberate conflict. Train, train, train.

Give Them a Break

Runaway and missing children episodes, except for nonfamily abductions,
are not the image a new recruit has when they hit the street. What comes to
mind is the bank robber, the rapist, and in today's world, the terrorist. The
old-time veteran may see the runaway and missing child, except for nonfamily abductions, as a nuisance to police work, if not just a waste of time. The
author can sympathize with both types of officers.

As an entry-level officer you want to fight crime, and book and lodge
criminals. As a veteran officer, you have already seen plenty of runaways and
missing children (other than nonfamily abduction) about whom you have
taken reports and have returned them to their parents, and they have eventually run away again. Other than nonfamily abductions, you may want to
minimize any missing child as a runaway and do the minimum to investigate their episode.

Many runaway and missing children are put in harm's way when they are
not thoroughly investigated and located. Yes, they may be wrong for running
away or not communicating their whereabouts to their parents and going
missing, but as law enforcement officers, you have taken an oath to protect
and serve, and to take it to a higher level, to investigate and recover any missing or runaway child, with no exceptions.

Research shows that runaways and missing children may be endangered
(71% of runaways may be endangered runaways)[*] while on the streets. They
are exposed to all kinds of criminal intent and those who will take advantage of them. NISMART-2 data show that "Alarming numbers of runaways/
thrownaways are in the company of violent, sexually exploiting, or drug abusing companions or suffer an actual or attempted assault away from home."

---

[*] NISMART-2 Runaway/Thrownaway Children: National Estimates and Characteristics:
https://www.ncjrs.gov/html/ojjdp/NISMART-2/04/

The perception was that we thought that we understood and knew how to handle runaways and missing children, but what I found out as a trainer and while researching material for this book, is that we really did not know the complexity of runaways and missing children. You may ask yourself, "Why does a child run away or a child become missing?"

Data show that runaways and thrownaways typically have a reason to leave home. They are running away from something, to something better, or so they think. About half of them have been sexually or physically abused or neglected. As a last resort to escape such abuse, many kids resort to running away or a parent or guardian gets tired of them and throws them out.

There is more to it than just taking the report of a runaway or missing child, locating that child, and returning that child to the environment from which they chose to run away. Law enforcement has a duty to investigate the reasons *why* the child chose to runaway and then take appropriate action to resolve or prosecute any crimes that may have been committed against the child. If law enforcement fails to do so, they find themselves in court justifying why they returned a child to a dangerous home environment. Such foreseeable police actions are called *police negligence*.

While the vast majority of all missing and runaway children eventually return home, many do not. These children, who are not located or refuse to return home, resort to finding some way—any way—of making a living on their own at an early age. These children may resort to "survival sex" to earn money to live day to day, or they may become involved in *sex tourism*, prostitution, using and/or selling drugs, and other crimes (i.e., burglary, robbery, etc.) to survive.

As a result, they are exposed to sexually transmitted diseases, as well as other physical and psychological damage that can scar them for life or kill them. In this light, missing or runaway children cases are not victimless or status crimes. Runaways often become victims of their living conditions or their environment, whether at home or on the street.

Society has to pick up the cost of the manpower to locate these children, health care, and placing these children in a safe environment, such as foster care homes, and sometimes detention. An emphasis is made here and reiterated that runaways and all missing children are not victimless or status crimes. The classification of missing children as runaways may be a status offense in itself, but what may have been done to them in their home prior to running away and becoming missing may have been a crime or a series of crimes committed against them.

A runaway and missing child is a law enforcement problem and response. The response to a runaway or missing child is more far-reaching than just taking a report and recovering the child. The response and investigation should include the reason *why* the child ran away or became missing, such as the following:

- Family conflict
  - Neglect
  - Abuse (physical/emotional)
- Domestic violence
- Thrown out
- Sexual assault

The Victim and the Offender

3

It takes a community to protect a child, but it takes a country and all of its resources to recover one lost or missing child.

Who are the victims and the offenders of runaway and missing children? Are there specific characteristics or traits that will assist the first responder/investigator in determining the type of missing child report to which they are responding?

The Victim

Are there model victims? Without knowing the complex dynamics of runaway and missing children, it is very difficult to say yes. The National Incidence Studies of Missing, Abducted, Runaway, and Thrownaway Children (NISMART-2)* identified seven distinctive types of missing children:

- Runaway
- Thrownaway
- Missing benign
- Missing involuntary, lost, or injured
- Family abduction
- Nonfamily abduction
- Stereotypical stranger abduction

Other types of missing children identified (through research) by the author and used in this book are:

- International abduction
- Internet abduction
- Infant abduction

These distinctive categories of missing children have become universal terminology for those who respond to and investigate missing children. Each missing child classification has its own dynamics and characteristics.

---

* NISMART-2 National Estimates of Missing Children: An Overview: https://www.ncjrs. gov/pdffiles1/ojjdp/196465.pdf

In today's world, every law enforcement agency and every officer must have knowledge of each of these classifications of missing children to adequately respond to, investigate, and recover a missing child.

When children are born, they pass through different stages of life and therefore become exposed to different types of risks and victimization. As they grow older they are at risk of becoming victims of different crimes due to age progression and less supervision by their parents.

Developmental Perspective Theory[*]

As law enforcement officers, we are always looking for information that will assist us in doing our job. Responding to and investigating missing and runaway children is no exception. Missing children calls can be as complicated as any other serious felony. Who, What, When, Where, Why, and sometimes How must be determined immediately.

Through his research on missing children, David Finkelhor PhD[†] identified the *Developmental Perspective Theory*. Dr. Finkelhor's Developmental Perspective Theory can assist the first responder/investigator in determining what type of missing child situation they may be responding to based on the missing child's age.

Dr. Finkelhor's Developmental Perspective Theory was covered in the Federal Bureau of Investigation's *FBI Bulletin* (April 2001).[‡] In this publication the author summarizes Dr. Finkelhor's theory.

> **A developmental perspective:** Contemporary analyses of nationally representative child abduction patterns demonstrate that law enforcement and criminal justice professionals can better understand the dynamics of child abduction by assessing child victimization from a developmental perspective [reference made here to Dr. David Finkelhor]. Simply put, as children progress through life they become more physically and emotionally mature, more independent, and more mobile. As they age, their attributes, vulnerabilities, and accessibility change, and they gain exposure to and become desired by different types of abductors who exploit them for different reasons. Younger, more constantly monitored children (birth to 5 years), for example, generally have a greater risk of victimization by parents or other trusted caregivers who have access to their protective confines. More independent school-age children who experience

---

[*] David Finkelhor PhD, "The Victimization of Children: A Developmental Perspective," *American Journal of Orthopsychiatry* 65, no. 2 (1995): 177–193.

[†] David Finkelhor, PhD, director, Crimes against Children Research Center, codirector, Family Research Laboratory, University of New Hampshire, 126 Horton Social Science Center.

[‡] Wayne D. Lord, Monique C. Boudreaux, and Kenneth V. Lanning, "Investigating Potential Child Abductions Cases," *FBI Bulletin* 70, no. 4 (2001), p. 2.

lapses in supervision by caretakers are more accessible and more often victimized by acquaintances or strangers outside their homes. Thus during their lives, children face different abduction and victimization scenarios and risks.

To put a developmental perspective in context and to assist the first responder/investigator in understanding the theory, a chart was created to show the types of classifications a missing child may be exposed to through their natural aging process (Table 3.1).

As Dr. Finkelhor's Development Perspective Theory and the probability chart displays, a child is exposed to different types of abduction and runaway episodes as they age. Development Perspective Theory not only applies to missing and runaway children, but can also be applied to all victimization and crimes committed against missing children and juveniles (i.e., pornography, Internet crimes, different degrees or exploitation, assaults, robbery, rape, etc.).

Not only does the Development Perspective Theory apply to the types of missing child, but it can explain why some missing children are reported more quickly than others. Elementary children (e.g., ten–eleven-year-olds) through high school teens are reported missing later than newborns through elementary children (e.g., six–nine-year-olds). So, the time it takes a parent to report their child missing may vary from immediate (infants and younger children) to within twenty-four hours (older children to teens).

Table 3.1 Missing Child Risk Awareness Chart

Newborns to toddlers (0–2 years)
High risk of infant abduction, family or international abduction, infanticide
Low risk of runaway, benign episode, lost or injured, nonfamily or stranger – Internet abduction

Preschool Children (3–5 years)
High risk of family or international abduction, infanticide
Low risk of runaway, benign episode, lost or injured, nonfamily or stranger – Internet abduction

Elementary Children (6–11 years)
High risk of family or international abduction, benign episode, lost or injured, stranger abduction
Moderate risk of benign episode, nonfamily abduction, infanticide
Low risk of runaway, Internet abduction

Middle School Children (12–14 years)
High risk of benign episode, injured or lost, stranger – Internet abduction
Moderate risk of runaway, nonfamily abduction
Low to moderate risk of family or international abduction

High School Children (15–17 years)
High risk of runaway, benign episode, nonfamily – Internet abduction
Moderate to high risk of injured or lost, stranger abduction
Low risk of family or international abduction

Speed, organization, and coordination (SOC) in the most serious missing child response is essential. The first responder or investigator needs to immediately activate any investigative personnel or resources when there is any suspected foul play involving a missing child.

The first thirty minutes are crucial to a successful recovery of a missing child. Understanding and using the development perspective may immediately assist the first responder/investigator in those first thirty minutes in the decision-making process or classification of what type of missing child they may have by age. The following is an example:

> If a missing child is four years old and the probability chart shows that the child has a low probability of running away, or a Internet abduction victim or involved in a benign episode, why would the first responder/investigator consider them in those classifications, unless evidence shows otherwise, in his/her initial assessment?

Is this theory foolproof? Probably not, but it gives that first responder a starting point, instead of approaching a missing child report in the dark and having no plan of action.

Parents, Family Members, Friends, and Communities as Victims

The secondary victims of runaways and missing children are parents, other family members, friends, and their communities. All one has to do is watch the news coverage of any missing child to see the emotional stress that the family and community goes through when a child is reported missing. Examples of these secondary victims and their emotional roller coaster rides include:

- Elizabeth Smart, Salt Lake City, Utah, June 2002
- Carlie Brucia, Sarasota, Florida, February 2001

The communities to which missing, abducted, and runaway children belong are victims too. The author of this book lived in Sarasota, Florida, when Carlie Brucia was abducted by a stranger and murdered. He and his family experienced personal anger, and the community was shocked, outraged, and felt violated. The entire community was instantly put in a state of fear for all of their children and was suspicious of almost everyone. Hundreds of volunteer citizens rallied to assist in searches and other tasks to find Carlie. Due to the professionalism of the Sarasota Sheriff's Department in its response, investigation, and daily press releases, those fears were lessened, but the anger over a missing child still remained. This prompt and thorough response and investigation into Carlie Brucia's abduction proved to be a positive contribution to the community and heightened the community's confidence in their sheriff's department.

Only until such a devastating event takes place in your own home town and jurisdiction do you come to realize what effect a missing child has on communities. This is why secondary victims are mentioned, because the first responder/investigator and the department they represent must understand the short- and long-term effects any missing child have on all parties involved, including the community and the responding department.

Types of Family Reactions to Missing Children or Abductions

The family and family members of a missing child are victims too. With that in mind, law enforcement must never forget the effects of missing children and abductions on family members:

- Anguish
- Hurt
- Terror
- Frustration
- How a parent of a missing child must be visualizing what their child must be going through

One can only imagine what Ed and Lois Smart must have experienced day after day and night after night during those agonizing nine months (June 5, 2002–March 12, 2003) that Elizabeth Smart was held captive.

During Elizabeth's nine-month abduction, the Smart family came to realize and identified two types of family reactions that law enforcement may encounter during a missing child case. The missing child's family may have an introverted or extroverted reaction to missing children or abductions.[*]

> **Introvert:** Family feels helpless and can do nothing but curl up into a fetal position and leave it up to law enforcement to search and investigate.
>
> **Extrovert:** Families will strike out to do something about the abduction. Some will not know where to start; others will be resourceful and will gather volunteers to help search, and in the process, re-create the wheel.

---

[*] Mr. Smart's presentation was given at the International Association of Directors of Law Enforcement Standards and Training (I ADLEST), Salt Lake City, Utah, 2004.

Whichever type of family the responding agency encounters, introvert or extrovert, the families will initially put their trust in the responding agencies' hands. This trust will trigger the following:

- Immediate response in compliance with the National Child Search Assistance Act of 1990
- Proper classification of their missing child
- Activation of an AMBER Alert when appropriate
- Investigation of their missing child's case with all readily available resources at their disposal

The introvert family may take this posture: "We have reported our missing child to the police and they will do everything from this point on." The introvert family will most likely not distribute their own news releases, but only at the direction of the police. They will solely rely on the police to continue the investigation, keep them updated, and keep public awareness at an elevated level.

Ed and Lois Smart's family was an extrovert family that never gave up on their missing child. The Smarts were extremely resourceful in maintaining a relationship with law enforcement and the media to keep national focus and attention on Elizabeth's abduction. The Smart family sought out volunteers and organized searches. Being an extrovert reactionary family paid off. Elizabeth was found alive after nine months of being held captive. They never gave up!

The Liaison

The responding department responsible for the investigation must always keep in mind to assign a liaison person to the family of the missing child. This liaison officer is responsible for the following:

- Updating the family as to the progression of the investigation
- Keeping an open atmosphere of cooperation and dialogue

This liaison should continue from the beginning of the case until its resolution.

This liaison officer may be the most essential conduit between the parents of a missing child and the department investigating the missing child episode. Whether the parents are introvert or extrovert, they will rely on the liaison officer to keep them updated on their missing child's investigation.

The first responder/investigator or liaison officer must guard against giving too much information or minimal feedback to the parents about the ongoing investigation. There is always a fine line between what should be released or even told to the parents of a missing child and what should not. Information and feedback to parents and family of a missing child are always very time sensitive and delicate; calls should be highly scrutinized by the investigating agency. One of the greatest concerns in updating the family is the family's urgency to know what is going on compared to the investigating agency's time-sensitive release of information. Tough call—balancing the demands from the parents against the agency's need to avoid jeopardizing its investigation.

Another aspect of the liaison officer and the investigating department is to protect the confidentiality and integrity of the investigation, including the statements or alibis of all people interviewed. Statements and alibis should not be leaked to the news media, other investigators, other departments, or friends or relatives of the missing child.

The Community

Law enforcement must never forget that the communities of a missing child are victims. Therefore, they should be treated accordingly with continuous updates and assurances that everything humanly possible is being done to find the missing child. These updates are at the discretion of the responding investigation department and should be tailored to meet the needs of the investigation and what the news media and community should be told. In no way should these updates jeopardize any response or investigation.

It has been shown through case histories of nonfamily abductions and AMBER Alerts that those communities will rally together and volunteer their time to assist law enforcement in locating a missing child. For this reason alone, a close liaison with the community should be maintained. The timing and sensitivity of any media releases should be solely at the discretion of the responding department and according to what the investigation dictates at the time.

The liaisons among law enforcement, the family, and the community will either be short or long term. The liaison and public exposure will depend on what type of missing child incident has occurred and what type of media coverage it gets. A runaway will most likely not receive the resources or media attention that an abducted child would. Even law enforcement resources and media attention on an abducted child will diminish as time goes on and the child is not located or recovered. David Smart (Elizabeth Smart's uncle) addressed this manpower and news coverage by observing:[*]

> Law enforcement gave all its resources, around the clock, to the investigation, but as we all know, law enforcement does not have the manpower resources to continue an in-depth investigation forever, so after a month, which is a lengthy time, the resources diminished.

[*] Elizabeth Smart's Abduction. Presentation by David Smart, Elizabeth Smart's uncle.

The liaisons among law enforcement, parents, and the community of a missing child, even after a missing child case turns into a long-term case or cold case, should continue with periodic updates and disposition of the child's missing status.

The Offender

3% of most child molesters will be apprehended, but most are able to molest dozens of children before getting caught

5% or fewer of molested children will tell someone[*]

What can one say about a person who commits crimes against a child? There are numerous studies and articles written about this type of offender. When one researches the area of *child offenders* they find volumes of literature pertaining to child offenders, child molesters, and child abductors. Yet with all of this valuable information, crimes against children continue by those who desire to prey on children.

There is a lot of valuable information about those who commit crimes against children, but most of this information is decentralized. What does being decentralized mean? The research, studies, and data pertaining to all missing children is dispersed and there is no one-stop source. If the research, studies, and data pertaining to all missing children were *centralized*, there would be invaluable information and resources to assist law enforcement in responding to and investigating runaway and missing children.

What does being centralized mean? It means to consolidate this information under a single, central authority for law enforcement to refer to when a child runs away or goes missing. Chapter 24, "Missing Children Resources," presents such data for the reader's future research and to be used by them when they receive a report of a missing or runaway child. The resources in Chapter 24 are not all-inclusive, but it is a starting point.

One outstanding resource is the National Center for Missing and Exploited Children (NCMEC). NCMEC will be referred to from time to time throughout this book as the best resource available in those first crucial hours of a missing child.

The offender who commits a crime against *any* child, regardless of their age, is a dangerous and unpredictable person. This is an offender who is a *lethal child sex predator*. Thank God for those universities, professors, and

---

[*] Understanding and Protecting Your Children From Child Molesters and Predators By Cory Jewell Jensen, M.S. and Steve Jensen, M.A., http://www.cacecm.org/understanding %20%26%20protecting%20your%20children.pdf

researchers who have documented well the traits and characteristics of this type of offender. NISMART-2 (refer to Appendix U) and the Attorney General of Washington Study (refer to Appendix U) have brought together what is probably the most current information about the runaway, abducted child, and the offender.

It is fully understood that the offender who commits crimes against children is a complex person and that complexity will be left to those who have far greater credentials in this subject. Studies such as NISMART-2, the Attorney General of Washington Study, and others have produced information that may assist the first responder/investigator regarding probabilities, traits, and characteristics of an offender who may abduct children.

Are there *model* child abductors or offenders who commit crimes against children? As stated previously, much material is written on this subject. In those volumes, the who, what, when, where, why, and sometimes how of police work can be found. Without beating a dead horse, NISMART-2 and the Attorney General of Washington Study do that, but when a missing child incident happens and the investigators rely on such studies, there is always that oddball case where the offender only has a few of the elements or characteristics and falls outside of the study's predictions and probabilities. It is not one single event or characteristic or trait, but a *cluster* of characteristics and traits that rises to the level of reasonable suspicion or probable cause to believe a person is a suspect, a person of interest, or the focus of attention in a response or investigation.

An offender in a runaway (if child is enticed/solicited) or abducted child case can come in all shapes, sizes, colors, genders, economic statuses, and could be the most inconspicuous person. We really do not know who the offender or abductor will be or who has either enticed a child to run away by the use of the Internet or other means. It could be the father, the mother, an uncle, an aunt, a family member, the neighbor, a friend (close or slight acquaintance), a person of trust, or a stranger. The offender/abductor may be a person known or unknown. Who really knows? (Only the offender does.)

There is no doubt that everyone in a missing child investigation is a suspect until proven differently. The offender in such crimes is a sneaky complex offender who has hidden his or her desires for some time and has chosen to act on those desires. The following chapters are written to give the responding officer, the investigator, and his or her department some insight and tools to start with and use throughout their investigations of a runaway or missing child in identifying a victim or offender.

Federal and State Statutes

Runaway and Missing Children

4

Know the Law

There are federal and state statutes that govern runaway and missing children. *All fifty states have made it a crime to kidnap or abduct a child.* First responders and investigators of missing and runaway children should have knowledge of federal and state statutes and any related laws that may be associated with missing and runaway children. If the first responder/investigator does not know the federal or state statutes that pertain to runaway and missing children, they should consult with their local and federal prosecutors.

Federal Statutes

Undoubtedly the most important federal statute for law enforcement regarding runaway and missing children is the *National Child Search Assistance Act of 1990* (42 U.S.C. 5780). Due to its significance and federally mandated context to responding and investigating runaway and missing children, the state requirements (42 U.S.C 5780) are offered here in their entirety.

National Child Search Assistance Act (42 U.S.C. 5780) of 1990

Each state reporting under the provisions of this title shall:

(1) ensure that no law enforcement agency with the State establishes or maintains any policy that requires the observance of any waiting period before accepting a missing child or unidentified person report;

(2) ensure that no law enforcement agency within the State establishes or maintains any policy that requires the removal of a missing person entry from its State law enforcement system or the National Crime Information Center computer database based solely on the age of the person; and

(3) provide that each such report and all necessary, available information, which, with respect to each missing child, shall include—

(A) the name, date of birth, sex, race, height, weight, eye color and hair color of the child;

(B) the date and location of the last known contact with the child; and

(C) the category under which the child is reported missing; is entered within 2 hours into the State law enforcement system and the National Crime Information Center computer networks and made available to the Missing Children Information Clearinghouse within the State or other agency designated within the State to receive such reports; and ...*

(D) prohibits the removal of a missing child report from NCIC when the child turns age 18 before being recovered, and ...*

(4) provide that after receiving reports as provided in paragraph (2) the law enforcement agency that entered the report into the National Crime Information Center shall—

(A) no later than 60 days after the original entry of the record into the State law enforcement system and National Crime Information Center computer networks, verify and update such record with any additional information, including, where available, medical and dental records;

(B) institute or assist with appropriate search and investigative procedures; and

(C) maintain close liaison with the National Center for Missing and Exploited Children for the exchange of information and technical assistance in the missing children cases.

The National Child Search Assistance Act is the guiding federal statute for reporting, responding to, advising other law enforcement agencies, investigating, seeking assistance, and updating current information regarding runaways and missing children in the United States.

The act mandates that every law enforcement agency shall (not *may*) have or maintain *no* waiting period before they accept a missing child or unidentified person report. The old analogy of a twenty-four- or forty-eight-hour waiting period for reporting a runaway or missing child that was used by law enforcement in the past for missing children no longer exists. The Act mandates that every law enforcement agency shall (not *may*) collect all necessary information on the missing child and enter that information within two hours into their state's computer system and in the National Crime Information Center (NCIC). The act mandates that every agency shall (not *may*) update the runaway or missing child's information no later than sixty

---

* The Adam Walsh law added items (C) and (D) to the Search Assistance Act.

days after the original report was taken. The Act prohibits the removal of a report of a missing child from NCIC who turns eighteen before being recovered. The Act further directs every agency to maintain a close liaison with the National Center for Missing and Exploited Children (NCMEC).

Nowhere in this act will you find the word *may,* which would give the responding agency discretion as to when to take a report, have an observance policy, when to collect information, when to enter the missing child into state computers or NCIC, and when to update a missing child's investigation. The National Child Search Assistance Act specifically directs all law enforcement agencies in this country regarding who, when, why, and how a missing child report will be handled, responded to, and investigated. There is *no* ambiguity in this Act. So the question to be asked is, "How well does law enforcement comply with the National Child Search Assistance Act?"

The Scripps Howard News Service (2005)˙ did a first-of-its-kind study of computer files at the NCMEC to determine law enforcement's compliance with the National Child Search Assistance Act. The study was based on 37,665 missing children reported to NCMEC between January 1, 2000, and December 31, 2004. The Scripps Howard News Service study brought to light that many agencies are not in compliance with the National Child Search Assistance Act for a variety of reasons (in part):

- Dozens of departments across the nation failed to report at least 4,498 runaway, lost, and abducted children, 17 of which are dead and 131 are still missing.
- Reporting and mishandling of missing children varied considerably from one city to the next; as low as 9% to a high of 61% failure rate.
- One city reported ten missing children to the FBI, but reported making 2,791 arrests of runaway children. Runaways were not counted as missing children.
- Another city claimed they were unaware that federal law requires that all missing children be reported immediately to state and federal authorities.
- Public agencies blame others for not reporting runaways and missing children (e.g., police department faults the department of social services and vice versa).
- Younger children are much less likely to be correctly reported under the Act.
- Racial and ethnic minorities are less likely to be correctly reported missing than nonminorities.

˙ Thomas Hargrove, "Missing: Children at Risk," study of police and National Child Search Assistance Act, Scripps Howard News Service, May 2005. http://www.sitnews. us/1205news/122005_shns_missing-police.html

There is no reason, but inexcusable rationalization, why runaway and missing children are not reported in accordance with the National Child Search Assistance Act by law enforcement agencies. In the Introduction there is a section referring to liability and police negligence. To be protected from such allegations and lawsuits, it best serves any agency and their officers responsible for receiving or investigating and reporting a runaway or missing child to follow the National Child Search Assistance Act.

The National Child Search Assistance Act is one of numerous federal laws pertaining to runaway and missing children. The following federal statutes may assist an officer when responding to a runaway or missing child. The statutes are presented in an overview fashion and are not all-inclusive.

Federal Criminal and Civil Laws Regarding Missing and Abducted Children*

The Juvenile Justice Delinquency Act (Section 223(a)(14)) Deinstitutionalization of Status Offenders (DSO)

Status offenders may not be held in secure detention or confinement. (Status offenses are offenses that only apply to children, such as skipping school, running away, breaking curfew, and possession or use of alcohol.) There are, however, several exceptions to this rule, including allowing some status offenders to be detained for up to twenty-four hours. The DSO provision seeks to ensure that status offenders who have not committed a criminal offense are not held in secure juvenile facilities for extended periods of time or in secure adult facilities for any length of time. These children, instead, should receive community-based services, such as day treatment or residential home treatment, counseling, mentoring, alternative education, and job development support.

Uniform Child Custody Jurisdiction Act (UCCJA), 9 ULA at 123

The Uniform Child Custody Jurisdiction Act (1968) creates guidelines to avoid jurisdictional competition and conflict with courts of other states in matters of child custody, promotes cooperation with the courts of other states, and facilitates the enforcement of custody decrees of other states.

---

* National Center for Missing Exploited Children website: Federal Laws. https://secure. missingkids.com/missingkids/servlet/PageServlet?LanguageCountry=en_US&PageId=161

The Uniform Child Custody Jurisdiction and Enforcement Act (UCCJEA), 9 ULA at 115 (Part 1)

This is a complete description of the uniform state law that replaces the Uniform Child Custody Jurisdiction Act. Almost every state has adopted the UCCJEA since it became available in 1997; the rest are considering it, and in all likelihood the UCCJEA will become the law of every state and the District of Columbia within a few years. It governs jurisdiction in interstate custody and visitation cases, requires interstate enforcement and nonmodification of sister-state custody orders, and authorizes public officials to play a role in civil child custody enforcement and cases involving The Hague Convention on the Civil Aspects of International Child Abduction.

Juvenile Justice and Delinquency Prevention Act

The Juvenile Justice and Delinquency Prevention Act (1974) has been amended numerous times; however, the overall purposes remain the same, including to provide technical assistance to public and private nonprofit juvenile-justice and delinquency-prevention programs, establish training programs for persons who work with delinquents or potential delinquents or whose work or activities relate to juvenile-delinquency programs, establish a federal assistance program to deal with the problems of runaway and home-less youth, and assist states and local communities to prevent youth from entering the justice system.

The Hague Convention on the Civil Aspects of International Child Abduction

The Hague Convention on the Civil Aspects of International Child Abduction (1980) establishes procedures to ensure the prompt return of children wrong-fully removed to or retained in a country other than that of their habitual residence.

International Child Abduction Remedies Act, 42 USC 11601 et seq.

The International Child Abduction Remedies Act (1988) implements The Hague Convention on the Civil Aspects of International Child Abduction and authorizes state and federal courts to hear cases under the Convention.

Parental Kidnapping Prevention Act (PKPA), 28 USC 1738 A

The Parental Kidnapping Prevention Act (1980) assures that full faith and credit is given to child-custody determinations. States may honor and enforce custody determinations made in other states as long as certain requirements listed by the Act are satisfied.

Missing Children Act, 28 USC 534

The Missing Children Act (1982) authorizes the attorney general to collect and exchange information that would assist in the identification of unidentified deceased individuals and the location of missing persons, including missing children.

Missing Children's Assistance Act, 42 USC 5771

The Missing Children's Assistance Act (1984) directs the administrator of the Office of Juvenile Justice and Delinquency Prevention to establish and operate a national toll-free telephone line for missing children and a national resource center and clearinghouse.

Adam Walsh Child Protection and Safety Act

The Adam Walsh Child Protection and Safety Act (2006) amended a portion of the National Child Search Assistance Act to mandate law enforcement entry of information about missing and abducted children into the National Crime Information Center (NCIC) database within two hours of receipt of the report and prohibits the removal of a missing child report from NCIC when the child turns age eighteen before being recovered.

International Parental Kidnapping Crime Act (IPKCA), 18 USC 1204

The International Parental Kidnapping Crime Act of 1993 makes it a federal crime to remove a child from the United States or retain a child, who has been in the United States, outside the United States with the intent to obstruct the lawful exercise of parental rights.

Jacob Wetterling Crimes against Children and Sexually Violent Offender Registration Act, 42 USC 14071

The Jacob Wetterling Crimes against Children and Sexually Violent Offender Registration Act (1994) prescribes a ten-year registration requirement for offenders convicted of sexually violent offenses or criminal offenses against a victim who is a minor. Sexually violent predators have additional registration requirements.

Trafficking Victims Protection Act of 2000

The purpose of this act is to combat trafficking in persons, a contemporary manifestation of slavery whose victims are predominantly women and children, to ensure just and effective punishment of traffickers, and to protect their victims.

Extradition Treaties Interpretation Act of 1998 (18 USC 3181)

Authorizes the United States to interpret extradition treaties listing "kidnapping" as encompassing the offense of parental kidnapping.

Mann Act, 18 U.S.C.

Sections 2421 to 2423 of the Act set forth several offenses including the offense of knowingly transporting any individual, male or female, in interstate or foreign commerce or in any territory or possession of the United States for the purpose of prostitution or sexual activity which is a criminal offense under the federal or state statute or local ordinance. Section 2423 is concerned solely with the transportation of minors under the age of 18 years and provides for an enhanced penalty. This section should generally be used when minors are victims, although the other two sections also cover minors ("any individual").

Unlawful Flight to Avoid Prosecution (UFAP) 18 U.S.C. SS 1073 (1994)

Enhances the ability of states to pursue abductors beyond state and national borders; Permits the FBI to investigate cases that would otherwise be under state jurisdiction and authorizes use of UFAP warrants in parental kidnapping cases.

Family Educational Rights and Privacy Act of 1974 (20 USC § 1232g)

The Family Educational Rights and Privacy Act (FERPA) allows parents, custodial and noncustodial, to obtain information contained in their child's school records. This makes it possible for a noncustodial parent to verify that the child is enrolled and attending a particular school, how the child is doing, and, most importantly, obtain the name and address of any other schools the records have been forwarded to in the event a parent abducts the child.

Protect Act of 2003

Passed in 2003 establishes the National Volunteer AMBER Alert Program, and a National AMBER Alert Coordinator. The Act comprehensively strengthens law enforcement's ability to prevent, investigate, prosecute and punish violent crimes committed against children. The Act:

- Comprehensively strengthens law enforcement's ability to prevent, investigate, prosecute and punish violent crimes committed against children.
- Makes clear there is no statute of limitations for crimes involving the abduction or physical or sexual abuse of a child, in virtually all cases.
- Makes it more difficult for defendants accused of serious crimes against children to obtain bail.
- Strengthens laws punishing offenders who travel abroad to prey on children ("sex tourism").
- Increased penalties for Nonfamily member child abduction.
- Increased penalties for sexual exploitation of children and child pornography.
- "Two Strikes" provision that requires life imprisonment for offenders who commit two serious sexual abuse offenses against a child.
- Strengthen the Laws Against Child Pornography.

State Statutes

Law enforcement's history and experience has demonstrated that knowing the federal and state statutes has many benefits when it comes to any law enforcement actions. Knowing the law in any police action protects the officer and their department from allegations that they they did not respond in a professional matter, protects the officer and department from civil lawsuits of police misconduct and negligence, and most of all, assists the first responding officer and investigators in the correct way of responding to and investigating a runaway or missing child report.

As stated previously, it is a crime in every state to abduct or kidnap a child. State laws pertaining to kidnapping and other crimes committed against children vary from state to state. Officers and their agencies who respond to a missing child report should consult with their local and federal prosecutors before detaining or arresting a possible suspect for the abduction or kidnapping of any child.

Missing Children Abduction Motives, Lures, and Tactics

5

Motives for Abducting Children

Any abduction and its components are complicated. As the first responder/ investigator you will have to immediately determine what classification of missing child case you are dealing with and the motive for the abduction (i.e., runaway, family abduction, stranger abduction, etc.). The motive for abducting a child can be one or more of the following:[*]

- **Nontraditional:** Very young children abducted predominately by a woman to fill a perceived void in the offender's life (i.e., infant abduction).
- **Ransom:** Children abducted to obtain financial benefit from the victim's family.
- **Profit:** Children abducted to obtain financial benefit from a third party. Most for-profit trafficking in children involves buying (not abducting) children from parents or legal guardians. Cases involving forcible abduction are rare in the United States.
- **Sexual:** Children abducted primarily for the sexual gratification of the offender.
- **Killing:** Children abducted to be killed by the offender. For some individuals the act of killing itself brings arousal and/or gratification.
- **Sex trafficking:** Child abducted primarily to be placed in servitude for labor or sex trade.
- **Political:** Children abducted for political or governmental gain or advantage. No known documented cases in the United States.
- **Revenge:** Children abducted primarily for retribution (i.e., gang activity, parental disputes, custody disputes, ex-boyfriends, etc.).
- **Miscellaneous:** Children abducted for a wide variety of reasons related to criminal activity (i.e., carjacking with a child inside, taking a child hostage to facilitate escape, etc.).

[*] Kenneth V. Lanning and Ann Wolbert Burgess, National Center for Missing and Exploited Children (NCMEC), "Child Molesters Who Abduct: Summary of the Case in Point Series," US Department of Justice, Office of Juvenile Justice Delinquency Prevention, March 1995.

- **Voluntarily missing:** Has the child voluntarily gone missing on their own (i.e., runaway, Internet-related missing, lost or otherwise missing, etc.)?
- **Nonvoluntarily missing:** Has the child gone missing due to foul play (i.e., Internet voluntarily related to offline meeting and then abducted, nonfamily abduction, etc.)?

During the initial interview of the parent(s), the first responder/investigator has to either include or exclude each of these motives and zero in on the one they think is the primary and/or secondary motive for the abduction. Once a primary motive(s) has been established, the first responder/investigator may want to consider and refer to the Developmental Perspective Theory[*] (see Chapter 3, "The Victims and the Offenders"). The Developmental Perspective Theory is another tool for the first responder/investigator to use to build probable cause to substantiate what classification of missing child they believe they have.

Understanding developmental perspective as an investigating tool and putting it into context with other information presented in this book (i.e., motives, lures, tactics, age, race, sex, etc.) will put the first responder or investigator in a better position to make the "best call" during the first thirty minutes of the missing child response.

As the first responder of a missing child, you will have to prove or disprove probable cause for each missing child classification and motive. Once you have established probable cause and focus in on the one classification and/or motive(s), you will find that your response and investigation will be productive.

Child Abductor Lures

[A] child abduction killer who lures the child away by asking for help locating a lost pet is very likely to lure away the next victim in a similar way.[†]

The lures and tactics used by child predators and molesters to gain control of a victim have been well identified by research and are very useful to the first

---

[*] David Finkelhor PhD, "A Developmental Perspective Theory," University of New Hampshire professor and Associate of the Office of Juvenile Justice and Delinquency Prevention Crimes Against Children

[†] K.M. Brown, R.D. Keppel, J. G. Weis, and M. E. Skeen, "Case Management for Missing Children Homicide Investigation: Report II," Bob McKenna, Attorney General of Washington & US Department of Justice, Office of Juvenile Justice and Delinquency Prevention, May 2006. The website is http://www.atg.wa.gov/uploadedFiles/Another/ Supporting_Law_Enforcement/Homicide_Investigation_Tracking_System_(HITS)/ Child_Abduction_Murder_Research/CMIIPDF.pdf

responder/investigator. When first responders and investigators are armed with this knowledge and information, they will be able to conduct an interview or neighborhood canvass that is more productive.

There are only a few ways a child abductor or molester can gain control of a child. They will either use force or a lure. Force can be either verbal (e.g., "Get into this car") or physical (i.e., snatch, grab, pull, carry away, etc.). A child abductor may attempt to use a lure first, and if that does not work, use force (e.g., "Do you need a ride?" The child refuses and the assailant gets out of the vehicle and grabs the child).

The author is the founder and president of Michigan Child Safety Advocates (MCSA). MCSA has tracked over 3,000 abductions or attempted abductions since 2004. MCSA's research, along with companion research and police experience, show that abductors use several different techniques to gain control of children and complete an abduction. MCSA found in its study that 51% of the abductions or attempted abductions were committed by using force only, 42% were committed by lure only, and 7% were committed by lure and force. Research has well documented child luring techniques that may be used by a child predator, including the following:[*]

- **Assistance Lure**
  - Help finding a pet
  - Need directions
  - Need a ride
  - Your parents sent me
- **Bribery Lure**
  - Candy
  - Ice cream
  - Money
  - Job/work
- **Threat Lure (Physical/Emotional/Lethal)**
  - Verbal, assault, weapon
  - Get into car
- **Authoritative Lure**
  - Police officer
  - Displaying a badge
  - Security guard
- **Emergency Situation Lure**
  - "Your Parent(s) have sent me to pick you up and take you to the hospital. They have been injured, come with me."

---

[*] Michigan Child Safety Advocates (http://www.michildsafety.com), Good Knight Child Empowerment (http://www.goodknight.org/), and Child Lures Prevention (http://www.childluresprevention.com).

- **Game Lure**
  - "I have videos at my house."
  - "Come with me to the video arcade."
- **Name Recognition Lure**
  - Knowing a child's name from their name on backpack may be enough to begin a conversation with a potential child victim.
- **Ego/Fame Lure**
  - "You are a great ball player. Would you like to . . .?"
  - "You're pretty. I am a photographer for a magazine that needs beautiful girls like you. Would you like to be in our magazine as a model?"
- **Hero Lure**
  - "You're better than . . ."
- **Pornography Lure**
  - "It's okay, everyone looks at this stuff."
- **Computer Lure**
  - Entice or coerce a child using the Internet.

Research has documented that most abductors are legitimately in the area at the time of the abduction (i.e., the abductor lives in area, is a construction worker, painter, attending social event, food delivery person, etc.).[*]

Using the Developmental Perspective Theory (see Chapter 3) helps you put into perspective the types of child lures that would be used on different age groups. Would a potential nonfamily child or a stranger abductor use a pet scheme on a fifteen- to seventeen-year-old? Most likely not, but more force may be used on the fifteen- to seventeen-year-old or the lure of ego and fame.

Could it be possible that the child abductor attempted to abduct another child before he fulfilled his desire? If so, when the first responder/investigator is canvassing a potential last known location and abduction location they may want to ask questions about any stranger that has been in the area attempting any of the previously mentioned child lures on their children. There may be a child who told a parent about a man who tried to bribe them, or said he was an officer, but the parent did not give it much thought or weight at the time and did not call the police. But because you knocked on the door and asked the question about any suspicious activity, that parent remembers that their child did tell them of man who was asking for help and you end up getting a description of a possible suspect or vehicle.

---

[*] Kenneth A. Hanfland, Robert D. Keppel, and Joseph G. Weis, "Case Management for Missing Children Homicide Investigation," Christine O. Gregoire, Attorney General of Washington and US Department of Justice Office of Juvenile Justice and Delinquency Prevention, 1997.

Keep in mind that abductors may be in the area of the abduction legitimately, so when canvassing a neighborhood you may want to ask these questions: "Have you seen anything out of the ordinary? or "Have you seen anything or anyone who is not ordinarily in the area?"*

Child Abductor Tactics

On October 6, 2002, a lone child predator trolled the streets of Richwood, Missouri, looking for an innocent lone victim to abduct. He found his victim riding a bike and abducted the eleven-year-old boy. The child predator took this child back to his apartment in Kirkwood, Missouri, and held him captive for four years. During those four years of captivity this child was sexually abused and terrorized.

On January 7, 2007, this same child predator roamed the rural areas of Beaufort, Missouri, following school buses and looking for another victim. The predator's modus operandi (MO) did not alter. He was looking for a lone victim. On January 8, 2007, he spotted a thirteen-year-old boy getting off a school bus. This thirteen-year-old victim was walking alone from the school bus stop to his home a short distance away. The predator wasted no time and abducted the victim at gun point.

The child predator took the victim back to the Kirkwood apartment (where he was holding the other boy, now fifteen years old) and sexually molested him. An adequate police response and AMBER Alert to the January 8, 2007 abduction led the police to the predator's apartment and both boys were rescued and the predator arrested.

Lethal child predators are devious stealth predators who generally operate alone to seek out a lone victim to satisfy their deviant sexually motivated desires. An estimated 85.7% of attempted child abductions are carried out when a child is alone.[†] The child predator's victims are usually *crimes of opportunity* with no apparent victim characteristics as a motivator.[‡] We know that child predators use tactics and select areas where children are most vulnerable, such as the following:[§]

- The abduction or attempted abduction will be a one-on-one confrontation.

---

[*] Hanfland, Keppel, and Weis, 1997.
[†] Michigan Child Safety Advocates, data involving 3,000 child abductions or attempted abductions.
[‡] Hanfland, Keppel, and Weis, 1997.
[§] National Center for Missing and Exploited Children and Michigan Child Safety Advocates.

- The abductor will use one or more child lures or the use of force, verbal or physically.
- The abduction or attempted abduction will occur more often when a child is going to and from school.
- The abduction or attempted abduction will occur when the child is alone and is most likely at their school bus stop.
- The victims are more often females than males.
- The age of the victim is most often between the ages of ten and fourteen.
- The predator is most often a male suspect.
- The abduction or attempted abduction usually involves a suspect using a motor vehicle.

Response and Initial Interview

6

Response

Time plays a critical role in the successful recovery of a missing child. Each passing minute may mean that a child is being moved farther away from home. Each passing minute may mean increasing danger to the child. Each passing minute may mean that a child is being victimized by the perpetrator. Each passing minute may mean that clues and leads to the child's whereabouts are being lost.[*]

The first responder/investigator response to any missing child should be in strict accordance with the National Child Search Assistance Act. Time is of the essence in the most serious missing children cases. One must remember that in a stereotypical stranger abduction, a child is most likely killed within three hours of their abduction, and it takes on average two hours before a parent contacts the police about their missing child. One must also remember that an overwhelming majority of the reported abducted children cases start out or are classified by the first responder/investigator as a runaway or otherwise missing child (i.e., Carlie Burcia abduction/murder).

Yes, time plays a critical role in any missing child response. The pressing dilemma for the first responder/investigator is determining how much time was lost before someone realized and reported the child missing to the responding agency.

Research[†] has documented and tells the first responder/investigator that a child who is abducted may be sexually abused and murdered within three hours of their abduction. A parent may take two hours before calling the police. These two elements add up to the fact that the first responder/investigator may only have one hour to do the following:

---

[*] John Walsh, "Reason to Hope: On the Front Lines with John Walsh," US Department of Justice, *Juvenile Justice* V, no. 1 (May 1998).

[†] Kenneth A. Hanfland, Robert D. Keppel, and Joseph G. Weis, "Case Management for Missing Children Homicide Investigation," Christine O. Gregoire, Attorney General of Washington and US Department of Justice Office of Juvenile Justice and Delinquency Prevention, 1997.

- Interview the parent/witnesses.
- Classify the missing child.
- Activate an AMBER Alert.
- Locate the missing child's last known location.
- Determine the abduction location.

Yes, time plays a critical role in missing children responses, and there is no time to be spinning your wheels considering whether a child is a runaway or otherwise missing child unless there is unsubstantiated proof that the missing child is a runaway or otherwise missing child. Unless that unsubstantiated proof is present, every first responder/investigator should consider every missing child as an abduction until proven differently. If the first responder/investigator doesn't think *abduction*, time is working against them that may cause a missing child's death. There should be no doubt in any first responder or investigator's mind that the first thirty minutes of a missing child response is the most critical as it relates to gathering information, disseminating information, and locating a missing child. During the first thirty minutes the first responder or investigator must accomplish the following:

- Immediate determination of missing child's classification (i.e., runaway, family abduction, stranger abduction, etc.).
- Determine the motive, including missing voluntarily or nonvoluntarily.
- Determine the risk endangerment assessment of missing child.
- Identify and secure the last known location of the missing child.
- Identify and secure the abduction location (when applicable) of the missing child.
- Begin be-on-the-lookout broadcasts.
- Canvass (not a search) the last known location and abduction location of the missing child for witnesses or the victim.
- Enter the missing child into NCIC and state computer systems.
- Implement a *child is missing alert*.
- Activate an AMBER Alert (only when local/state criteria are met).
- Contact the local FBI office for assistance and activation of FBI Child Abduction Rapid Deployment (CARD) team.
- Contact the National Center for Missing and Exploited Children (NCMEC) and activate Team Adam.

Refer to Appendix A ("Investigating Missing Children Timeline Guide Considerations").

Initial Interview

Time is of the essence every time a child goes missing; there is no room for error.[*]

The first responder's/investigator's initial interview can be the Achilles' heel of a missing or runaway child response or the robust element of the response or investigation. In the beginning, when parents or the custodial caretaker of a child become aware that a child is missing, they will most likely turn to their local law enforcement agency.

What is an interview? Speaking from a law enforcement perspective, it is designed to seek out information to determine who, what, where, when, why, and how something (a crime) happened. In police academies, seminars, and conferences throughout their careers, entry-level and in-service officers are trained in interviewing strategies so they become efficient at interviewing people. They learn ways of perceiving and telling the truth from fiction, either by verbal or nonverbal statements. Many books have been written on techniques of interviewing. Interviewing is a learned skill that comes with training and experience.

Can one imagine, in today's world of crime and terrorism, how skilled an interviewer must be? Could you imagine what it would be like to be the person responsible for the interrogation of Saddam Hussein and or one of his lieutenants? How about O. J. Simpson? How would you have conducted such interviews, with the whole world watching every step you took or question you asked? Not to mention the attorneys waiting for you to make one little mistake so they could take advantage of that mistake and exploit it in their client's favor.

The initial interview of a parent, custodial caretaker, or witness regarding a missing child is a critical event. How the first responder/investigator conducts the initial interview will require immediate evaluation of statements to determine the following:

- Are they truthful?
- Are they credible?
- Are they deceptive?
- Are they hiding something?
- Are they lying?
- Are they covering something up?
- Are they making a false report?

[*] Isabelle Zehnder. "Elizabeth Ennen Murder: Importance of Police Actions When Child Goes Missing," February 24, 2011, examiner.com, http://www.examiner.com/missing-persons-in-national/elizabeth-ennen-murder-importance-of-police-actions-when-child-goes-missing

Yes, the first thirty minutes of the initial interview of a missing child response or investigation is the most robust, significant, vital, imperative, essential, critical, and crucial aspect and should never become the Achilles' heel of a missing child case. The first responder/investigator will have to determine in this short time frame if there is going to be a full-blown response that will put into motion a lot of manpower, resources, and cost or not.

One of most common themes of this book is to plant in the reader's mind that it takes an average of two hours for a parent or custodial caretaker to contact police to report a child missing. In the worst-case scenario, when a child is abducted by a stranger, they are killed within three hours of the abduction. It takes an average of five hours for law enforcement to enter the missing child into NCIC and an average of six hours for an AMBER Alert activation. This alone demonstrates how critical the initial interview is. Time is of the essence and can be a missing child's and law enforcement's worst enemy!

Let us look back at the Preface of this book. The couple described there had the experience that a lot of parents have had in the initial realization that their child was missing. Did they consider calling the police immediately? No, they did not. Their concern was to make every effort to locate their child. From a police perspective, it could be argued that they should have called the police immediately at the time when they first became aware their child was missing, but is this reality? No! They chose to look for their child and did locate him. But what would have happened if they had not located the child, and would have called upon you, the police, to respond immediately and use every resource available to locate their child, even though they had known their child was missing for two hours? Where would you begin and how would you interview them, now that time is of the essence?

Law enforcement officers responding to missing and runaway children wonder why a parent acted the way they did when their child went missing. Why didn't they call right away? Why did they wait so long? These are valid questions. Law enforcement has the responsibility to find the answers to these questions. It could lead to a false report or the cover-up of a crime. But as law enforcement pursues answers to such questions, they must be sensitive to the tragedy that the parents are going through and take a posture of not prejudging the actions of the parents before their arrival. Each missing child or runaway will be different than the last one. That comes with the territory of being an officer. But what law enforcement must guard against is becoming cynical and prejudging a parent for what they did do or failed to do or delayed doing. If the department does not have personnel available to help support parents of a missing or runaway child, they could refer the parents to the National Center for Missing and Exploited Children (1-800-The-Lost).

When it comes to missing children and the response from the first responder/investigator, it is unlike any other type of call they will receive. Missing children responses are *time sensitive* and there is very little room for error when conducting the initial interview to determine the circumstances and classification of the missing child.

The ramifications of misclassifying a missing child during the initial interview (i.e., abducted child vs. runaway classification) can have devastating consequences and outcomes, such as:

- Delaying the immediate appropriate response and investigation of a missing child
- Delaying the dissemination of pertinent and valuable information regarding the missing child
- Destruction and contamination of crime scenes and evidence
- Delaying adequate and critical resources to locate the missing child
- Delays that can ultimately result in the missing child's death

The first responder/investigator in a missing child case will most likely be confronted with a hysterical and fearful family. The attitude displayed during the initial interview can be a comfort to a parent of a missing child, or an attitude that illustrates that the first responder/investigator may be the parents' and missing child's worst nightmare.

The first responder/investigator should consider the following prior to or during any initial interview of parent(s), family members, or witnesses (not all-inclusive):

- Have a plan of action prior to arrival.
- Attempt to put the parent, guardian, and family member at ease.
- Present an image that includes the following:
  - Friendliness
  - Patience
  - Support
  - Professionalism
  - Trust
  - Confidence
  - Concern
- When a child goes missing, the parent(s), guardian, family member, or witness may display any of the following:
  - Fear
  - Anguish
  - Anger
  - Stress
  - Hysteria
  - Confusion
  - Panic

- Advise parent(s) or guardian(s) of missing children of what to expect:
  - From the department
  - From the initial response
  - From the investigation
    - Conduct all interviews privately.
    - Do not make any promises you may not be able to keep.
    - Assign a liaison officer to the family.
    - Give the family the name and telephone number(s) of the liaison and advise them that the liaison officer can be contacted 24/7 until the missing child has been located or recovered.
- Be flexible, but in control.

The immediate primary goal of the initial interview of a parent, custodian, or guardian of a missing child is to identify the following:

- The information on the missing child as mandated in the National Child Search Assistance Act:
  - Name
  - Date of birth
  - Sex/race
  - Height/weight
  - Eye and hair color
  - Category in which the child is reported missing
- Additional identifiers of the missing child (i.e., clothing, scars, tattoos, etc.)
- Last known location
- Risk assessment of the missing child
- Voluntarily or nonvoluntarily missing
- Is foul play involved?
- Motive for the missing child
- Classification of the missing child (i.e., abducted, runaway, otherwise missing, etc.)
- Identifiers of suspect or suspect vehicle
- Tactic used by the abductor
- Circumstances of the disappearance
- Information needed for state AMBER Alert
- Relationship of abductor and missing child (i.e., family member, stranger, etc.)
- Citizenship of abductor and missing child, if international abduction is suspected

It cannot be overemphasized that all missing children incidents are time sensitive, even a runaway child. Once the most pertinent information is gathered during the initial interview, the Missing Child Assessment Checklist (Appendix T) should be completed and a classification of the missing child should be made. Once the missing child has been classified (e.g., runaway, stranger abduction, etc.) the Abduction/Missing Child Report Summary Worksheet should be completed. This worksheet can serve as a tool for collecting information until a formal case report is written. Refer to Appendix P.

After the initial interview is conducted and the Missing Child's Assessment Checklist and the Abduction/Missing Child Report Summary Worksheet are completed, it is time to get the information out on the missing child.

Missing Children Crime Scenes and Neighborhood Canvass

7

Immediately, without delay, identify known crime scenes of missing children.

Crime scenes of any missing child should be treated like any other serious violent felony crime. Identify them, secure them, and protect them. Missing children crime scenes are unique crime scenes. In most crime scenes you have a suspect and victim who come in contact with one another. A crime is committed at that location and creates a limited crime scene.

With missing children you may have multiple crime scenes over a period of time and distance. A child is taken, moved to an assault or murder location, and then disposed of. Each location is a crime scene.

Even in a runaway child response, the child's last known location should be treated as a crime scene and should be secured until the following is proven through a thorough investigation:

- The missing child left voluntarily.
- There was no foul play involved.
- That there was no crime committed against the child as a catalyst for them to choose to run away or go missing (i.e., child abuse, child neglect, incest, sexual assault, etc.).

If all missing children crime scenes are not treated like serious felonies, it will be too late to go back and reestablish a contaminated crime scene. Remember, a crime scene can always be made smaller, but it is almost impossible to make it larger. One does not have to imagine how the last known location or abduction location of a missing child can be contaminated, tampered with, or cleaned up to destroy evidence if not secured or protected. There are documented cases where a first responder/investigator has predetermined a missing child to be a runaway, when in fact the case proves to be an abduction and the investigator must return to a destroyed crime scene.

The following information is designed to immediately assist the first responder/investigator in identifying and securing crime scenes:[*]

- Caller location
  - This is the location of the person who reports the child missing.
    - The caller's location can also be the same as the child's last known location or the abduction location.
  - Examples of the caller's location:
    - Home
    - The home of a friend of the child
    - Relative's home
    - School
    - Other
  - Examples of case histories of the caller's location as the last known location and murder location:
    - Michigan, July 2005: A seven-year-old boy is reported missing or a runaway by his foster parents. Six months later the foster care father led police to the boy's skeletal remains in a rural area. The cause of death was from child neglect, physical abuse, and the child was killed in the home.
    - Colorado, December 1996: the mother of a six-year-old girl reported that the child had been abducted from her bedroom. Responding officers did not treat the home as a crime scene. Several hours later they located the child in the basement of the home. She had been strangled to death.
- Last known location
  - This is the last known location where the missing child was seen.
    - The last known location can also be the caller's location, the abduction location, or a runaway's last known location.
  - Examples of last known locations:
    - Child's home
    - Child's front yard
    - Neighbor's home
    - Neighbor's front yard
    - Friend's front yard
    - Street
    - Other

---

[*] Kenneth A. Hanfland, Robert D. Keppel, and Joseph G. Weis, "Case Management for Missing Children Homicide Investigation," Christine O. Gregoire, Attorney General of Washington and US Department of Justice Office of Juvenile Justice and Delinquency Prevention, 1997; author of this volume.

- Research and police experience has documented that the last known location can be a crime scene, as in one case in the western United States in 2011 where a sixteen-year-old babysitter was eventually sexually assaulted and murdered by a couple for whom she worked.
- Runaway, missing, initial contact, and abduction locations:
  - This is the location from which the child ran away or went missing or from which the child was abducted.
    - These crime scenes can also be the last known location and/or the caller's location.
  - Examples of these crime scenes:
    - Child's front yard
    - Neighbor's front yard
    - Friend's front yard
    - Street
    - Public place
    - Wooded area
    - Other
  - Facts about child abduction crime scenes:
    - They may be within one quarter to one mile of the missing child's home or their last known location.[*]
    - In the case of high school children and older teens (fifteen to seventeen years), they may be more than one mile from their last known location.[†]
    - The location is where the abductor reveals him- or herself to the victim.
    - The abduction location is the only missing child crime scene where the suspect and victim may be seen by witnesses.
    - An immediate neighborhood canvass of the abduction location may produce a witness who can give a description of the victim, suspect, and what happened.
- Assault location (if applicable)
  - The assault location is where the child is taken and assaulted (when/if applicable).
  - The assault location will most likely not be the caller's location, the last known location, or the abduction location.

---

[*] Hanfland, Keppel, and Weis, 1997, this book's author, and the National Incident Studies of Missing, Runaway, and Thrownaway Children (NISMART-2), October 2002.

[†] Wayne D. Lord, PhD, Monique C. Boudreaux, PhD, and Kenneth B. Lanning, MS, "Investigating Potential Child Abduction Cases: A Developmental Perspective," *FBI Bulletin* 70, no. 4 (April 2001).

- Examples of assault locations:
  - Abductor's residence
  - Abductor's vehicle
  - Vacant homes
  - Vacant warehouses
  - Fields
  - Wooded areas
  - Other
- The assault location may produce witnesses or discarded evidence that will put the suspect and victim together.
- Return location
  - The return location for all missing children, with the exception of stereotypical stranger murder abductions is as follows:
    - Research and police experience has determined that runaways and missing children may be or will be returned to the caller's location or the last known location.
    - Abductors in family abductions and/or nonfamily abductions may return the victim to their last known location or abduction location.
- Murder location:
  - This is the site where the missing or abducted child was murdered.
  - This crime scene can also be one of the following:
    - Abduction location (i.e, crime committed in a home invasion, etc.)
    - Assault location
    - Disposal location
- Disposal location
  - This is the site where the missing child or abducted murdered child's body was taken for disposal.
  - This crime scene can also be one of the following:
    - Abduction location
    - Assault location
    - Murder location
  - Facts about the disposal location:
    - Possibly within three city blocks of the murder location[*]
    - In cases where the offender kills the victim, the remains of younger school-age children are generally recovered within one mile of the abduction location.[†]

[*] Hanfland, Keppel, and Weis, 1997, this book's author, and the National Incident Studies of Missing, Runaway, and Thrownaway Children (NISMART-2), October 2002.
[†] Lord, Boudreaux, and Lanning, 2001.

- Older school-age children are recovered from distant sites
  (i.e., as few as ten or more than thirty miles away)[*]
- In cases of infant abductions, the offender typically disposes of the victims close to their home (within one mile
  of the offender's residence) in a secure location familiar to
  the offender.[†]
- In cases of infant abductions, the remains of most victims
  are found outside, hidden or buried, and in many cases the
  offender has placed the child in some type of container (e.g.,
  plastic bag, box) prior to disposal.[‡]
- In cases involving high school students or older teens (fifteen to seventeen years), when the offender kills the victim, they typically dis-
  pose of the remains within five miles of the abduction site.[§]

The Importance of Immediately Identifying Crime Scenes of Missing Children

Research completed by public and private organizations regarding missing children and police experience have shown that a child involved in an
attempted abduction or abduction is within 200 feet to one mile of their last
known location. The last known location is the starting point of a missing
child investigation.

Immediately identifying and securing the last known location may assist
the first responder/investigator in the following:

- Implementing a neighborhood canvass
- Identifying the abduction location
- Identifying witnesses or unknown witnesses who may have seen if
  the missing child was taken by direct physical force, was lured away,
  or left voluntarily
- Confirming the type of missing child classification (i.e., runaway,
  abduction, etc.)
- Interviewing the last person to see the missing child and identifying
  where the missing child was known to be going
- Implementing a full-blown search for the missing child

[*] Lord, Boudreaux, and Lanning, 2001.
[†] Lord, Boudreaux, and Lanning, 2001.
[‡] Lord, Boudreaux, and Lanning, 2001.
[§] Lord, Boudreaux, and Lanning, 2001.

- When the last known location and abduction locations are known, the solvability rate of a missing child case increases; if these locations are not known the solvability decreases drastically.*

Hanfland, Keppel, and Weis (1997) determined that the murder location and the disposal location are less than 200 feet (1/2 of an average block) apart.

Unfortunately, the site of the actual murder is known less frequently than any other missing child site. For investigative effectiveness, without the murder site, the police have less evidence to tie to the killer. "Case Management for Missing Children Homicide Investigation: Report II,"* indicates that the murder site is the richest site in terms of physical evidence collection. It is second in importance only to the actual body of the victim for evidence that is connected to the killer.†

For response and investigative effectiveness, understanding the close proximity of the murder location and disposal location may assist the investigation and prosecution in several ways:[29]

- When the murder location is not known, the disposal location may lead police to the murder location.
- The murder location and disposal location are the richest in evidence of the victim and murder.
- The murder location and disposal location may reveal evidence discarded by the abductor (i.e., discarded evidence thrown from a vehicle before or after assault, murder, or disposal of the body, etc.).
- The suspect in an abduction may return to the disposal location before it is made public.

Neighborhood Canvassing and Searching

The neighborhood canvass constitutes one of the most productive investigative tools.‡

Neighborhood canvass means the checking, by police, around the area of the victim's last know location and/or the location to which the victim was known to be going, or around any site determined to be important to the investigation, in an effort to locate witnesses or to obtain facts about the

---

* K.M. Brown, R.D. Keppel, J. G. Weis, and M. E. Skeen, "Case Management for Missing Children Homicide Investigation: Report II," Bob McKenna, Attorney General of Washington & US Department of Justice, Office of Juvenile Justice and Delinquency Prevention, May 2006.

† Brown, Keppel, Weis, and Skeen, 2006.

‡ Gary Fothewell, DPA, "Notes for the Occasional Major Case Manager," *FBI Law Enforcement Bulletin* 75, no. 1 (January 2006).

circumstances. This typically involves going from door to door, person to person. An area search differs from a neighborhood canvass in that the latter typically involves going from door to door to contact potential witnesses, while the former is more likely part of the actual search for the victim and/or physical evidence. These two activities may occur simultaneously or separately, depending on circumstances.[*]

Where does the first responder/investigator start their investigation when there is no probable cause or reason to believe that foul play is involved in a missing child's response or investigation? Many missing children are initially reported as *missing* or *runaway*.

Unless there are extenuating circumstances that indicate a missing child is not a runaway, benign episode, or lost/injured child, how would the first responder/investigator confirm the status of a missing child in the shortest amount of time? Remember, missing child responses are time sensitive. One response or investigative tool is to immediately locate the last known location of the missing child and conduct a neighborhood canvass, with a minimum of a three-block radius.

Data was taken from the Hanfland, Keppel, and Weis study (1997) of potential crime scenes to create a first responder/investigator canvass and search radius guide (Figure 7.1).

This Canvass and Search Radius Guide was created to assist the first responder/investigator in creating a starting point for the neighborhood

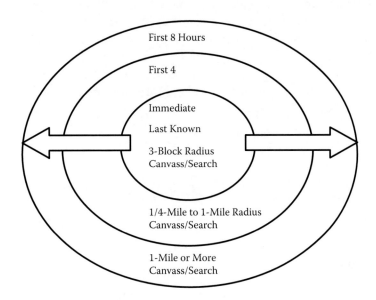

First 8 Hours

First 4

Immediate

Last Known

3-Block Radius
Canvass/Search

1/4-Mile to 1-Mile Radius
Canvass/Search

1-Mile or More
Canvass/Search

Figure 7.1 First responder/investigator canvass and search radius guide.

[*] Brown, Keppel, Weis, and Skeen, 2006.

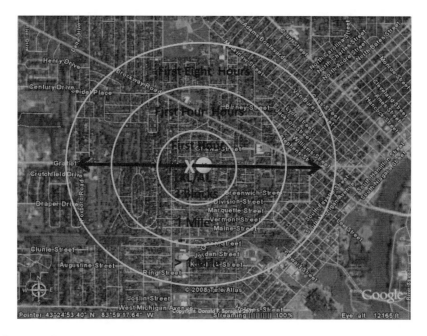

Figure 7. 2 First responder/investigator canvass and search radius overlay.

canvass. In a missing child response and investigation, the last known location must be identified immediately. Once this location has been identified, a neighborhood canvass can be implemented using the timelines and radius of the First Responder/Investigator Canvass and Search Radius Diagram.

Another response or investigative tool is to take the information from Figure 7.1 and use it as an overlay on an aerial map. This information can be used to identify the radius areas of the last known location and potential neighborhood canvass or search to determine size, density, terrain, manpower needed, and so on. Refer to Figure 7.2.

When canvassing or searching any area for a missing child, particular attention should given to areas such as the following:

- Vacant houses
- Vacant apartments
- Vacant warehouses
- Vacant vehicles
- Sewer Systems
- Ponds/lakes
- Other

The first responder/investigator may draw from a variety of different people who wish to assist in locating the missing child. These people can be fellow officers who are supporting the investigation, outside agency personnel, police reserves, police auxiliary personnel, police cadets, civilian volunteers, and so on.

All of these people can be used in different segments of a response and investigation of a missing child, which can include a neighborhood canvass, going door to door seeking information about the missing child. How would one control what information is being sought and what questions are being asked? One tool that can be used in controlling the actions, information gathering, and questions being asked is a printed questionnaire for all involved personnel. This questionnaire creates uniformity in the information being sought and guides all those involved in the neighborhood canvass.

A Neighborhood Canvass Questionnaire has been created to assist in neighborhood canvasses and investigation of a missing child. The Missing Child Neighborhood Canvass Questionnaire is found in Appendix Q.

Missing Children Endangerment Risk Assessment (ERA)

8

Seventy-one percent of the total estimated runaways/thrownaways may be endangered during their episode.[*]

It is important for the first responder/investigator to realize that all missing children are at risk and are endangered during their episode, whether short term or long term.

During the initial first responder/investigator interview, information will be collected regarding the who, what, where, when, why, and how about a missing child. An additional important element is an *endangerment risk assessment* (ERA) of the missing child's welfare.

The endangerment risk assessment information that is acquired at the initial interview could be most important to the well-being of a missing child. After the initial interview is conducted, an immediate classification is made, which sets in motion the type of response or investigation that will follow. Conducting an immediate ERA of a missing child will aggregate the classification phase and will assist in the determination of the level of the investigation that will follow.

There is no definition of an endangerment risk assessment, other than determining if a missing child is endangered during their episode. With that being stated, the author has chosen the National Center for Missing and Exploited Children (NCMEC) definition for voluntarily missing children and runaways to be used for all classifications of missing children presented in this book. The NCMEC defines endangerment as:

A child who is voluntarily missing, between the ages of 11 and 17, who has run away and is considered to be at risk because of his/her use of, or involvement with, these endangerments:

- Drugs, alcohol, prostitution
- Telephone chat line enticement, online enticement
- Gang-related activity
- Weapons, or any medical problems (i.e., kidney, asthma, health problems, depression, suicidal tendencies, etc.)

---

[*] National Center for Missing and Exploited Children.

- Has been missing for thirty days or more
- If law enforcement or social services is calling in the report, a child is considered endangered automatically.

The first responder/investigator and their department should consider the following when assessing the potential of endangerment for a runaway/thrownaway child:

- A staggering estimate from the National Runaway Switchboard:[*] "between 1.3 and 2.8 million runaway and homeless youth live on the streets each day, where they will be exposed to drugs, disease and prostitution. Five thousand of them will die this year as a result of assault, illness or suicide."
- The National Runaway Switchboard further reports that 75% of runaways who remain at large for two or more weeks will become involved in theft, drugs, or pornography, while one out of every three teens on the street will be lured into prostitution within 48 hours of leaving home. Gay or bisexual youth are even more likely to be involved in prostitution.
- Findings from a study titled "The Commercial Sexual Exploitation of Children in the U.S., Canada, and Mexico" states that 325,000 children are reported as being sexually exploited in the United States annually. Of that figure, 121,911 ran away from home and 51,602 were thrown out of their homes by a parent or guardian.

Refer to Appendix E for the Endangerment Risk Assessment (ERA) Checklist.

---

[*] National Runaway Switchboard: http://www.1800runaway.org. The Commercial Sexual Exploitation of Children in the U.S., Canada, and Mexico, Full Report, by Richard J. Estes and Neil Alan Weiner: http://www.scribd.com/doc/78886345/The-Commercial-Sexual-Exploitation-of-Children-In-the-U-S-Canada-and-Mexico-Complete-CSEC-020220

Getting the Information Out

9

Research and police experience emphasize the critical importance of communicating and alerting federal, state, local law enforcement, and the public immediately so that missing children are found as quickly as possible.

Time is critical when responding to reports of missing children. How information is rapidly communicated in real time is important and can mean the difference between life and death for many missing children.

A review of the history of communications in law enforcement would probably show that law enforcement has always attempted to communicate with other law enforcement agencies, the media, and the community. This has been done on a face-to-face basis, in one-on-one communications, via the pony express, the stage coach, wanted posters, the telegraph, the telephone, car radios, the National Crime Information Center (NCIC) teletype system, and in today's world, the computer. Oh, yes, let's not forget the era when officers had *call boxes* and rapping and tapping their police batons on the cement to communicate with each other.

There has been an everlasting attempt by law enforcement to create ways to communicate in real time and prevent deadly time gaps in communication among federal, state, and local police agencies concerning:

- Crimes
- Victims
- Suspects
- Preventing crime
- Apprehending suspects/criminals

Communication is an essential element in the prevention, response, investigation, and recovery of any missing child. It is well documented that *deadly time gaps* and the *lack of real-time communication* can be a missing or runaway child's worst enemy—perhaps deadliest.

What is a deadly time gap? A *deadly time gap* is the time period during which there is a lack of information being disseminated; from the time a child is reported missing and the time the information is put into the National

Figure 9.1 A deadly time gap is demonstrated in this figure and indicated by the "No Information Going Out" arrow.

Crime Information Center (NCIC) and state computers and an AMBER Alert is activated. These deadly time gaps may become a life-or-death situation for a missing or runaway child.

Presently there are many different ways that law enforcement agencies can communicate with each other, the media, and public. Prior to the Adam Walsh abduction and murder, law enforcement throughout the nation had nothing in place to disseminate important information regarding any type of missing child.

The NCIC and statewide teletype systems were in place at the time of Adam Walsh's abduction, but the entry of a missing child was not mandatory until the National Child Search Assistance Act of 1990 was enacted. In this legislation, Congress also mandated that the National Center for Missing and Exploited Children (NCMEC) be created as the nation's repository for information on missing children. As presented throughout this book, NCMEC plays a vital role in any missing child case; since its creation, NCMEC has played a primary role in disseminating vital information regarding missing children to and between law enforcement agencies, the media, and communities. Every law enforcement agency that responds to and investigates a missing child case should take advantage of NCMEC's resources and technical advances to disseminate information on a missing child.

Modern-day communication systems are available at no cost to law enforcement, the media, and communities to disseminate pertinent information in real time and minimize deadly time gaps. These systems include the following:

- NCIC
- Statewide teletype and computer systems
- A Child Is Missing Alert
- NCMEC's LOCATER program
- National and state AMBER Alert activations

Used properly, rapidly, and accurately, these communications systems can be used in real time and can decrease deadly time gaps, which can be the difference between life and death for a missing child.

Overview of Law Enforcement Communications Systems and Missing Children

NCIC and Statewide Teletype Systems

The NCIC and statewide teletype systems allow law enforcement to disseminate and share information immediately. These two communication systems are well known to law enforcement and do not need an in-depth explanation. If used properly and in conjunction with the National Child Search Assistance Act of 1990, these systems will be the first line of communications that will be used to disseminate information about a missing or runaway child to other police agencies and NCMEC.

The NCIC and statewide teletype systems only have the capability to disseminate text-based information. With this deficiency, how would an agency distribute photos and pertinent information beyond the capability of the these systems? When a missing or runaway child does not immediately meet the criteria for photo distribution or an AMBER Alert, a potentially deadly time gap exists.

So, what is available for law enforcement to fill this potentially deadly time gap and keep the flow of information going?

The NCMEC LOCATER System

As we have learned since the creation of the AMBER Alert, alerting the public about an abducted child has saved the lives of many children. The activation of an AMBER Alert gets the public involved; they become law enforcement's eyes and ears and have assisted in solving child abductions and other missing children cases. But not all missing or runaway children reach the level of an AMBER Alert (discussed later in this chapter). When appropriate, how can a law enforcement agency get pertinent information out to other agencies, the media, and the public regarding a missing or runaway child who does not meet the criteria for an AMBER Alert?

In 2001 the NCMEC was mandated by Congress to create a state-of-the-art program to assist law enforcement with the immediate dissemination of images and information to hasten the recovery of missing and abducted children. In compliance with that mandate, NCMEC launched the Lost Child Alert Technology Resource (LOCATER) program to assist law enforcement with advanced technology to create and quickly distribute information and posters of missing children locally, statewide, or nationwide (see Appendix C).

The LOCATER program is a valuable tool for law enforcement to fill in the potentially deadly time gaps. The LOCATER program keeps other agencies up to date regarding critical information about a missing child or runaway. The LOCATER program keeps the media and public aware of a missing or runaway child. It maintains a partnership with the police and the public, allowing them be the eyes and ears of the investigation and to help in the recovery of a missing or runaway child. For all practical purposes, LOCATER is a local AMBER Alert, but at the agencies' discretion and according to local criteria.

Law enforcement agencies that choose to participate in NCMEC's LOCATER program can quickly create their own missing-person posters. Once created, high-quality copies can be printed for distribution at roll calls, at incident command posts, and to the community. Posters can also be electronically transmitted to other agencies, the media, and the public via the Internet or through a broadcast fax service.*

NCMEC's LOCATER program is a vital tool for law enforcement to have at their fingertips. The LOCATER program should be in every agency's arsenal to help in the response, investigation, and recovery of a missing or runaway child.

If any police department does not have NCMEC's LOCATER program, it only has to contact NCMEC (1-800-THE-LOST/Locater Division) or go online to http://www.missingkids.com (Law enforcement) and request an application or complete an online application to participate in NCMEC's LOCATER program. It may be the tool you need to get the information out about a missing or runaway child that may save their lives. There is no cost.

There are approximately 17,800 full-time police departments nationwide. Could you imagine the impact if all the police agencies in the United States would tie into NCMEC's LOCATER and AMBER Alert programs? We can!

Now you know that LOCATER is a local AMBER Alert program that can fill in that potentially deadly time gap. Now let's learn about the A Child Is Missing Alert, another local AMBER Alert program.

A Child Is Missing Alert

Time is ticking! A child is missing! Is foul play involved? Did the child go missing voluntarily or nonvoluntarily? All that is known is that a child is missing. What type of communication system is available to law enforcement with the fewest criteria to get the word out that a child is missing?

A Child Is Missing (ACIM) is a Fort Lauderdale, FL-based nonprofit organization founded in 1997. It was created because no community-based program existed for locating missing children, the disabled, and the elderly (often with Alzheimer's) during the crucial first hours of disappearance. Unlike an AMBER Alert, police can utilize the system anytime they believe a child is in danger, even if it's because the child has simply wandered off. The

---

* National Center for Missing Exploited Children (NCMEC) LOCATER program website http://www.missingkids.com

system can also be used to alert the public when an adult, such as one with Alzheimer's, goes missing.*

ACIM can place *1,000 calls in sixty seconds*, can process multiple cases simultaneously, and can work without jurisdictional boundaries.* Imagine 1,000 calls every sixty seconds being placed to homeowners, parents, grandparents, and cell phones that a child is missing. That is a whole lot of eyes and ears looking for a missing child. This is known in the law enforcement community as a *community effort* and all at the expense of making a phone call. And yes, the cost to a department to use ACIM is zero.

Here is how it works:

- A child is reported missing.
- Only law enforcement can activate the program.
- The program can also be used in these cases:
  - Any person who has gone missing, including adults
  - As a sexual offender/predator alert program: This program provides law enforcement with the capability of delivering public service messages to neighborhoods where a registered sexual offender/predator has moved.
  - School lockdowns/evacuations: When law enforcement needs to communicate with students' parents
- The responding agency calls A Child Is Missing and gives them the pertinent information they request. By the time you hang up, the information is going out to 1,000 homes in your jurisdiction, every sixty seconds.

A Child Is Missing is another tool in the law enforcement arsenal to get information out to the community in real time, so its eyes and ears can be working for you.

Now you know that LOCATER and ACIM are miniature or local AMBER Alerts that can fill in that potentially deadly time gap. Now let's learn about the AMBER Alert.

AMBER Alert

As a nation, we rejoice each time one of our children is brought home safely after enduring the trauma of an abduction. The AMBER Alert program has proven to be a vital, successful tool in returning these innocent children to their families.

—*Former Attorney General John Ashcroft*

---

* *A Child Is Missing Headquarters*, 500 SE 17th St., # 101, Ft Lauderdale, FL 33316, Phone: (954) 763-1288; toll-free: (888) 875-2246; fax: (954) 763-4569; pager: (954) 492-4778, http://www.achildismissing.org

One of the most vital tools to recover an abducted or missing child who is endangered is the national or state AMBER (America Missing Broadcast Emergency Response) Alert program. The national AMBER Alert system began in 1996 when Dallas-Fort Worth broadcasters teamed with local police to develop an early-warning system to help find abducted children. The plan was created as a legacy to nine-year-old Amber Hagerman, who was kidnapped while riding her bicycle in Arlington, Texas, and then brutally murdered.[*]

The national and state AMBER Alert plans are voluntary partnerships among law enforcement agencies, state transportation entities, state emergency management offices, NCMEC, and national and local broadcasters to activate an urgent bulletin in the most serious child abductions.

AMBER Alert broadcasts alert private citizens about an abducted child by getting the news media, radio, and TV involved by broadcasting the fact that a child has been abducted, along with a description of the child, suspect, and vehicle. Some states have already begun to use electronic highway signs. The PROTECT Act of 2003 allotted federal funds to be used in such areas to enhance the ability of law enforcement to get pertinent information of child abductions out to the community.

The goal of AMBER Alert systems is to galvanize private citizens (the community) and arm them with information about an abducted child using basic broadcasting technology to shrink windows of opportunity for the abductor to commit crimes against or murder abducted children.

History has shown that arming citizens with information has been helpful to law enforcement in the recovery of missing children and crime prevention in a variety of ways.

- Elizabeth Smart (abduction, Salt Lake City, Utah, 2003): Two couples spotted a scruffy drifter on the streets and reported this suspicious subject and rescued a teen who was wearing a wig and a scarf as a disguise. The teen was Elizabeth Smart.
- October 2003: The snipers who terrorized the Washington, DC region for weeks were captured after keen-eyed motorists spotted a blue Chevy sought by authorities at a roadside rest stop.
- July 2003: Amid several highly publicized child abductions, including that of Elizabeth Smart, swift-footed neighbors in California prevented another kidnapping. After a man scaled a backyard fence and grabbed a five-year old boy, neighbors who heard the screams of the child's mother chased and captured the abductor.
- California, 2003: Two teen girls were abducted from two separate cars at a "lover's lane." The boyfriends were gagged and tied up and

[*] Press Release, US Department of Justice, September 4, 2003.

placed in the trunk of the car. An AMBER Alert was initiated including photos of both girls and a description of the white Ford Bronco used by the abductor. Messages went out over the airways and on electronic freeway signs throughout the state. An animal control worker heard a radio AMBER Alert and called authorities, which led them to the abductor, vehicle, and the two girls. A standoff ensued resulting in the suspect being shot and killed by law enforcement and the two girls rescued.

• The AMBER Alert program in California has been so successful that every child whose disappearance was announced via the AMBER Alert activation has been returned safely.[*]

An AMBER Alert activation or request should be used very sparingly and should follow strict local, state, and federal guidelines and procedures. Each state can adopt its own policy and procedures regarding the actual activation of AMBER Alerts. The NCMEC has established AMBER Alert minimum guidelines that should be considered or incorporated in any federal or state criteria:

• Law enforcement confirms that a child has been abducted.
• Law enforcement believes that circumstances surrounding the abduction indicate that the child is in danger of serious bodily harm or death.
• There is enough descriptive information about the child, abductor, and/ or suspect's vehicle to believe an immediate broadcast alert will help.

Here is a telling story by abducted child Tamara Brooks[†] who was kidnapped at gunpoint in California:

"I knew that he was going to kill us!" abducted teenager Tamara Brooks said after her rescue. A year after she and another teenage girl were kidnapped at gunpoint, Ms. Brooks, age 17, is still thankful for the program that she credits with saving their lives. After an AMBER Alert was issued in California, drivers spotted a Ford Bronco, allowing police and sheriff's deputies north of Los Angeles to narrow their search for Ms. Brooks and Jacqueline Marris, then 17, who were kidnapped out of separate cars and then bound, gagged, and abducted.

Ms. Brooks recounted the story of her 13 hour struggle to remain alive. Together, both Tamara and Jacqueline tried to fight back and were assaulted. They both knew that they had only minutes left when they were rescued—a rescue, Tamara says, that was the result of an AMBER Alert.

---

[*] KlaasKids Foundation, "Monitoring the New Amber Alert Plan System," *Klaas Action Review* 9, no. 2 (summer 2003).
[†] Tamara Brooks abduction: http://tamarabrooks.org

Communications are essential in the recovery of an abducted child. In the Polly Klaas abduction and murder case, two deputies had Polly's killer in their grasp within an hour, yet they were unaware that a crime had been committed.* How tragic this was was due to a lack of communication.

The technology available today will hopefully bring about a change. Most patrol cars now have computers, a fast high-frequency radio system, *National Law Enforcement Telecommunications System (*NLETS), NCIC, NCMEC's state of the art LOCATER, Internet alerts, and the AMBER Alert system. Today, not only can we have fast, almost real-time communication and get information out about a missing child to law enforcement agencies, but we can galvanize communities to assist in looking for and locating an abducted child.

In this book we have repeatedly stated that *on average* it takes a parent two hours to contact the police regarding their missing child. We have also demonstrated that 74% of the abducted child murder victims are killed within three hours.† So there should be no doubt in anyone's mind that, time is of the essence, and the method law enforcement chooses to put out information regarding a missing or abducted child is time sensitive and a critical factor in the life or death of that child and the apprehension of the suspect.

Regardless, if the abductor can drive through several states from the crime scene before police get involved, AMBER Alerts travel faster. There is a saying in police work: "A wanted suspect can never outrun a police radio." Many criminals have tried and most of them have failed. The same analogy applies to an abducted child—the abductor can never outrun an AMBER Alert, because it is a nationwide program.

NCMEC's initiative to promote a nationwide AMBER Alert system in 1996 has brought about a revolutionary way for law enforcement to disseminate information about abducted children. Knowing that AMBER Alerts could be abused and used incorrectly, intentionally or unintentionally, the following should be part of any policy or procedure for an AMBER Alert activation:

- An AMBER Alert may be activated only by law enforcement agencies.
- An AMBER Alert is intended only for the most serious, time-critical child abduction cases.
- An AMBER Alert is not intended for cases involving runaways or parental abduction, except in life-threatening situations.

---

* KlaasKids Foundation, "Monitoring The New Amber Alert Plan System," *Klaas Action Review* 9, no. 2 (summer 2003).
† Kenneth A. Hanfland, Robert D. Keppel, and Joseph G. Weis, "Case Management for Missing Children Homicide Investigation," Christine O. Gregoire, Attorney General of Washington and US Department of Justice Office of Juvenile Justice and Delinquency Prevention, 1997.

To avoid any abuse of AMBER Alert activations, law enforcement must operate, implement, and activate AMBER Alert activations under strict scrutiny, guidelines, policies, and procedures. This is the basis for protecting the integrity of AMBER Alerts, to which all participants—local, state, and federal—in any AMBER Alert program must strictly adhere.

Getting the information out regarding missing or runaway children is essential in their recovery and to prevent harm to them. Use of the methods of communication mentioned in this chapter will ensure the immediate dissemination of vital information. Refer to Appendix D for the AMBER Alert Checklist.

Incident Command Center and Civilian Volunteers

10

The Incident Command Center is the nerve center for any response or investigation of any missing child incident.

Incident Command Center

There is an old saying in police work that the veteran officer knows and that is emphasized in most police academies: "The first responder to any case will either make it or break it." That is so true when it comes to missing children.

When responding to a missing child incident, the first responder/investigator will be responsible for setting up the first *Incident Command Center*. It will most likely be their patrol or detective car. There have been many departments nationwide that have placed the first incident command center at the caller's location and later determined the caller's location to be the last known location or abduction location, and unintentionally contaminated potential crime scenes. These departments have also identified the abduction location during a neighborhood canvass and set up the Incident Command Center there with the same results.

This is the story of one such disaster involving a wrongfully placed Incident Command Center:

In one missing child case in the South the responding department placed the Incident Command Center in the front yard of the missing child's home. Later it was learned that the missing child's home was identified as the caller's location, the last known location, and the abduction location.

To make matters worse, further investigation revealed that the assailant took the child 150 yards across the street, which was determined to be the assault location, murder location, and disposal location.

The assailant approached and entered the home through the front yard and front door. To make the investigation worse, when K-9 units were called in to do a track, due to crime scene contamination, the K-9s hit on scents that were tracked back to the Incident Command Center, which was parked in the front yard.

When considering an incident command center, other than a police vehicle, the first responder/investigator should identify the last known location or abduction location of a missing child. Once this has been accomplished, immediately set up the Incident Command Center away from those locations. The primary incident command center should not be within one mile of the last known location of a missing child.

As illustrated in a missing child case in the western United States, the first responder/investigator immediately identified the caller location and proceeded to determine the last known location of the missing child in an apartment complex. The first responder's patrol car was the initial incident command center at the caller's location until the last known location was determined. Once the last known location was identified, the first responder's patrol car ceased to be the initial incident command center and a primary mobile Incident Command Center was established one mile from the last known location.

During the next forty-eight hours of the missing child investigation the abduction location was determined, and then the assault location was identified in an apartment complex, which led to the discovery of the murder location and disposal location. Once the murder location and disposal location were identified, the responding department moved the Incident Command Center to the front entrance of the apartment complex.

With this type of response and movement of the incident command center, the integrity of the investigation and all investigative aspects were intact and no contamination of the missing child crime scenes occurred.

The progression of the investigation will dictate the movement and placement of an Incident Command Center. It is critical to protect the integrity of the overall missing child investigation and crime scenes. Recklessly placing an Incident Command Center at any of the recognized crime scenes addressed in this book, until they are processed would be disastrous. Trying to move it later will be almost impossible due to some of the following issues:

- News media and press releases
- Public sentiment
- Volunteers
- The progress of the investigation

A mobile or fixed Incident Command Center is a designated centralized area from which the operations and decision-making process of any police investigation is directed. See Figure 10.1 for examples.

Selecting the primary Incident Command Center can be just as important as any other process in a missing child investigation. First responders and investigators should consider the following when selecting a site for an Incident Command Center:

- It should never be in or directly adjacent to the missing child crime scene(s).

- Mobile types of Incident Command Centers can be:

- Fixed types of Incident Command Centers can be:

Figure 10.1 Examples of Incident Command Centers.

- It should be far enough away from a missing child crime scene(s) that it will not interfere with any response or any portion of the investigation. Remember, it has been statistically proven that a child is usually abducted within one mile of his or her last known location.
- It should have a large enough area to accommodate the following:
  - Incident Command Center
  - Parking for officers and volunteers
  - Separation of command post, news media, volunteers, etc.

There should be a lot of thought given to the logistics of the Incident Command Center and the following should always be available:

- Electricity
- Drinking water
- Bathroom facilities—male and female
- Access to telephone lines
- Ability to monitor television broadcasts
- Staging areas for law enforcement personnel and civilian volunteers

Figure 10.2 illustrates the layout of an Incident Command Center.

Civilian Volunteers

Skip and Joan Downs, a married couple who live in Crystal River, Florida, were watching a local television station on a Friday morning when a news broadcaster announced that a child was missing in their city.

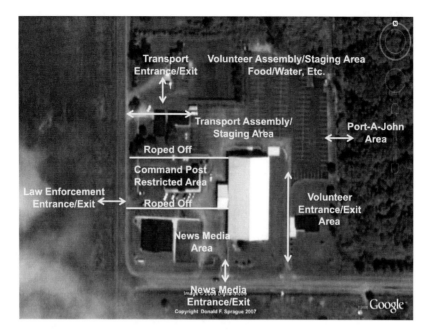

Figure 10.2 Layout of an Incident Command Center.

Wanting to help and willing to do anything they could to assist in finding the missing child, they decided to volunteer their time. The following day they drove to the volunteer staging area and were surprised to learn that they were two of 540 volunteers.

Anticipating that they would have to produce some sort of identification and possibly be subject to a background check, they were surprised to learn that there was no requirement to produce any sort of identification nor would they have to submit to a minimum background check.

Not ever having been involved in an incident like this, they expected clear cut directions and coordination from the law enforcement agency in charge of the investigation. Not knowing police procedures, they anticipated receiving explicit directions and a well-organized operation. They were, however, taken aback with such things as:

- The Incident-Command Center was easily accessible to the volunteers, cars, and news media.
- When advised to search and during the search through palmetto terrain, they were not given anything to probe with; in fact, they had to supply their own stick or find an object they could use to probe.
- Mr. and Mrs. Downs thought that K-9 units should have been used before the volunteers searched a designated area.
- They were also surprised that no medical personnel were assigned to individual volunteer search teams, but were only at the Incident Command Center.

The Downs and all of the other volunteers had two common interests in volunteering their time to find this missing child. The first was to help find the child, but the second, an emotional issue, was that no one wanted to be the person who would find the missing child's body. This is one of several reasons they believe that only adult volunteers should participate in such incidents.*

When a child goes missing, everyone should be concerned, even if it is a runaway who is distraught over their living environment. Remember those milk cartons with missing children on them? The intent of putting missing children on those cartons was to solicit the eyes of 100,000 unsuspecting volunteers to look for a runaway or otherwise missing child.

When a child goes missing and is classified as an abduction and the news media broadcasts the child abduction, concerned volunteers will show up and volunteer to assist in finding that missing child. One only has to look at the abductions of Elizabeth Smart, Carlia Brucia, and Jessica Lunsford to realize the compassion people have for missing children and how they will volunteer their time and services to help locate a missing child.

Why should law enforcement be concerned about civilian volunteers investigating missing children? What should the first responder/investigator know about the potential volunteers and how should they be utilized?

Research shows that, on average, it takes a parent two hours to contact law enforcement to report their child missing. During this two-hour delay, what is that parent doing about their missing child? Are they waiting for the child's return not fearing that any foul play is involved? Are they searching for their missing child and making phone calls? Have they called family members, relatives, or friends to help find their missing child? Probably all of these are possible. But, it is likely that volunteers are already involved before the first responder/investigator gets the call or arrives at the scene.

Let there be no mistake: in any missing child response or investigation, law enforcement and civilian volunteers will have to work together to locate or recover a missing child. The response of civilian volunteers will depend on the classification (i.e., stranger abduction vs. family abduction) and the intensity of news media coverage (Elizabeth Smart vs. Jahessye Shockley). A runaway child will most likely not receive the news coverage of a child who has been abducted by a stranger or a missing child who does not meet the criteria of an AMBER alert, resulting in a far smaller civilian volunteer response. A runaway may have family, relatives, or friends volunteer their time who may post flyers or posters throughout their city in an attempt to locate the runaway.

Many different people will volunteer their time, services, and expertise when a child is reported missing until that child is located. Missing children

---

* Personal interview with Skip and Joan Downs, Crystal River, Florida, Jessica Lunsford's abduction murder.

volunteers come from all walks of life; they are white, black, Hispanic, Asian, and from every economic status.

Research and law enforcement experience has shown that many of these volunteers are honest citizens with good intentions—but some are not. The same research and law enforcement experience has shown that criminals and even the abductor have attempted to get involved as volunteers.

Every precaution should be taken to exclude volunteers who may have criminal records or other reasons to participate (i.e., even plant themselves into the missing child investigation to learn the progress of the investigation). These efforts should include the following:

- Designate an officer in charge of volunteers.
- The officer in charge should be specifically assigned to perform the following tasks (not all-inclusive):
  - Processing:
    - All volunteers should be required to sign a waiver exonerating the department for any claim of workers compensation in case of injury.
    - All volunteers should be required to produce valid identification (i.e., driver's license, state identification, etc.).
    - All volunteers should be required to (signed waiver) submit to a limited background check.
    - A national search should be conducted for any potential outstanding warrants.
    - A national registered sex offender check should be done.
    - A search for a national, state, or local criminal record should be done.
  - To shorten the time that could be involved in approving volunteers, the officer in charge may consider their local county emergency management organizations. These agencies should have an established certified list of volunteers for activation during disasters who have gone through security and background checks.
- Training: A minimum amount of training should be implemented for these volunteers as it relates to:
  - Chain of command
  - Purpose of their participation
  - Evidence preservation and collection:
    - What to do if evidence is located
    - Who to contact if evidence is located
    - What to do if the missing child is located alive or deceased
  - Searches
    - Type of search pattern (i.e., grid, etc.)
    - Type of terrain to be searched (i.e., flat, hilly, undergrowth, etc.)

- Difference between searching private property and public property (i.e., volunteers should not enter private property, but should contact the officer in charge, etc.)
- Clothing: Type of clothing and shoes/boots to be worn
- Weather
  - Hyperthermia in cold weather
  - Heat exhaustion in hot weather
- Logistics
  - The location of the volunteer site should be different than the location of the Incident Command Center.
  - There should be a sign-in and sign-out location and directions for how to sign in and out.
  - Training building for volunteers
    - Location
    - Time/date
  - Electricity
  - Heating/air conditioning
  - Water
  - Restroom facilities
  - Parking
  - Shelter
    - At search areas
    - Staging area
    - For adverse weather
  - Search material
    - Walking/probing sticks
    - Type of terrain to be searched
  - Food/drinks
  - Daily briefings and debriefing
  - Communications
    - During active search
    - Prior to searches (i.e., cancellation, need for more volunteers, etc.)
  - Transportation
    - How transportation will be supplied to and from assignments
    - Officer in charge of volunteers may consider contacting schools for the use of their school buses, etc.
  - Other considerations
    - Relief
    - Health of volunteer
    - Medical personnel for physical and emotional problems
    - Civil liability and workers compensation, if injured
- Suggestion box for officers and volunteers

Coordinating, assigning, and using volunteers in the most efficient and effective manner during a missing child investigation is not an easy task and should be taken seriously. There is no doubt that under the right conditions and the right missing child case, there will be volunteers. There may be a few to a few thousand, and they will be looking for direction from the first responder/investigator to the commander in charge.

To assist in processing volunteers, a worksheet has been created. Refer to Appendix R for the Volunteer Background Check form.

Long-Term and Cold Cases

11

No police officer, investigator, chief, or prosecutor ever envisions or wants a case to become long term or the dreaded "cold case." But, due to leads drying up, lack of continuous news media coverage, and possibly budgetary and personnel problems, many cases do turn into long-term and become cold cases. Missing children cases are not exempt.

Preparing and collecting evidence and the preservation of evidence and statements starts at the beginning of any active missing child case. From the first responder to the last investigator who works on the active case, they must remember that a missing child case may become long-term or cold. Many missing children cases have ended up this way. There are probably investigators who can attest to the fact that long-term or cold case integrity was compromised by failure to properly preserve evidence, failure to acquire the proper DNA and blood samples, failure to transcribe statements and original taped statements, and on and on.

How many missing children long-term or cold cases are there? No one really knows. As an example, the National Center for Missing and Exploited Children (NCMEC) website lists 2,719 active short-term, long-term, and cold cases.[*] These are missing children who meet NCMEC's criteria of missing. But what about missing children who are in the federal, state, and local systems that do not meet the broad term of *missing* or who are classified as crimes other than a missing child (i.e., homicide, etc.). No one knows that number. The point is, treat every missing child case as if it could become a long-term or cold case. That way you help ensure that if your case goes cold, when another investigator reactivates the case and reviews it in the future, you have done all you can do to assist and help recover or bring closure to your original missing child case. Many cold cases have a good chance of being handed down to future generations of investigators, who will have to rely on your original response and investigation.

A murder might never be solved because evidence was destroyed in an unsolved slaying.

It was 1972 when a shy teenager from a housing project walked to a nearby convenience store to buy a carton of Oleo and two bottles of Pepsi for her mother.

---

[*] National Center for Missing Exploited Children website, http://www.missingkids.com, quick research for missing children over the past 40 years, October 2011.

She had pleaded to go alone.

Nine days later, her body was found in some bushes just blocks away from home. She'd been raped and beaten. Her head was smashed in with a brick.

Police collected evidence: a brick and a chunk of concrete that had blood stains and hair strands on it, a prayer book that was found near Laura's body, also stained with blood, and her clothing. They also recovered the items she got at the store—margarine, a bottle of pop, and the receipt.

Nearly four decades later her family still has no answers.

Short of a confession, it's likely they'll never know who killed the 16-year-old because all of the evidence was destroyed or lost.

Her bloodstained clothing was ordered destroyed in 1977; the Pepsi bottle followed in 1978. A brick and a chunk of concrete marked with blood and hair strands were destroyed in 1984. The fingernail scrapings and rape evidence—swabs taken during the autopsy—are nowhere to be found.

Since the teenager's death, at least two of the officers who investigated the case have died. So have her parents.

This story illustrates what legal experts say is a pervasive problem nation-wide—the mishandling of criminal evidence.

Law enforcement doesn't track how often evidence gets lost or destroyed, but experts concede it's not uncommon.

The above story is true—where it happened or what department was involved is not the reason for its inclusion here. The point is, an abducted child case went cold and evidence was not preserved and was eventually destroyed over the years. There will be no arrest, no prosecution, and the most tragic thing is the parents have gone to their grave not knowing who raped and killed their daughter.

To assist in this vital area of long-term and cold cases, a guide has been created for the first responder/investigator to use in preparing for the possibility of a long-term or cold case of a missing child. Refer to Appendix B for the Long-Term and Cold Case Checklist.

Reunification

12

One of the main response objectives for law enforcement is the notification of death, recovery, or reuniting of the missing child and the parents. To the author's knowledge, there is no such training for entry-level officers or for the veteran, nor does the author know of any policy or procedure written to guide officers in the notification of death, recovery, or reuniting of a missing child and the parents. Yet, it is the conclusion of a missing child case.

When a child is located alive, or in the worst-case scenario dead, it will be the responsibility of the investigating police department to notify the parents, news media, and community. Each classification of missing children discussed in this book has different complex strategies for reuniting a missing child with their parents and family. An example of this is the reunification of a runaway with the parents compared to a nonfamily stranger abduction. The runaway compared to the nonfamily stranger abduction has totally different dynamics and circumstances that require different reunification strategies.

At times, the reunification of a missing child will be way beyond any department's capability to handle, given their own personnel and resources. The length of time a child is missing (and under what conditions) may be short or long, and legally complex (civil or criminal).

The reader only has to remember that Elizabeth Smart's abduction lasted nine months. When she was located, the Salt Lake City Police Department found themselves in a reunification scenario that they were not prepared for. Let us also recall Shawn Hornbeck who was abducted and held captive in Missouri for four years.

Team Approach

The process for reuniting missing children and their families starts long before a child goes missing. It should be the policy of any department that the best interest of the child comes first. Once this is recognized, police agencies have to address missing children reunification in their policies and procedures. These policies and procedures should not only direct an officer on how to accomplish this, but create a team approach.*

The National Center for Missing and Exploited Children (NCMEC) has a specific division within their organization that will assist any law enforcement agency in reuniting a missing child with their family. NCMEC also has a manual (free of charge) that addresses the recovery and reunification of missing children. This document is the only written material that the author could locate to assist in the notification or reunification of a missing child with their parents.

The reunification of a missing child should be a team approach. An effective missing child reunification team, which will have the best interests of the child at heart, will include:

- A specially trained, on-call law enforcement officer
- A specially trained, on-call mental health professional
- Participation of child welfare or social services professional
- Participation of victim/witness advocates
- Participation of family or dependency court professional
- Participation of a local prosecutor

Reuniting a child with their family is not just taking the child back home, but may involve skills of many different professionals. When a missing child has been located, the officer will not know what type of emotional stress the child has been under or what they have been subjected to. Examples of these situations:

- A runaway may have been assaulted physically or sexually at home and chose to run from that environment.
- A family-abducted child may have been taken out of state or out of this country and has lived a life of concealment.
- A nonfamily-abducted child may have been subject to physical and sexual abuse. The stereotypical abducted child is often deceased when located.

There should be no doubt that a missing child reunification team of professionals should be put in place and consist of individuals in the following fields:

- Law enforcement
- Social service
- Prosecutor
- Medical
- Mental Health

---

* Kathryn M. Turman, ed., "Recovery and Reunification of Missing Children: A Team Approach," National Center for Missing and Exploited Children, Office of Juvenile Justice and Delinquency Prevention, March 1995.

It is strongly suggested that an on-call local prosecutor participate on any missing child reunification team to legally protect the child and the department. Many legal issues and questions can evolve in missing children reunification cases. Examples of these legal issues are as follows:

- A child who has been physically or sexually abused in a home: Should that child be returned to their parent or guardian, and if not, where should that child be placed? What crimes should be pursued and prosecuted against the offender?
- A child is abducted from their home by a parent and there are allegations of physical abuse, sexual abuse, and maltreatment: Should that child be returned to their parents or guardian and if not, where should that child be placed? What crimes should be pursued and prosecuted against the offender?
- A child is a victim of a nonfamily abduction: What criminal procedures should be followed based on the investigation, interviews, suspect, and evidence?
- When the best interest of a child is the main focus of a reunification and because legal or conflicting circumstances prevent such reunification, who will have legal responsibility and authority to place the child in a protective custody environment?

The Response

When a missing child or runaway is located, the police will most likely be the first responder. With this responsibility, police agencies should have policies and procedures in place.

Guidelines for the reunification of a missing child have been created to assist the first responder/investigator. These guidelines are not all-inclusive, but were created to give guidance in the process of reunification. These guidelines are not in any particular order and may vary from one missing child or runaway to another. Refer to Appendix S for the Reunification Checklist.

False Police Reports

13

Officers with any experience will attest to the fact that people do lie and make false reports to police for numerous reasons. They may be covering up a crime, be frightened, or may want to mislead the police.

It takes a skilled officer to detect false police reports, and sometimes it is just a gut instinct that something is fishy about the report. False missing children reports may take a few minutes to decipher or it may take hours or months. The following examples are only a few of such false reports of missing children:

- July 7, 2011, Fayetteville, NC: Shaniya Davis's mother[*] (Antoinette Davis) was indicted on murder and other charges. The mother of five-year-old Shaniya Davis was indicted on charges of first-degree murder, rape of a child, and human trafficking. A grand jury also indicted Antoinette Davis, 27, on charges of taking indecent liberties with a child, committing a sexual offense, sexual servitude, and making a false police report, authorities said.
- March 21, 2011, Asheboro, NC: A woman[†] who told police her child was nearly abducted on Sunday will be charged with filing a false police report, police said on Tuesday. The woman lost sight of her child and panicked, which led her to make up the kidnapping story.
- February 14, 2011, Lake County, FL, deputies:[‡] Girl fabricated Clermont attempted abduction: A fourteen-year-old girl who told Lake County deputies a man tried to grab her at the bus stop last week admitted that she fabricated the story. She admitted she invented the tale because she did not want to get in trouble for losing her eyeglasses.

Typically a parent or guardian participates in these types of reports, but as previously shown, even a child or teenager or a respected person can

---

[*] Shaniya Davis' mother indicted on murder, other charges, Fayobserver, July 7, 2011: http://fayobserver.com/articles/2011/07/06/1106653?sac=Home
[†] Asheboro Police: Mother Made Up Kidnapping Story, March 21, 2011: http://www.digtriad.com/news/local/article/167415/57/Asheboro-Police-Mother-Made-Up-Kidnapping-Story.
[‡] Deputies: Girl fabricated Clermont attempted abduction, *Orlando Sentinel*, February 14, 2011: http://articles.orlandosentinel.com/2011-02-14/news/os-girl-14-attempted-abduction-clermo20110210_1_false-police-report-abduction-detectives

initiate a false police report. The bad thing about a false police report is that it requires resources that could be used in other areas.

A review of two cases will underscore how much time, energy, and resources are wasted in false police reports, if they are not identified early in a missing and runaway child report.

- October 1994: Susan Smith,* a South Carolina woman, killed her two boys by driving her auto into a lake while the children slept in their car seats. She reported that a black man had taken her children to mislead police in their investigation. This case made national news with Smith pleading with the abductor, "I would like to say to whoever has my children that they please, I mean please bring 'em home to us where they belong."
- July 2, 2005: Tim and Lisa Holland† reported their seven-year-old adopted son was missing and had possibly run away. An intense investigation and search was conducted. On January 2, 2006, Tim Holland told detectives that Lisa killed Ricky Holland with two blows from a hammer to his head. Tim Holland also admitted to disposing of the body at Lisa Holland's direction. Tim Holland admitted to staging Ricky's room to make it appear as if he had run away as in previous cases, again at Lisa Holland's direction.

Can you imagine the resources and time that were put into these cases? Law enforcement is charged with either proving or disproving such reports by thoroughly investigating any allegations. Agencies have limited resources and budgets they must manage, but these cases are examples that received immediate national recognition. They put into motion all the resources both of these departments could muster to thoroughly investigate the allegations.

These departments were put under a microscope as to what they were going to do and how they were going to do it. In the Susan Smith case, a white mother accused a black male of taking her children. Not only did the police have to deal with a possible child abduction, but also public perception. In the Ricky Holland case, hours, days, weeks, and months of police resources and manpower at the local, state, and federal level were devoted to the case.

The first responder/investigator of a missing or runaway child will be exposed to such false reports and will have to evaluate not only what type of missing child incident they may have, but also the credibility of the report itself. There are documented cases of parents, boyfriends, girlfriends, and

---

* Susan Smith: Child Murderer or Victim?: http://www.trutv.com/library/crime/notorious_murders/famous/smith/susan_3.html
† Ricky Holland timeline, *Lansing State Journal:* http://www.lansingstatejournal.com/article/20071201/NEWS01/60630003/Ricky-Holland-timeline.

guardians who have killed their children and reported them missing to cover up their crimes. There are documented cases of parents who have sexually abused their children or told them to leave and made false reports that they were runaways or even abducted.

The first responder/investigator is the first officer on the scene and will be confronted with the impression, or gut feeling, of a fishy report. These instincts should not be ignored and should be communicated to the supervisor and those who will be conducting the investigation.

Yes, it will take time, patience, resources, and a thorough investigation to expose the facts of and identify a false report, but that is the nature of the beast in law enforcement. False missing children reports are somewhat irregular, but they do exist.

Runaways and Thrownaways

14

One out of every seven children will run away before the age of eighteen.

Runaway/thrownaway and benign episodes account for 84% of all children who are reported missing.

In this chapter, runaways/thrownaways, benign episodes, and lost, injured, and otherwise missing children will be discussed. When it comes to missing children, research and statistics show that runaways, thrownaways, benign episodes, and lost, injured, or otherwise missing will be the most frequent calls for a police response to a missing child. The National Runaway Switchboard estimates that more than 1,200 children in the United States run away from home each day. This staggering estimate amplifies that runaways alone are high volume calls for law enforcement.

Missing children definitions and classifications are not uniform and have caused much controversy. Prior to the National Incidence Studies of Missing, Abducted, Runaway, and Thrownaway Children (NISMART) 1 and 2 studies, a missing child was either classified as a runaway or just missing. Law enforcement did not classify a missing child as they do today (due to NISMART-2). There should be no wonder why law enforcement missed the ball when defining or classifying a missing child before NISMART-2. They just did not know the difference and did not recognize the complexity of a missing child case. As stated in the introduction, NISMART-2 identified and defined seven classifications of missing children that have become universal. For continuity, those classifications are used in this book.

First Responder/Investigator: Runaways (RAs)/Thrownaways (TAs)

There are an estimated[*] 1,682,900 runaways per year of which 70% are not reported. There are an estimated[†] 127,100 thrownaways per year of which 70% are not reported.

[*] NISMART-2 Runaway/Thrownaway Children: National Estimates and Characteristics: https://www.ncjrs.gov/html/ojjdp/NISMART-2/04/
[†] NISMART-2 Runaway/Thrownaway Children: National Estimates and Characteristics: https://www.ncjrs.gov/html/ojjdp/NISMART-2/04/

NISMART-2 defines a runaway and thrownaway episodes as follows:

- A runaway episode is one that meets any one of the following criteria:
  A child leaves home without permission and stays away overnight.
  A child fourteen years old or younger (or older and mentally incompetent) who is away from home, chooses not to come home when expected to, and stays away overnight.
  A child fifteen years old or older who is away from home chooses not to come home and stays away two nights.
- A thrownaway episode is one that meets either of these criteria:
  A child is asked or told to leave home by a parent or other household adult, no adequate alternative care is arranged for the child by a household adult, and the child is out of the household overnight.
  A child who is away from home is prevented from returning home by a parent or other household adult, no adequate alternative care is arranged for the child by a household adult, and the child is out of the household overnight

The first responder/investigator has to be conscious of parents who throw their children out of the home and report them as runaways. It may vary from state to state, but throwing one's child out of their home before the age of legal adulthood is a crime (i.e., child abandonment, child neglect, etc.).

Runaway/thrownaway children and their individual circumstances are unique and complex. Their problems leading up to running away or becoming a thrownaway are not usually a single event. Rather, over time, multiple abuse or neglect episodes or a combination of living conditions trigger their decision to run away or be thrown out by their parents. There is no one typical runaway or thrownaway child. Potential runaways and thrownaways come from every type of family, economic status, all neighborhoods, and all races.

A child will not run away from a home where they are loved or feel safe unless there is a reason. A runaway child is running away *from* something to something they think is better. As an example, research and studies have documented that the following:

- Less than 25% of the estimated runaways have been physically and/ or sexually assaulted in their own home.[*]

[*] Heather Hammer, David Finkelhor, and Andrea Sedlak, "Runaway/Thrownaway Children: National Estimates and Characteristics," NISMART–2, Washington, DC: US Department of Justice, Office of Justice Programs, Office of Juvenile Justice and Delinquency Prevention, October 2002.

- Runaways and thrownaways commonly describe a significant family conflict that led to their departure.[*]
- In many situations, family conflict has existed for a period of some time, resulting in a series of episodes, some where the youth clearly ran away, others where the parent clearly threw the child out of the house.[†]

So in reality, whether law enforcement or society wants to accept it, runaways and thrownaways can be victims of crimes before they choose to run away. The assailants are the people whom they trust the most—a parent, foster parent, siblings, and relatives.

What is tragic about runaways and thrownaways is that law enforcement in general does not respond to a runaway or thrownaway for the purpose of finding out *why* the child chose to run away or was thrown out. They take the report, locate the runaway or thrownaway, and return them to the same environment they chose to run away from without determining the *why*.

Unless there are extenuating circumstances that may indicate that foul play is involved, the missing child will most likely be classified as a runaway or otherwise missing child. Is this the appropriate classification of a missing child? Probably not, but in the eyes of law enforcement, unless there is evidence otherwise (i.e., witness or surveillance tape of an abduction or ransom note, etc.), this will be the only reasonable suspicion the first responder/investigator will have at the time.

Upon the arrival of the first responder/investigator, parents of missing children will have hunches or will adamantly state that their child did not run away. As in the case of Carlie Brucia (Sarasota, Florida, abducted by a stranger and caught on surveillance tape), Carlie's mother, on the arrival of the police, continually stated that her daughter had not run away. Carlie had no history of any past runaway episodes. There was no evidence of abduction at the time. The responding agency continued their investigation into Carlie's disappearance (downgraded from a possible abduction) until the next day when the surveillance tape was discovered. Once the evidence of Carlie being abducted was discovered and the responding department proved that the person in the surveillance tape was not a family member or friend, they upgraded her disappearance to a stranger abduction.

Carlie's abduction is illustrated here to show how difficult the initial response to a missing child can be. Here, the first responder was confronted with a missing child only. There was no evidence to consider other than Carlie's

[*] "Why They Run: An In-Depth Look at America's Runaway Youth," National Runaway Switchboard, May 2010. This study is an analysis of runaways and thrownaways over the period 2000–2009.
[†] "Why They Run," May 2010.

mother stating that Carlie was not a runaway. In this case she was right. But in how many cases in the past has a parent had such feelings and they were wrong?

When responding to missing children cases like Carlie Brucia's, it is like rolling dice. Has the missing child been abducted? Has the child been a victim of foul play? Was the child kicked out of their home? Has the child been taken by an estranged parent? Is the child at someone else's home and failed to tell their parent where they are? Is the missing child injured and lying in a hospital somewhere? Or, did the child run away or was the child thrown out of their home?

Yes, it is like rolling dice when that first responder/investigator only has information that a child is missing and nothing else. But if there is any doubt or you have an adamant parent who states, "I know my child and I know she/he did not run away," it may behoove you to think *possible abduction*. Does this mean that all the resources and manpower available should be used immediately as though it were a child abduction? The author thinks not, but the process of eliminating a missing child as a runaway, thrownaway, or child abduction will be put into motion. Think abduction!

In the Carlie Brucia case, the Sarasota Sheriff's Department responded to a missing child. They had very little to no information or evidence to exclude Carlie as a runaway or an abducted child. Although through the nighttime hours they reduced the number of officers involved in looking for her, they did not just classify her as a runaway and let time take its course. Throughout those critical nighttime hours, they continued to look for Carlie.

The sheriff's department continued their effort to locate Carlie the following morning. In an effort to find a witness or to determine the circumstances of Carlie's disappearance, the sheriff's department conducted a neighborhood canvass of the area Carlie may have used to walk home. Through this neighborhood canvass the deputies located a local car wash owner. They asked the owner to review his surveillance tape of the previous days. During his review of the surveillance tape, Carlie's abduction was recorded. Once the sheriff's department realized they had a possible stranger child abduction, they kicked the investigation into high gear.

In hindsight one can only ask, "Could the first responder have responded differently and immediately classified Carlie as a child abduction?" In hindsight the answer would be an unequivocal yes. But, as in any police response, they will have to be judged in the context of what was presented to them at the time of arrival.

In Carlie Brucia's abduction, the first responder had no witness or evidence to give him any reasonable suspicion that foul play was involved in her disappearance. In this case the mother was right, Carlie did not run away. Carlie's case and the first responder's actions taken that night when he knocked on Carlie's front door and interviewed Carlie's mother is what officers are confronted with when responding to a missing child. Did the child runaway or has the child been abducted?

Runaways or Thrownaways Located and Returned

Once a runaway or thrownaway is located, he or she will most likely be returned home with no follow-up investigation as to the reason *why* the child ran away. The returned runaway or thrownaway will be returned to a lifestyle and environment from which they chose to run away. The returned runaway or thrownaway may relive their experience over and over again and may be revictimized until they decide to run away or be thrown out again. The National Runaway Switchboard (2004)* reported that 41% of the runaways had a previous runaway episode. Even though the National Runaway Switchboard statistic does not reveal the reason why the child had a previous runaway episode, wouldn't it behoove law enforcement to thoroughly investigate the reason why the child ran away in the first place and then take appropriate action to resolve the child's problem and prevent call backs and repeat episodes? The author thinks yes.

Even though this book is written to assist police officers in the initial response to missing children, it is their responsibility to investigate any missing child as thoroughly as any other case. A runaway missing child is not just the act of taking a runaway report and entering the runaway into National Communications Information Center (NCIC), locating them, and returning them to their home. It should call for a response, an investigation, and a determination of what forced a child to run away from their home. After a thorough investigation, if there is probable cause to believe that there were associated catalyst crimes (i.e., child neglect/abuse, sexual abuse, incest, etc.) committed against the child that forced them to run away, then those offenders and the crimes discovered should be prosecuted to the fullest extent of the law.

Crimes committed against children who run away are well documented in research and studies:

- Michigan Family Impact Seminars, "Prostituted Teens: More Than a Runaway Problem," Briefing Report No. 2002-2, Michigan State University and Wayne State University, states that, "ninety percent of runaway-prostitutes are survivors of sexual violence such as incest and sexual assault."
- "Prostitution of Children and Child Sex Tourism: An Analysis of Domestic and International Responses," US Department of Justice, Office of Juvenile Justice and Delinquency Prevention (OJJDP) and the National Center for Missing and Exploited Children (NCMEC), p. 3, April 1999: "Among runaway and homeless youth, up to one-third report engaging in street prostitution—or survival

---

* National Runaway Switchboard: http://www.1800runaway.org.

sex—to achieve the basic necessities of life. . . . Sex abuse appears to indirectly increase the chance of prostitution by increasing the risk of running away. It is not so much that sexual abuse leads to prostitution as it is that running away leads to prostitution."

- "Female Juvenile Prostitution: Problem and Response," OJJDP/NCMEC, December 1992, Preface, p. v: "Some of these children leave home to escape physical or sexual abuse or neglect. Without legitimate means of support and a safe place to stay, they are often victimized again through pornography, sexual exploitation, and drugs."
- "Forced Labor: The Prostitution of Children," US Department of Labor, Bureau of International Labor Affairs, 1996, p. 42: "We have a huge problem on both coasts with thousands of runaway children and thrownaway children engaging in prostitution."
- Les B. Whitbesk, Danny R. Hoyt, Kurt D. Johnson, "Midwest Longitudinal Study of Homeless Adolescents," University of Nebraska–Lincoln, April 2002, p. 3: "Physical and sexual abuse by an adult caretaker is often a precipitous event to running away from home. Sexual abuse was significantly more prevalent among adolescent girls."
- National Incident-Based Reporting System (NIBRS) data (1999): "70% of forcible sex offenses and 97% of non-forcible sex offenses occurred against persons ages 0 through seventeen."
- Statistics show that one in five girls and one in ten boys are sexually exploited before they reach adulthood, yet less than 35% of those child sexual assaults are reported to authorities.[*]

A Story of a Runaway

Christine

"Something Less Than Human"

In 1981, I became a statistic: I became a runaway teen, escaping sexual and physical abuse. When I ran away, I no longer had a place to live with my parents nor did I have a living relative who would take me in. Filled with a sense of bravado, invincibility, and bravery, I left, figuring that my life couldn't be in any more jeopardy than it already was at what I'd called home. In leaving I hoped there would be no more broken bones, no more sexual abuse, no more rationalizations of molestation and cruelty. When I left that day, I had no more than a change of clothes and under one hundred dollars. No longer did my name, childhood identity, school, or grades matter. All became irrelevant in the world I was about to enter.

[*] National Center for Missing and Exploited Children (NCMEC): http://missingkids.com

As a runaway teen, your old concerns quickly disappeared and are replaced by new, life threatening ones. There were no familiar faces and no one who wanted to talk to a teenage girl who was homeless; even my name became irrelevant. Instead, my concerns are more pragmatic, involving finding food, shelter, and water, and passing time without the money to financially support these needs. I'd resorted to sleeping in cemeteries, and stealing food out of dumpsters and from convenience stores in order to eat. Getting drinking water and a chance to wash my face became quests of endurance. I had to hide from security guards, store and restaurant employees and others who didn't want a homeless girl "loitering." As a runaway teen, I was viewed as something less than human. Still, it was safer than going home.

"Into my hunger, loneliness and desperation came a man named Bruce."

Attractive, well dressed, and very charismatic, he approached me in a suburban mall and offered to "help" me. He could provide me with food, shelter, clothing, work—and I really wanted to work. I wanted desperately to be off the street and to have something—to do. In essence he knew exactly how to manipulate a desperate teenage girl with his promises to fulfill all my needs. The manipulation began within minutes of meeting him. When I questioned whether or not this "work" was prostitution, he retracted the offer and began to walk away. Desperate, I ran after him, pleading with him to give another chance and to forgive my insult.

Source: Excerpted from Leighton and DePasquale (1999)

Christine was a victim of crimes in the one place she had no choice to be—her home! The place that most of us take for granted as a safe haven, one of love, one of caring parents and family. We can only imagine the horror Christine, and many others like her, live in and go through. Before Christine and so many like her chose to run away, how many times were the police or social service agencies called to their home but did not recognize the signs of a neglected or abused child (physically, emotionally, or sexually) and just wrote it off as a family dispute or a distraught child?

Christine's episode happened in 1981, but fast forward to the present day and the symptoms, causation, and abuse of runway children has not changed. The neglect and abuse will continue until someone intervenes for them—before they decide on the "final solution" to their survival problem and run away. The author wonders who that person might be. Could it be you, the first responder/investigator?

Breaking the Cycle of a Runaway/Thrownaway

For whatever reason the child has chosen to run away, they believe they have made the right choice!

Figure 14.1 illustrates the cycle of a runaway or thrownaway, what they may go through, and how law enforcement may participate in that cycle. When it comes to family issues, nobody knows for sure what goes on behind closed doors. Law enforcement has a duty, within legal boundaries, to (1) attempt to find out what happened behind those closed doors that caused a child to run away, and (2) prevent suspected crimes or child abuse and neglect that may be inflicted on a child and/or other members of a family.

The most common reason for running away is physical or sexual abuse at home or fear of abuse upon return.

Phase 1: Stress Building

Despite being victimized more often than other age groups, teens are the least likely to report their victimization.

Phase 1 may take months or years of neglect or abuse. A child is exposed, or is a victim of violence or abuse in their household. The illustrated stress-building examples (see Figure 14.1) are not all-inclusive, but are only for illustrative purposes. A child may be exposed to far worse things than are listed.

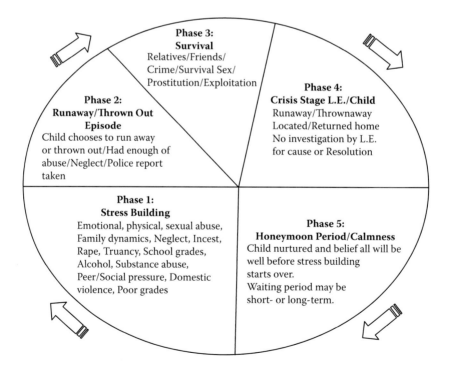

Figure 14.1 Cycle of a runaway or thrownaway.

When child neglect or abuse is the catalyst for a runaway, the perpetrator can be anyone:

- Father
- Mother
- Brother
- Sister
- Grandparent
- Aunt
- Uncle
- Close friend
- Slight acquaintance

The author has been asked, "Why doesn't the abused or neglected child report the abuse or neglect?" There are many reasons why a child would tolerate and not report such crimes committed against them:

- Shame
- Loyalty to the family
- Fear
- Guilt
- Family dynamics

Much research has been done in this area trying to explain the child's actions. This exceeds the scope of this book, but is the beginning phase of a cycle that may build to a child to running away.

Phase 2: Runaway/Thrownaway Episode

A child that runs away should be a signal to the first responder/investigator that something may be wrong in that child's personal life.

In this phase of the cycle, the runaway has tolerated enough of the stress-building phase and decides to run away. At the time law enforcement is called, it may not be understood why the child chose to run away. But for whatever reasons a juvenile decides to run away, they believe their decision is the right, rational, and sound thing to do. As stated before in this book, a runaway is running away *from* something *to* something they think is better. This phase is where law enforcement begins its investigation not only into the runaway, but into the causes in Phase 1.

Phase 3: Survival

In this phase of the cycle, when a runaway has made the decision to run away, he or she may or may not have thought about how they will survive away from home. The survival phase of a runaway/thrownaway will include how to get food, shelter, and how to get money to meet their basic needs. In the early phases of their runaway incident, a family member or friend may assist in these priorities. As time goes on and there are no family members or friends left to rely on, the runaway may resort to crime, prostitution, survival sex, or sex tourism. This is a high-risk phase for child exploitation from predators, pimps, and all of the sexual and other diseases that are related to such exploitation and crimes.

Phase 4: Crisis Stage for Law Enforcement and Runaway/Thrownaway Child

> Runaways "may leave on impulse, protesting a family quarrel over a rule or an isolated incident." But the main motivation for running away seems to be neglect or abuse at home. They decide that their only chance to survive is to run away.[*]

This phase of the cycle is probably second only to the stress-building phase in importance. This does not mean that any of the other phases should be minimized. In this phase the child and law enforcement can begin to communicate. Through interaction, they can determine the core reasons and issues of *why* the child ran away. Once the *why* has been determined (i.e., neglect/abuse, etc.), proper placement of a runaway may be considered.

A runaway or thrownaway, after being located, may not voluntarily open up to the officer. There often is no real attempt on the officer's part to communicate with the runaway or thrownaway and determine the causes that led up to the juvenile choosing to run away.

However, it could be that the runaway or thrownaway is hoping that the officer will ask them why they left their home. Are they too embarrassed or frightened to open up to the officer? With a little care, compassion, and persuasion the child may trust that officer and tell them what has been taking place behind closed doors.

---

[*] Laurie Schaffner, *Teenage Runaways: Broken Hearts and Bad Attitudes* (New York: Haworth Press, 1999).

Phase 5: Honeymoon Period/Calmness

This phase of the cycle begins when the runaway or thrownaway child is returned home. In this phase the parent(s) of a child who chose to run away or was thrown out, may exhibit any of these behaviors:

- Apologetic to the child
- Shower them with kindness and gifts
- Tell them that the abuse or neglect will stop
- Tell them everything will okay
- Tell them everything can be worked out.

This may be true for a lot of returned runaways and thrownaways. Others know from past experience that the cycle may start over.

In Phase 4 the reason why a child ran away or was thrown out may have been discovered, but what will happen to a runaway or thrownaway child on the return home? Law enforcement and research recognizes that half of all runaways will likely run two or more times.[*] Again, why is there a high recidivism rate? The opportunity for law enforcement exists in modern research to understand the honeymoon phase and what, if anything, changed after a runaway or thrownaway has been located and returned home.

The following data from the National Runaway Switchboard (NRS) will assist law enforcement to better understand what may happen during the honeymoon phase to a child and family when a child is located and returned home. The youth surveyed stated the following:[†]

- Things did not get better (48.5%)
- Things were worse (22.1%)
- Things were better at first but then were worse (10.3%)
- Things were better (8.8%)
- Sometimes better and sometimes worse (2.9%)
- Things were worse at first but got better (1.5%)
- Unknown (5.9%)

Phase 5, the honeymoon period of the cycle of a runaway/thrownaway, is very similar to the honeymoon phase of a domestic violence cycle. As an example, in the honeymoon phase of domestic violence the assailant showers the victim with gifts and promises that all will be okay. But depending on how violent the stress phase is, violence in the domestic violence cycle

---

[*] "Why They Run," May 2010.
[†] "Why They Run," May 2010.

depends on how quickly the domestic violence cycle starts over. The more violence there is, the quicker the cycle starts over.

Only 10.3% of the runaways or thrownaways surveyed in the NRS analysis stated that things were better (8.8%) or things were worse at first but got better (1.5%). The survey showed that 80.9% of runaways or thrownaways reported that things remained the same (which is to say bad) or became worse.[*] With these staggering statistics the honeymoon period of a runaway or thrownawy appears to be short lived. As an example, if 70.6% of NRS respondents stated that things did not get better or things got worse, how long will the honeymoon period be before the cycle of a runaway/thrownaway starts over?

The return of a runaway or thrownaway child to a parent is complicated. It calls for an investigation of why the child ran away or was thrown out, but also what will happen to them on their return.

Characteristics and Traits of Runaways and Thrownaway Children

Runaway/thrownaway children constitute 37% of children missing from their caretakers for any reason and 21% of all missing children reported to authorities.[†] Runaway/thrownaway children have similar characteristics and traits including:[‡]

- Age: twelve to seventeen years
- Gender: male or female
- Race: white
- Number of miles traveled from home: more than one mile and no more than fifty miles
- Duration of time missing: twenty-four hours but less than one week
- Reason for runaway/thrownaway status: physical or sexually abused and substance abuse

Refer to Appendices F and G for additional characteristics and traits of a runaway.

---

[*] "Why They Run," May 2010.
[†] Heather Hammer, Daniel Finkelhor, and Andrea Sedlack, "Runaway/Thrownaway Children: National Estimates and Characteristics," National Incidence Studies of Missing, Abducted, Runaway, and Thrownaway Children (NISMART–2) series, Washington, DC: US Department of Justice, Office of Justice Programs, Office of Juvenile Justice and Delinquency Prevention, October 2002.
[‡] NISMART-2 Runaway/Thrownaway Children: National Estimates and Characteristics: https://www.ncjrs.gov/html/ojjdp/NISMART-2/04/

Missing Benign Episode (MBE)

15

There are an estimated 374,700 missing benign episodes per year.[*]

Second to runaways, a missing benign episode, and the lost, injured, or otherwise missing child are the types of missing child cases that law enforcement will be called upon to handle. Understanding the dynamics of a missing benign episode will assist the first responder/investigator in their evaluation of these two classifications of a missing child.

The National Incidence Studies of Children Missing Involuntarily, or for Benign Reasons (NISMART-2) defines a missing benign episode (MBE) as follows:

> A missing benign episode occurs when a child's whereabouts are unknown to the child's caretaker, who either contacts law enforcement or a missing children's agency to locate the missing child or
>
> (1) the child becomes missing for at least an hour,
> (2) the caretaker tries to locate the child, and
> (3) contacts the police about the episode for any reason, as long as the child was not lost, injured, abducted, victimized, or classified as runaway/thrownaway.

Here are two examples of an MBE:[†]

- A thirteen-year-old boy skipped school without permission. The school called the police when the boy's absence was discovered, and both the police and the boy's frantic mother searched for him. At the time, the mother was convinced that her son was either injured or kidnapped because this had never happened before. The boy was gone for three hours before he returned home safely.

[*] Andrea J. Sedlak, Daniel Finkelhor, and Heather Hammer, "National Estimates of Children Missing Involuntarily of for Benign Reasons," National Incidence Studies of Missing, Abducted, Runaway, and Thrownaway Children (NISMART–2) series, Washington, DC: US Department of Justice, Office of Justice Programs, Office of Juvenile Justice and Delinquency Prevention, July 2005.

[†] NISMART-2 National Estimates of Children Missing Involuntarily, or for Benign Reasons: https://secure.missingkids.com/en_US/documents/NISMART_national_estimates_missing_invol.pdf

- A seven-year-old boy was supposed to be watching television in the living room. His mother called him for dinner and discovered he was not there. Instead, the boy had gone outside to play and fallen asleep in the corner of the detached garage on their property. It was dark outside, and the parents searched for the boy with the assistance of their neighbors. When they could not find him, the neighbors called the police to assist in locating the missing child. The episode lasted forty-five minutes.

Other MBE considerations are as follows:

- Communication failures among parents, guardians, family members, and the missing child
- Forgetfulness either by parent, guardian, or child
- Unexpected delays
- The child forgetting the time
- Flat tire
- Missing a ride
- Helping a friend
- Talked into something by a friend
- Pranks
- Out partying
- Anger at parents and "I will show them"
- Misunderstandings between parents and children about when the child would return or where they would be

The response to an MBE is totally different from the response to a missing or runaway child. There is no probable cause or reasonable suspicion to believe the child has run away or has been abducted nor is there any reason to expect foul play in their missing status.

The responding officer should make every attempt to locate the child before resorting to options such as a LOCATER or AMBER Alert (discussed in Chapter 9), but remember that any child who is experiencing an MBE still falls under the National Child Search Assistance Act and every effort should be made to comply with that Act. First responders and investigators have two hours from the time they take a missing child report to enter the MBE missing child into the National Communications Information Center (NCIC) system.

The A Child Is Missing Alert, discussed in Chapter 9 ("Getting the Information Out"), is a resource that fits perfectly in MBEs. At no cost to the law enforcement agency, 1,000 citizens can be contacted every sixty seconds* to assist them in locating a MBE child by using A Child Is Missing Alert.

Refer to Appendices F and H for additional characteristics and traits of an MBE.

* A Child is Missing Alert brochure.

Missing Involuntary, Lost, or Injured (MILI) 16

There are an estimated[*] 204,503 lost, injured, or otherwise missing episodes per year.

The National Incidence Studies of Children Missing Involuntarily, or for Benign Reasons (NISMART-2) defines MILI as follows:

> A missing involuntary, lost, or injured episode occurs when a child's whereabouts are unknown to the child's caretaker, who either contacts law enforcement or a missing children's agency to locate the missing child or becomes alarmed for at least one hour and tries to locate the child, and one of the following conditions applies:
>
> (1) the child was trying to get home or make contact with the caretaker but was unable to do so because the child was lost, stranded, or injured (defined as physical harm that required medical attention or resulted in injuries that were evident the next day, e.g., cuts, bruises, or sprains), or
>
> (2) the child was too young to know how to return home or make contact with the caretaker.

Here are two examples of MILI:[†]

- A sixteen-year-old girl accompanied her friend to the doctor's office, and on the way home their car was involved in an accident. An ambulance transported the pair to the hospital, where they were examined and the girl was treated for a dislocation and a stress-induced asthma attack. The girl's mother became alarmed when she could not reach her daughter on her pager and called the girl's father and friends to find the girl. Nobody contacted the mother about her

---

[*] Andrea J. Sedlak, Daniel Finkelhor, and Heather Hammer, "National Estimates of Children Missing Involuntarily of for Benign Reasons," National Incidence Studies of Missing, Abducted, Runaway, and Thrownaway Children (NISMART–2) series, Washington, DC: US Department of Justice, Office of Justice Programs, Office of Juvenile Justice and Delinquency Prevention, July 2005.

[†] NISMART-2 National Estimates of Children Missing Involuntarily, or for Benign Reasons: https://secure.missingkids.com/en_US/documents/NISMART_national_estimates_missing_invol.pdf

daughter's whereabouts until five hours after she became alarmed. The child was returned home two hours after she was located at the hospital. The episode lasted seven hours.

- A fourteen-year-old girl and her ten-year-old brother were hiking in a park with their father. With his permission, they went ahead on the trail and inadvertently got separated from him and lost. Losing sight of his children caused the father to be very alarmed, and he immediately retraced their steps in search of them, asking any person he came across for help, and flagged down cars to ask where the trails ended. While he was searching for the children, they were trying to find him, and it took an hour before the father found his children unharmed.

Other MILI considerations are as follows:

- Immediate medical attention without parent knowing
- Disability
- Absence due to injury
- Wandering off

MILI children constitute 16% of children missing from their caretakers for any reason and 9% of all missing children reported to authorities. MILI missing children have a high probability of characteristics and traits similar to MBE missing children:[*]

- Age: twelve to seventeen years
- Gender: male
- Race: white
- Time missing: one to six hours
- Reason for disappearance: failed to come home

Refer to Appendices F and I for additional characteristics and traits of an MILI.

---

[*] Sedlak, Finkelhor, and Hammer, 2005.

Family Child Abduction (FCA)

17

350,000 children will be victims of a family child abduction per year.[*]
44,900 children will be victims of attempted family child abductions per year.
82% of the reported abducted children in the United States are FCAs.[†]

The National Incidence Studies of Children Abducted By Family Members (NISMART-2) defines family child abduction as follows:

- [T]he taking or keeping of a child by a family member in violation of a custody order, a decree, or other legitimate custodial rights, where the taking or keeping involved some element of concealment, flight, or intent to deprive a lawful custodian indefinitely of custodial privileges.
- Some of the specific definitional elements are as follows:

  Taking: Child was taken by a family member in violation of a custody order or decree or other legitimate custodial right.

  Keeping: Child was not returned or given over by a family member in violation of a custody order or decree or other legitimate custodial right.

  Concealment: Family member attempted to conceal the taking or whereabouts of the child with the intent to prevent return, contact, or visitation.

  Flight: Family member transported or had the intent to transport the child from the state for the purpose of making recovery more difficult.

  Intent to deprive indefinitely: Family member indicated an intent to prevent contact with the child on an indefinite basis or to affect custodial privileges indefinitely.

---

[*] Heather Hammer, Daniel Finkelhor, and Andrea J. Sedlak, "Children Abducted by Family Members: National Estimates and Characteristics, National Incidence Studies of Missing, Abducted, Runaway, and Thrownaway Children (NISMART–2) series, Washington, DC: US Department of Justice, Office of Justice Programs, Office of Juvenile Justice and Delinquency Prevention, October 2002.

[†] NISMART-2 NISMART-2 Children Abducted By Family Members: National Estimates and Characteristics: http://www.missingkids.com/en_US/documents/NISMART-22_family abduction.pdf

Child: Person under eighteen years of age. For a child fifteen or older, there needed to be evidence that the family member used some kind of force or threat to take or to detain the child, unless the child was mentally disabled.

Family member: A biological, adoptive, or foster family member; someone acting on behalf of such a family member; or the romantic partner of a family member.

As a law enforcement officer you will be called upon to respond to domestic violence calls. History and experience has shown that this one specific area of calls for service has been an officer safety concern. Many officers have either been injured or killed during their response to such calls. In police academies throughout the nation, blocks of instruction are set aside with specific curriculum for entry-level police officers, training them for their response to domestic violence incidents. The research completed prior to the establishment of the curriculum for domestic violence training identified three specific areas:

1. The law
2. The dynamics of domestic violence
3. The officer's response

Since the evolution of specific training for entry-level officers in how to respond to domestic violence, and having knowledge of the dynamics of a family experiencing domestic violence (plus knowing the laws), the assaults and killings of officers have diminished. In other words, we are better prepared *today* to handle domestic violence through training than we were ten years ago.

The same situation exists in the handling of FCAs. Law enforcement has a long way to go to be adequately trained to handle FCAs. The *Office of Juvenile Justice and Delinquency Prevention Bulletin* states:[*]

- The majority of law enforcement agencies reported that they did not have written policies and procedures governing parental abduction cases, and they did not receive formal training on the handling of parental abduction cases.
- [M]any federal, state, and local law enforcement agencies and prosecutors cited a general lack of knowledge and protocol in dealing with family abductions as the Achilles' heel in their ability to quickly and effectively carry out their responsibilities.

[*] The Uniform Child-Custody Jurisdiction and Enforcement Act, by Patricia M. Hoff, Office of Juvenile Justice and Delinquency Prevention Bulletin, December 2001: https://www.ncjrs.gov/html/ojjdp/jjbul2001_12_2/contents.html

With this information, it is hoped that this book will fill the void in training and assist the first responder/investigator in an FCA. The same curriculum theory that has been used nationally to train law enforcement in handling domestic violence calls is presented in this chapter for handling an FCA:

- The law
- The motives
- The dynamics of FCAs
- The response

The Law

The response by law enforcement to an FCA is mandated by the Federal Child Search Assistance Act of 1990. Refer to the Federal Statutes (Chapter 4) for compliance with the National Child Search Assistance Act.

FCAs encompass the taking, retention, or concealment of a child by a parent, other family member, or their agent, in derogation of the custody rights, including visitation rights, of another parent or family member. Because of the harmful effects on children, parental kidnapping has been characterized as a form of child abuse.

Intrastate FCAs

All fifty states have made it a crime for a noncustodial parent (adoptive or natural) or family member to take a child, or retain that child with the intent to detain or conceal the child from any parent or legal guardian who has legal custody or parental custody rights pursuant to a lawful court order at the time of the abduction or kidnapping. Although every state has made parental kidnapping a crime, not every state has made such a crime a felony. Depending on the circumstances, the abductor can be charged with a misdemeanor or a felony.

When a child is a victim of an FCA and the abducting parent or offender stays within the state of the abduction, all state laws and court decrees (civil/criminal) will be in effect and subject to that state court's jurisdiction.

Because each state may have different degrees of FCA statutes, and before a person is charged with an FCA crime, the first responder or investigator should consult with the local prosecutor.

Interstate FCAs: Federal Laws and Obstacles

Interstate custody disputes and FCA crimes are enforced under the Uniform Child Custody Jurisdiction Act, Uniform Child Custody Jurisdiction and

Enforcement Act, and Parental Kidnapping Prevention Act of 1990 (refer to Chapter 4, "Federal Criminal and Civil Laws Regarding Missing and Abducted Children").

When first responders and their departments handle such missing child cases, they should immediately contact and maintain a close liaison with the Federal Bureau of Investigation (FBI) and the local federal prosecutor for assistance and legal advice.

The responding law enforcement agency faces heightened challenges when an FCA child is taken out of the state or country. Family child abductions that involve interstate abductions can be complex and may have legal (civil/criminal) obstacles. When a child is transported across state lines or out of the country, the complexity becomes more intense. Documented studies, point to many obstacles in handling FCA cases, such as the following:[*]

- Verifying custody orders, overcoming the poor documentation available on custody orders, and dealing with custody orders subject to varying interpretations.
- Deciphering the deceptive and contradictory information provided by the left-behind and/or abducting parents.
- Interpreting vague laws or statutes regarding custody and child abduction.
- Clarifying law enforcement and prosecutor roles in other jurisdictions.
- Overcoming lack of cooperation among judges (in enforcing civil custody orders).
- Having to rely on less than cooperative law enforcement authorities in other jurisdictions to assist in the return of the child and the abductor.

All states have laws that make parental abduction, often called *criminal custodial interference*, a crime. These laws vary from state to state as to whether they cover abductions that occur before a custody order has been issued and abductions involving joint custodial parents. In some states, abduction is a felony only if the child is taken across state lines.[†]

If a state felony warrant has been issued in a case of parental abduction and the abductor has fled the state, then it is possible to obtain a warrant for unlawful flight to avoid prosecution (UFAP) under the Federal Fugitive Felon Act. Obtaining a UFAP warrant is an important step toward

---

[*] OJJDP: Parental Abduction: A Review of the Literature, Collins, J.J, 1993, Law Enforcement Policies and Practices Regarding Missing Children and Homeless Youth.

[†] Janet Chiancone, Linda Girdner, and Patricia Hoff, "Issues in Resolving Cases of International Child Abduction by Parents," *Office of Juvenile Justice and Delinquency Prevention (OJJP) Juvenile Justice Bulletin*, December 2001. https://www.ncjrs.gov/html/ojjdp/190074/index.html

possibly gaining greater law enforcement assistance with the case, such as involvement of the FBI.

When the first responder/investigator classifies a victim of an FCA and has reasonable suspicion that the child will be transported across state lines, they should immediately contact their local FBI office and ask for assistance. The two federal laws mentioned previously will take precedence over any disputes involving any interpretation of any court decree (civil/criminal) and should alleviate any potential civil obstacles or disputes of the home state court orders.

Motives of FCA

Motives for abducting children were discussed in Chapter 5 and those motives should be considered in an FCA response and investigation, but further consideration should be given to reasons why parents abduct their children:[*]

- The parent confuses their own frustration or disgust with the relationship as meaning that the other parent is bad for the child.
- The parent fears losing custody or visitation rights.
- The parent is "getting back at" the other parent by taking away something the other parent wants (i.e., the child).
- The parent is removing the child from real physical and/or emotional threat or injury by the other parent.
- The parent is removing the child from *perceived* physical and/or emotional threat or injury by the other parent.
- The parent fears the values, influence, and/or behavior to which the other parent may expose the child.
- The parent may have never intended to involve the other parent in raising the child, and is "eliminating" them by leaving and taking the child.
- The parent is trying to force a reconciliation or contact with the left-behind parent.
- The parent wants to be more important in the child's life or wants the child to be more dependent on them.

Having knowledge of why parents abduct their children, will give law enforcement additional awareness of the complex dynamics of FCAs.

---

[*] Liss Haviv and Janet Brodsky LICSW, "Why Parents Abduct Their Children," Take Root, a national 501 (c) (3) non-profit organization, http://www.takeroot.org/pubs/Why_Parents_Abduct.pdf

Dynamics of FCA

Many parents abduct their child because they truly believe that the other parent is abusing, molesting, or neglecting the child.

Family abduction is a type of crime and child welfare problem for which only limited statistical information has been available[*] and little is known when it comes to the dynamics of FCA. A general attitude that FCAs are custody battles, civil issues, not a law enforcement problem, or just a family problem are widely accepted by many law enforcement agencies. How far from the truth these preconceived opinions are. FCAs are just that—abductions.

Police officers and the law enforcement community have little to no knowledge, education, or training in the dynamics of FCAs. To the author's knowledge, there is no formal training for the first responder/investigator regarding FCAs. To put it simply, they (the police, first responder or investigator) are not trained in the dynamics of FCAs. The author, through his research and law enforcement experience, have identified three stages of the dynamics of FCAs:

1. Dynamics before an FCA
2. Dynamics during an FCA
3. Dynamics after an FCA

Dynamics before an FCA

Before a parent decides to abduct their child or children, there is usually some catalyst that moves the parent to resort to abduction. What happened behind closed doors to motivate a parent to abduct? Is there a dark family secret that only those living behind closed doors know?

Family domestic violence and family domestic disturbances are well known in our society and the law enforcement community. Law enforcement personnel are trained in the cycle of domestic violence and its phases:

- Phase 1: Stress, tension building
- Phase 2: Violent, take action
- Phase 3: Honeymoon, all will be okay

The law enforcement community understands that the more violent phase 2 is, the faster the cycle of domestic violence starts again. How many times do two parents go through the cycle of domestic violence before phase 2 becomes a *take action phase* and they abduct their child(ren)? An example

[*] Hammer, Finkelhor, and Sedlak, 2002.

of living in the domestic violence cycle and being a victim of family child abduction is expressed by one child, Carolyn:[*]

> I had lived with both my parents and three siblings in Chicago until the abduction. My parents married when my mother was sixteen or seventeen, he was older than her by thirteen years. My mother had been born and raised in Chicago; she married to escape a strict religious upbringing. My father was born and raised in rural Mississippi and had dropped out of school in the second grade to help his parents run their small farm. Though I am glad they married and gave life to me and my siblings, their marriage should never have taken place. My five years with them is remembered by violent fights and little else. We all learned to fear my father and to keep our distance when he was around. I believe at the time my father abducted the four of us my mother had been threatening to divorce him and he decided to seek his revenge by abducting us one night after she had left for work.

Carolyn's story is one of many testimonies that surface when one tries to understand the dynamics of FCAs before an FCA becomes the "final solution."

Dynamics during an FCA

During his law enforcement service and training, the author of this book was never trained to understand what a child victim of an FCA goes through during their FCA experience. To even attempt to describe what happens to a child during an FCA incident would be a disservice to all of the victims of FCAs, but this excerpt was taken from experts in this field who were victims of an FCA:[†]

> During the abduction, the child is also taught to deal with life very differently. For example, they frequently begin taking on adult burdens and responsibilities, often becoming an emotional caretaker for the taking parent. The child may find themselves with a parent who is incapable of providing parental guidance and orders them not to reveal their situation to anyone else, leaving the child to fend for themselves. In an effort to avoid detection the child may be forbidden to answer the door, told not to play outside, to close the blinds, to hide when riding in a car, to avoid authority or evade personal questions or lie. In such situations, hiding, secrecy, and distrust or fear of authority may become the norm.
>
> Some children are taken deep underground. In an attempt to conceal the child, the taking parent may not allow the child access to proper educational,

[*] Take Root, a national 501 (c) (3) non-profit organization, "The Missing Side: Carolyn," http://www.takeroot.org

[†] Liss Haviv and Janet Brodsky, LICSW, "How Children Experience Abductions," Take Root, a national 501 (c) (3) non-profit organization, http://www.takeroot.org/pubs/Child's_Experience.pdf

medical, and social services and support. Some abducted children are physically and/or sexually abused or forced into domestic servitude, while some are neglected and many are emotionally abused. This makes the abduction that much more complex for the child. The child is dependent on the abusive or neglectful parent and does not have a safe caregiver to turn to for protection. Although family abduction is almost always devastating for the child, the health, safety, and welfare of the child become particularly compromised in these situations.

So what does this mean to the first responder/investigator of an FCA? If the officer thoroughly understands the dynamics and trauma that a victim of an FCA goes through, he or she may be better able to meet the challenge of response, investigation, recovery, and reunification of the child with their family. What a challenge!

Dynamics after an FCA

"We don't expect you to need any additional help once you are found."[*] From a law enforcement perspective, how true this statement may be.

Every recovered missing child will be reunited with their parent(s) and family. When a child is located alive or dead, it will be the responsibility of the investigating police department to notify the parents, news media, and community of the disposition of the missing child. Who will do that?

The reunification of a missing child may be way beyond any department's capability to handle with their own personnel and resources. The longer a child is missing and under what conditions makes this a complex situation. Are the first responder or investigator and the department they represent equipped or trained to handle the reunification? Most likely not. An effective missing child reunification team, which will have the best interest of the child at heart, will include the following:[†]

- A specially trained, on-call law enforcement officer
- A specially trained, on-call mental health professional
- Participation of a child welfare or social services professional
- Participation of victim and witness advocates
- Participation of a family or dependency court professional
- Participation of a local prosecutor

---

[*] Liss Haviv, Janet Brodsky, LICSW, and Sam McClain, "The Myth of the Magic Bullet," Take Root, a national 501 (c) (3) non-profit organization, http://www.takeroot.org/pubs/Magic_Bullet.pdf.

[†] Kathryn M. Turman, ed., "Recovery and Reunification of Missing Children: A Team Approach," National Center for Missing and Exploited Children, Office of Juvenile Justice and Delinquency Prevention, March 1995.

The Response

> Family Child Abductions may be the final solution to domestic violence. Beware! Beware! Beware!

FCAs should be taken seriously by law enforcement, as they may be the "final solution" to past or present domestic violence. They have the same ingredients, elements, risks, and hazards. The abducting parent has made a deliberate, conscious decision to abduct the child(ren). They have most likely picked the time and place when the abduction will occur. They have chosen the method and type of force that will be used, possibly including killing the parent (or even the first responder/investigator). History, research, and experience have also shown that these abducting parents may even kill their own children. Here are only a few family child abduction examples that ended up tragically:*

- Agena and Aliyah Battle and Cedric Harrington (March 31, 2006 and June 5, 2004–March 19, 2008): Twins Agena and Aliyah, along with their brother Cedric, were abducted by their noncustodial father on March 5, 2008. They were all found dead on March 19, 2008. Their father is believed to have killed them before killing himself. He was reportedly jealous of their mother's fiancée.
- Aja Danelle Johnson (January 5, 2003–January 24, 2010): Aja was abducted by her noncustodial stepfather, Lester Hobbs, after the murder of her mother. They were both found deceased on March 30, 2010. He killed Aja and then himself.
- Luis Osvaldo Cisernos (July 16, 1998–February 24, 2003): Luis was abducted along with his sister Mariana by their noncustodial mother, Martha Patlan and her boyfriend Genero Derantes on June 18, 2002. (A sibling, Claudia, was left behind.) Their father reported them missing but the police said the joint custody agreement they had let the mother be with the children. Luis was found murdered on February 20, 2003. His body showed signs of extensive torture. Genero Espinosa Dorantes and Martha Patlan were arrested for his murder and sentenced to life in prison. Mariana was found alive on February 25, 2006.

As with domestic violence, it is well known and documented that FCAs are dangerous, not only for the first responder or investigator, but for family members who are present, and at times for those family members that are not present. There are many documented instances where a parent abducts their child(ren), murdered their spouse, and murdered other family members.

---

* The Victims of Family Abduction, For the Lost Blog, http://forthelost.wordpress.com

FCAs should be perceived as a high-risk response for law enforcement and not be perceived as a low-priority call. Any FCA should be responded to like any other domestic violence call. They are dangerous and the response should follow law enforcement practices and be within local policies and procedures. As in domestic violence, you do not know what has taken place. You do not know if the abductor is in the residence. You do not know if weapons are involved. You do not know the state of mind of the parties involved. You just don't know! You do not know what happened prior to your arrival *behind those closed doors.*

The emotional scarring caused by this event requires that law enforcement officers recognize that family abduction not as a harmless offense (two parents are arguing over who "loves the child more"), but instead as an insidious form of child abuse. The history of the issue has also demonstrated that law enforcement has a much broader responsibility than the simple act of retrieval. By responding promptly, professionally, and efficiently to reports of a family abduction, officers and the agencies they represent become, in effect, a means of protection for the child.[*]

Law enforcement is often the first place that victim families turn to after an abduction or when they detect a threat. First responders and investigators have the opportunity and responsibility to aid in the recovery of the child and to recognize and discourage behavior by family members considering abduction. By understanding the dynamics before, during, and after an FCA and recognizing that family abduction is a serious crime, first responders/investigators can become the first line of defense for children at risk of family abduction.[†]

Many law enforcement agencies still consider family abductions a domestic issue that should be worked out between parents and their lawyers. Many believe that a child is not in grave danger if the abductor is a family member. Unfortunately, this is not true, and these assumptions continue to endanger our children's lives.

The Victim (The Abducted Child)

To be a child with parents that quarrel and display violence toward each other is tragic in itself. A child who is at high risk of being kidnapped by one of their parents will most likely have no preconceived idea that their father or mother is going to abduct them. They may not even know they have been

---

[*] US Department of Justice, *A Law Enforcement Guide on International Parental Kidnapping* (Washington, DC: Office of Juvenile Justice and Delinquents Prevention, October 2002).

[†] Stop Family Abductions Now, a project of the Polly Klaas® Foundation, http://www.stop-familyabductionsnow.org

abducted for days, weeks, months, or years. The abducting parent lives in a deceptive world. They deceive and lie to their children they have kidnapped.

The abducting parent may deceive or lie about the left-behind parent to convince the abducted child that the abductor did nothing wrong and to cover up the fact that they have abducted the child. To deceive a family abducted child, the abducting parent may use the 3-D's indentified by Take Root.[*] Knowledge of the 3-D's may assist law enforcement in understanding the dynamics of FCA. The 3-D's are as follows, along with examples of the kinds of deceptions used by the abductor:[†]

- The missing parent is dead.
  - Was killed in a car accident
  - Committed suicide
  - Also includes complete omission, in which the child is told nothing at all about missing family and either doesn't remember or knows better than to ask; the missing family "does not exist."
- The missing parent is disinterested.
  - Walked out on you
  - Gave you to me
  - Sold you to me
  - Never loved or wanted you
- The missing parent is dangerous.
  - Crazy
  - Abusive
  - Mean
  - Bad
  - A drug addict
  - A prostitute
  - Plotting against us
  - Planning to hurt you
  - Planning to separate us
  - A thief
  - Demonized

When any police officer responds to a domestic disturbance, domestic violence, or runaway, and the child states one of the 3-D's as the reason why their mother or father does not live with them—think abduction.

---

[*] Liss Haviv and Janet Brodsky, LICSW, "Re-Framing Family Abduction," Take Root, a national 501 (c) (3) non-profit organization, http://www.takeroot.org/pubs/Reframing_Family_Abduction.pdf.
[†] Haviv and Brodsky, "Re-Framing Family Abduction."

Can you imagine how the abducting parent and child(ren) must live? The abducting parent and the abducted child live on the run and in isolation to prevent being located. No friends, no permanent residence. The children wonder what happened to their left-behind parent. They may be deprived of education to avoid being detected or located through school records. The abducting parent and the abducted child live in a transient world in hiding and on the run. They are, in essence, on the run from the law. The following are testimonies from children who were the victims of an FCA:[*]

We went underground for six months and changed our names. My father worked nights and home schooled me. We were living in a motel and I stayed inside with no outside contact & I knew there was something wrong, but I spoke up for him in court, so my dad said I was agreeing with him taking me. And that was that.

—Charlene, abducted at ages seven and eight

If I close my eyes, I can still see my mother waving goodbye to us from the parking lot of our apartment building as we watched her from the rear window of my father's truck. Little did we know that it would be close to a year before we would see her again.

—Kelly, abducted at age nine

My recollection is fuzzy about what we were told had happened to our mom. I think at first we were told we were going on vacation with our dad, and then later, I believe he told us that our mom had died & meanwhile, back in Pittsburgh, our poor mother was going crazy trying to find us.

—Sam, abducted at age six

The hardest thing to deal with was that my father had led me to feel that my mother was somehow dangerous to me. He couldn't get over his feelings about the divorce and let them go, and dragged me into his problems and tried to make me feel guilty about wanting a normal life that included a mom.

—Sarah Cecile, abducted at age four

The situation was long and grueling, and I found myself trying to become anything but the person I was now, and glancing back at the door, hoping that someone would find me and take me back to my father. I used to think that if I could just make it through one more day in the life I was in, that they would find me the next.

—Jen, abducted at age seven

[*] Testimonies taken from StopFamilyAbductionsNow.com

Law Enforcement's Attitude

Although all fifty states have parental kidnapping statutes, with some clas-sified as felonies and others as misdemeanors, most FCAs may be looked upon by law enforcement as being a nonpolice function (i.e., family dispute, family problem, civil in nature, and civil custodial battles). With that being said, history and experience tell us that many law enforcement agencies see FCAs as a low-priority response and investigation, and give very little or no credence to the circumstances or to the abduction itself.

Such policies, procedures, or practices by law enforcement are in direct conflict with the National Child Search Assistance Act which states, "no law enforcement agency within the State establishes or maintains any policy that requires the observance of any waiting period before accepting a missing child or unidentified person report." The Act does not discriminate against FCAs, nor does the Act distinguish FCAs from any other missing child response that is reported to law enforcement. Only the first responder/inves-tigator and the agency they represent do!

A recent poll was taken that showed that an overwhelming proportion of Americans consider stranger abductions to be more dangerous than, or equally as dangerous as, family abductions.* With this in mind, it would behoove the first responder/investigator and the department they represent to take FCA calls, responses, and investigations seriously. Society and par-ents do, so shouldn't you as the first responder?

Protect yourself and your agency from embarrassment and potential civil litigation. Treat all missing child reports the same. Respond in accor-dance with the National Child Search Assistance Act and your department's policies and procedures.

Refer to Chapter 18, "International Family Child Abduction (IFCA)," Table 18.1, for characteristics, traits, and a comparison of family abductions and international family abductions. For additional characteristics and traits of family abductions, refer to Appendices F and J.

---

* Poll conducted by Harris Interactive, Inc. in January 2004 for the Polly Klaas Foundation: http://www.stopfamilyabductionsnow.org/1_exec_sum_poll.html

International Family Child Abduction (IFCA)

18

One thousand children will be victims of an international family child abduction per year. Additionally, a recent prediction is that in the future international family abduction will* grow by 20% per year, due to the number of foreigners immigrating into the US. In addition research illustrates that more than 150,000 US residents marry foreign citizens each year.

National Incidence Studies of Missing, Abducted, Runaway, and Thrownaway Children (NISMART-2) definitions were used in this book for missing children, but NISMART-2 does not define an IFCA. For the purpose of this book the following definition will be used to define an IFCA:[†]

> International parental kidnapping encompasses taking, retaining, or concealing a child outside the country in which the child normally resides by a parent, his or her agent, or other person in derogation of another's parental rights, including custody and visitation rights. These rights may arise by operation of law, by legally binding agreement of the parties, or by court order.

US Attorney General John Ashcroft is quoted as saying, "The abduction of a child is a tragic and traumatic event. It is also a serious crime. When the abductor is a parent and the child is taken to another country, the emotional trauma to the child and left-behind parent can be great, as can the challenge to law enforcement."[‡]

What does the law enforcement community know about this type of abduction? When such abductions occur, to whom does the first responder/investigator turn? Who does the detective turn to when they get the case? What is the response to the demand by the left-behind parent for action to be taken? Who does the prosecutor turn to when the officer, detective, or

---

* US Department of Justice, *A Law Enforcement Guide on International Parental Kidnapping* (Washington, DC: Office of Juvenile Justice and Delinquents Prevention, October 2002).

† Janet Chiancone, Linda Girdner, and Patricia Hoff, "Issues in Resolving Cases of International Child Abduction by Parents," US Department of Justice, Office of Juvenile Justice and Delinquency Prevention, *OJJP Juvenile Justice Bulletin*, December 2001.

‡ US Department of Justice, *A Law Enforcement Guide on International Parental Kidnapping*, 2002.

the chief wants guidance in this kidnapping? What do any of these criminal justice officials know about the criminal or civil procedure when it comes to the investigation, seeking a warrant, prosecuting, and most of all the locating and recovering of a child who has been abducted or kidnapped by one of their parents and taken out of the United States?

In the previous chapter you learned about family child abductions. In this chapter we will discuss international family child abductions (IFCA), a direct derivative of FCAs. All of the state and federal statutes that were discussed regarding FCAs would most likely apply to IFCAs, but IFCAs involve additional federal statutes. The characteristics and traits of IFCAs may have the same or similar characteristics and traits as FCAs, but also have different family dynamics, due to cultural and religious differences.

IFCAs are very difficult cases for law enforcement agencies and are possibly the least well known. As an example, how many law enforcement agencies, prosecutors or local judges have any knowledge of The Hague Convention? In the examples available, very few. Probably the only criminal justice practitioner with such knowledge would be a federal agency (i.e., Federal Bureau of Investigations [FBI], US State Department, etc.).

IFCA is not taught in any police academy, and not likely to be taught in any in-service training. So, who does law enforcement turn to when an IFCA is committed in their jurisdiction? IFCA is a federal offense (International Parental Kidnapping Crime Act of 1993, refer to Chapter 4), so it is logical that the Federal Bureau of Investigations (FBI) would participate in any IFCA. The FBI, once notified, will either be the lead law enforcement agency or act as consultants.

Another resource that could assist any law enforcement agency in these IFCAs is the National Center for Missing and Exploited Children (NCMEC).

The NCMEC is a multifaceted organization available to any law enforcement agency in any missing and exploited child case, *at no cost*. It has a specific division that will assist any agency that has an IFCA. The International Section of NCMEC will advise, consult, and if need be walk any agency through an IFCA from the beginning of an investigation, warrant issuing, prosecuting, recovery, and reunification of the child with the left-behind parent.

The processes and procedures to recover a child from abroad are very complex and difficult because laws and treaties of other countries are involved. One of the most important ways that NCMEC can assist an agency involved in an IFCA is in the proper protocol and procedural process of The Hague Convention Act (refer to Chapter 4).

Inadequate Response Opinions from the Left-Behind Parent

Research shows that left-behind parents (victims) of IFCAs will have a high probability of dissatisfaction with the law enforcement response to their request for assistance, investigation, prosecution, and recovery of their abducted child. Left-behind parents expressed the following types of dissatisfaction:[*]

- "they received little or no assistance from the first law enforcement official they spoke with."
- "unsatisfactory response included being told that the child had to be missing for a prescribed period of time before police could take action."
- "that the police could not do anything unless there was evidence that the child had left the state."
- "law enforcement officials would not take information about their cases because the officials saw the abduction as a domestic situation."
  - It should be noted here that this is contrary to the National Child Search Assistance Act (42 U.S.C. 5779 and 5780, section (1) "Ensure that no law enforcement within the State establishes or maintains any policy that requires the observance of any waiting period before accepting a missing child or unidentified person report...."
- Many law enforcement agencies clearly were uninformed regarding the National Child Search Assistance Act, which mandates that law enforcement must enter the description of a missing child in the National Crime Information Center (NCIC) Missing Person File without a waiting period.
- Delayed response by law enforcement may have contributed to the success of abductions.
- Many law enforcement officials seemed unaware of their obligation to investigate the whereabouts of the abductor and child.
- At the other end of the spectrum are those law enforcement officials who responded immediately, offering support and referring parents to additional resources. Although present in only a minority of cases, this quick response clearly made a difference in how parents viewed the investigation and gave them confidence in the overall law enforcement effort.

The left-behind parent's vigilance and determination to search for their abducted child can be one of the most significant, persistent, and driving factors in locating and recovering their child. The extrovert family[†] will be persistent in a continuous effort to exert any private or public pressure on the investigating department to recover their child. The only way the responding department can dispel any of the previously mentioned perceptions is to take IFCAs seriously and respond and investigate the case to their utmost

---

[*] Janet Chiancone, Linda Girdner, and Patricia Hoff, December 2001.
[†] David Smart's definition of introvert and extrovert families; see Chapter 3.

ability. This includes dedicating the resources and manpower that they have available, immediately getting the FBI involved, and immediately contacting NCMEC for assistance and resources.

Local and State Police Agency Obstacles and IFCA

Local and state police encounter the following types of obstacles in IFCA cases.

- Lack of knowledge of the following:
  - IFCA and its complexity
  - Federal laws
  - The Hague Convention Treaty[*]
    - What countries are treaty partners of the United States?
    - When is removal or retention "wrongful" under The Hague Convention?
    - What is the return obligation, and are there any exceptions?
    - What is a Central Authority?
  - Foreign government criminal and civil laws
  - Foreign country customs, policies, and practices
  - Arrest, extradition, prosecution, locating abducted child, recovery of abducted child, and reunification
- Working in conjunction with the following:
  - Federal law enforcement agencies
  - Foreign law enforcement agencies
  - US State Department
- State and local prosecutors may forego criminal charges for these reasons:[†]
  - The cost involved in seeking international extradition of the fugitive abducting parents
  - Translating legal documents
  - Paying to transport the abductor and escort officers back to the United States

---

[*] "Family Abduction: Prevention and Response," National Center for Missing and Exploited Children (NCMEC), 2009.
[†] "A Report to the Attorney General on International Parental Kidnapping," Subcommittee on International Child Abduction of the Federal Agency Task Force on Missing and Exploited Children and the Policy Group on International Parental Kidnapping, April 1999, https://www.ncjrs.gov/pdffiles1/ojjdp/189382.pdf

Why the FBI and NCMEC?

First responders/investigators should immediately contact their local FBI office and NCMEC for assistance.

When a child is abducted from or wrongfully detained outside of the United States, state and local law enforcement and the left-behind parent and their advocates naturally turn to the federal government for help. The FBI is the law enforcement agency tasked with investigating international parental kidnapping cases under federal law.

We know from police experience and missing children studies that time is of the essence during any missing child's incident. We know that it takes, on average, two hours for a parent to report their child missing. We know that 74% of the children who are abducted by a stranger are murdered within three hours of their abduction. We know that it takes an average of five hours for a department to enter a missing child into the NCIC. And we also know that it takes an average of six and a half hours for an AMBER Alert to be activated.[*]

Through police experience and studies of IFCA, we know that the offender has most probably planned the abduction and the means to immediately get the child out of the country. IFCAs are time sensitive. It is imperative that the first responders immediately classify a victim of an IFCA and coordinate local, state, and federal agencies to recover the child and abductor before they leave the United States. If the offender is successful in getting out of the United States, it will be difficult to locate and recover the abducted child from another country.

Entering the offender and abducted child into NCIC immediately and getting the FBI and NCMEC involved may prevent the offender from successfully leaving the country. The FBI has more authority and resources immediately available to prevent an offender of an IFCA from leaving the country. However, they cannot use these resources if they are not requested to do so by the first responder/investigator. The FBI can assist by doing the following:

- Assuming federal jurisdiction
- Issuing a federal unlawful flight to avoid prosecution warrant
- Contacting other federal agencies
- Contacting all US debarkation sites, with a be-on-the-lookout (BOLO) for the offender and abducted child

[*] National Center for Missing and Exploited Children (NCMEC) and Kenneth A. Hanfland, Robert D. Keppel, and Joseph G. Weis, "Case Management for Missing Children Homicide Investigation," Christine O. Gregoire, Attorney General of Washington and US Department of Justice Office of Juvenile Justice and Delinquency Prevention, 1997.

Low Priority

As pointed out in the beginning of this chapter, law enforcement may give family child abductions low priority in their response and investigations. IFCAs are no different. The first responder/investigator may perceive IFCAs as being complicated (they are), and will most likely have no idea as to the proper protocol, laws, or procedures that have to be followed in IFCA incidents. Law enforcement may not prevent an IFCA from occurring, but police involvement in their initial response may stop a parent from leaving the country with the child.

So, what are some of the reasons to categorize a IFCA as a low priority? Recent research and data suggests that IFCAs are given a low priority response and classification by law enforcement for the following reasons:

- Lack of knowledge and expertise in this type of crime
- Lack of resources (available or unavailable) that will be contributed to this type crime
- Cost (the average cost just to the left-behind parent is $10,000– $270,000). One can only imagine what it would cost the taxpayer for an all-out response, investigation, recovery, and reunification of a child.

It should be noted that the cost to get NCMEC immediately involved in an IFCA is *zero*. NCMEC will assist any department in an IFCA at no cost and will walk the department through any process or consult with them in what steps to take in the investigation, in The Hague Convention procedural matters, and so on.

When an abducted child is classified as an IFCA, law enforcement should immediately kick the response and investigation into high gear and enter the abductor and abducted child into NCIC and contact the FBI for assistance. Time is of the essence and any unreasonable delay will put the abducted child at risk of being removed from the country. Once the abducted child is removed from the country, the federal government has limited power to respond to international abductions once the abductor and child reach a foreign country[*]

Taking action without delay and promptly entering the missing child and the abductor into NCIC will improve the chances for detecting and detaining the missing child and abductor in the United States. Every effort by the First Responder should be made to prevent the abducted child and abductor from leaving the U.S. due to, "As few as 24 percent of all children abducted abroad

---

[*] "A Report to the Attorney General on International Parental Kidnapping," April 1999.

are ever returned to the United States."[*] Once the abducted child and abductor get out of the U.S. it will be extremely hard to get the abducted child back to the left-behind-parent.

How important is it for the first responder/investigator to immediately enter an abducted child of an IFCA into NCIC? A quote from "A Report to the Attorney General on International Parental Kidnapping"[†] is worth noting:

> In the United States, absent a criminal warrant or facts supporting probable cause to arrest, it is unlikely that an abduction in progress can be stopped and a child intercepted. However, if a child is identified at a land border or at an airport in the United States as a result of an NCIC inquiry, FBI and FIS personnel may detain the child at least temporarily, even if there is no criminal warrant for the abductor, pending questioning of the suspected abductor to determine whether the International Parental Kidnapping Crime Act (IPKCA) or Fugitive Felon Act statute is being violated. If the person accompanying the child is ultimately detained on this basis, agents and inspectors may be able to detain the child temporarily until the relevant State authorities arrive. If, upon further investigation, the facts do not support a violation of IPKCA or the Fugitive Felon Act by the person accompanying the child, there is no basis under Federal criminal law to continue to detain the child.

The Victim

Can you imagine what an abducted or wrongfully retained child of an IFCA must experience—the fear, anguish, and lifelong mental and physical scars? One would assume being abducted by a family member in the United States is tragic enough, but to be abducted and then taken to a country of which the victim has no knowledge? The victim child of an IFCA is wrested from a familiar life, cut off from one parent, and thrust involuntarily into a new world. IFCAs take an emotional toll on all involved—the child, the left-behind parent, the estranged abducting parent, and the rest of the family.

An immediate response, classification, and notifications to proper federal agencies for assistance may prevent anguish for the victim of IFCA. But you may also prevent the abducted child from being removed from the United States.

Table 18.1 is a comparison of the high-probability characteristics of a child victim of family child abduction (FCA) and IFCA.

---

[*] A Law Enforcement Guide on International Parental Kidnapping: http://www.scribd.com/doc/51536529/A-Law-Enforcement-Guide-on-International-Parental-Kidnapping, p. 15.
[†] "A Report to the Attorney General on International Parental Kidnapping," April 1999.

Table 18.1 Family Child Abduction and International Family Child Abduction Victim Characteristics Comparison

Family Child Abduction[a]	International Family Child Abduction[b,c]
Age : Birth to 11 years	Age: Birth to 12 years
Average Age: 5 years	Average Age: 5 years
Gender: Male/Female	Gender: Male/Female
Race: White	Race: Same as abductor
Family structure: Single parent	Family structure: Married/Single parent
Abductor: Father	Abductor: Father
Abductor's age: 30–40 years	Age: 25–35 years
Child taken out of state: No	Child taken out of country: Yes
Duration of time missing: 24 hours–1 month	Duration of time missing: More than 6 months
Nationality: American	Nationality of abductor: Citizen of the country to which the child is taken

[a] Heather Hammer, Daniel Finkelhor, and Andrea Sedlack, "Child Abduction by Family Members: National Estimates and Characteristics," National Incidence Studies of Missing, Abducted, Runaway, and Thrownaway Children (NISMART–2) series, Washington, DC: US Department of Justice, Office of Justice Programs, Office of Juvenile Justice and Delinquency Prevention, October 2002.

[b] Janet Chiancone, Linda Girdner, and Patricia Hoff, December 2001.

[c] Linda Girdner, Janet Chiancone, and Janet Johnston, "International Child Abductors: Profile of the Abductors Most Likely to Succeed," paper presented at the Second World Congress on Family Law and the Rights of Children and Youth, June 3, 1997, San Francisco, CA.

The Abductor

The abductor may have ties and support from their native country. The abduction will most likely be planned and premeditated. The abduction may occur before or after a divorce decree or occur during a court-ordered visitation. Male abductors have a tendency to abduct a child before the decree and female abductors after a decree has been granted.

Refer to Appendices F and K for additional characteristics of IFCAs.

Nonfamily Child Abduction (NFCA)

19

58,200 children will be victims of nonfamily child abductions per year.[*]
114,600 children will be victims of attempted nonfamily child abductions per year
40% of the nonfamily child abductions are not reported.

The National Incidence Studies of Children Abducted By Family Members (NISMART-2) defines nonfamily child abduction as follows:[†]

(1) An episode in which a nonfamily perpetrator takes a child by the use of physical force or threat of bodily harm or detains the child for a substantial period of time (at least one hour) in an isolated place by the use of physical force or threat of bodily harm without lawful authority or parental permission, or

(2) an episode in which a child younger than fifteen or mentally incompetent, and without lawful authority or parental permission, is taken or detained or voluntarily accompanies a nonfamily perpetrator who conceals the child's whereabouts, demands ransom, or expresses the intention to keep the child permanently.

- **Stereotypical kidnapping:** A nonfamily abduction perpetrated by a slight acquaintance or stranger in which a child is detained overnight, transported at least fifty miles, held for ransom or abducted with intent to keep the child permanently, or killed. (See Chapter 20.)
- **Stranger:** A perpetrator whom the child or families do not know, or a perpetrator of unknown identity. (See Chapter 20.)
- **Slight acquaintance:** A nonfamily perpetrator whose name is unknown to the child or family prior to the abduction and whom the child or family did not know well enough to speak to, or a recent

[*] Daniel Finkelhor, Heather Hammer, and Andrea Sedlack, "Nonfamily Abducted Children: National Estimates and Characteristics," National Incidence Studies of Missing, Abducted, Runaway, and Thrownaway Children (NISMART–2) series, Washington, DC: US Department of Justice, Office of Justice Programs, Office of Juvenile Justice and Delinquency Prevention, October 2002.

[†] NISMART-2 Nonfamily Abductions: National Estimates and Characteristics: http://www.missingkids.com/en_US/documents/NISMART-22_nonfamily.pdf

acquaintance who the child or family have known for less than six months, or someone the family or child have known for longer than six months but seen less than once a month.

It is universally known that the *first line of defense* in preventing any child abduction is educating parents and children against abductions, but this alone will not prevent the child sexual predator from striking.

As stated, the best way to prevent any harm to our children is to educate them. But even with all the education on child safety and abduction prevention, we know that child abductions cannot be prevented. So the *second line of defense* for child abductions is speed, organization, and coordination (SOC) by law enforcement in the response, classification, and recovery of the missing child.

NFCA is a frightening crime for the victims, parents, and family. The panic, fear, and helplessness that come with the knowledge that a child is missing or has been abducted are overwhelming. Responding to an NFCA will be a challenge for the first responder/investigator and they will have to deal with the panic and the feeling of helplessness that will be expressed by the parents, friends, and family. The first responder/investigator will have to have a plan of action at the time they receive the call and when they knock on the door of a panic-driven parent.

A Parent's Worst Fear

In one missing child study, nearly 75% of parents said they feared their children might be abducted. One-third of parents said this was a frequent worry—a degree of fear greater than that held for any other concern, including car accidents, sports injuries, or drug addiction.[*]

Nothing is scarier for a parent than to have their child go missing. Here are a few examples:

- Before a child runs away from home, the parents, in most cases, have noticed a change in the behavior of the child. The parents in this type of missing child case are worried about the safety and well-being of the child, but to some degree know they *may be* safe.
- When a parent takes a child in the case of a family child abduction, the left-behind parent will be in a panic and in a helpless state of

[*] 1998 study of parents' worries by pediatricians at the Mayo Clinic in Rochester, Minnesota. Yellow Dyno, Protecting Children from Predators, Abduction Facts, Study of Parents Worries, by Co-Author Dr. Gunnar Stickler, Pediatrician at Mayo Clinic in Rochester, Minnesota, 1998.

mind, with deep concern as to whether they will ever see their child again, but to some degree know they *may be* safe.

- When it comes to an international family child abduction, the left-behind parent has a greater fear that they will never see their child again than they would in a family child abduction. They perceive that the task of getting their child back will be lengthy and difficult, but they too must feel that their child is *somewhat* safe.

- The involuntary missing, injured, or lost child or a child on a benign episode must be a terrible episode for a parent to experience. In these circumstances they do not know where their child is or what has happened to them. Have they been hurt in some way, are they out there all alone, or has someone taken their child? This must be the closest thing to an NFCA and a stereotypical stranger child abduction scenario that a parent can relate to. They just don't know the whereabouts or level of safety of their missing child.

What Is Known About NFCA?

Research studies and police experience have identified components of NFCAs that may assist the first responder/investigator:[*,†,‡,§]

- NFCAs are short term in nature, and most often less than three hours in duration from abduction through assault and release.

- Acquaintance abductions are not necessarily crime episodes of long duration or ones in which a child is officially declared missing. They could involve episodes during which a child was transported a short distance or into a building or car in order to accomplish a sexual assault or robbery.

[*] David Finkelhor and Richard Ormrod, "Kidnapping of Juveniles: Patterns from NIBRS," US Department of Justice, Office of Justice Programs, Office of Juvenile Justice and Delinquency Prevention, Juvenile Justice Bulletin, June 2000; Http://www.missingkids.com/en_US/documents/kidnapping_juveniles.pdf

[†] David Finkelhor and Richard Ormrod, "Homicides of Children and Youth," US Department of Justice, Office of Justice Programs, Office of Juvenile Justice and Delinquency Prevention, Juvenile Justice Bulletin, October 2001: https://www.ncjrs.gov/pdffiles1/ojjdp/187239.pdf

[‡] NISMART-2 Nonfamily Abductions: National Estimates and Characteristics: http://www.missingkids.com/en_US/documents/NISMART-22_nonfamily.pdf

[§] Investigating Potential Child Abduction Cases: A Developmental Perspective, by Wayne D. Lord, PhD, Monique C. Boudreaux, PhD, and Kenneth B. Lanning, MS, " FBI Bulletin 70, no. 4 (April 2001): http://www.fbi.gov/stats-services/publications/law-enforcement-bulletin/2001-pdfs/apr01leb.pdf

- Acquaintance abduction involves a comparatively high percentage of juvenile perpetrators.
- Acquaintance abduction victimizes youth ages twelve to seventeen years.
- Acquaintance abduction is the predominate problem for teenagers.
- The largest percentage of victims is female.
- NFCAs are more often associated with other crimes (especially sexual and physical assault).
- Acquaintance abductions are more likely to occur at a home or residence, but a substantial number also occur in outside locations.
- Acquaintance abductions have the highest percentage of injured victims.
- Acquaintance abductions at schools are unusual.
- Acquaintance abductions are, for the most part, weaponless crimes.
- Acquaintance abductions are more likely to occur during evening hours.
- Most children are abducted by people they know: family friends, adult associates, babysitters, boyfriends/ex-boyfriends, classmates, and neighbors.
- Offenders were usually males, and the great majority of them are under age thirty.

Primary Nonfamily Child Abduction Motives[*][†]

- Female victims
  - Sexual assault
  - Seek revenge for being spurned
  - Forced reconciliation
  - Prevent parents from breaking up their relationship
  - Gang activity
- Male victims
  - Robbery
  - Assault
- Male and female victims
  - Gang activity
    - Intimidation
    - Recruitment
  - Retaliation

[*] Finkelhor, Hammer, and Sedlack, October 2002.
[†] Finkelhor and Ormrod, June 2000.

Difference between Nonfamily Child Abductions and Stereotypical Child Abductions

NFCAs and stereotypical nonfamily child abductions are similar in motives and characteristics, but differences exist between them: NFCAs involve lesser degrees of force, movement, and detention than stereotypical nonfamily child abductions, which involve higher degrees of force and movement, and often result in murder.[*]

Refer to Chapter 20, "Stereotypical Stranger Child Abduction (SSCA)," Table 20.1, for a comparison of the characteristics of nonfamily child abductions and stereotypical stranger child adductions. For additional characteristics of nonfamily child abductions, refer to Appendices F and L.

---

[*] National Incident-Based Reporting System (NIBRS): The US Department of Justice is supplanting its Uniform Crime Report (UCR) system with the more comprehensive NIBRS data. NIBRS is far from a national system, but holds great promise.

Stereotypical Stranger Child Abduction (SSCA) 20

40 to 170 children will be victims of stereotypical nonfamily child abductions per year.[*]/[†]

Forty percent of the victims of stereotypical abductions are killed, and another 4% are not recovered.[‡]

National Incidence Studies of Missing, Abducted, Runaway, and Thrownaway Children (NISMART-2) defines stereotypical nonfamily child abduction as follows:

- **Stereotypical abduction:** A nonfamily abduction perpetrated by a slight acquaintance or stranger in which a child is detained overnight, transported at least fifty miles, held for ransom or abducted with intent to keep the child permanently, or killed.
- **Stranger:** A perpetrator whom the child or family does not know, or a perpetrator of unknown identity.
- **Slight acquaintance:** A nonfamily perpetrator whose name is unknown to the child or family prior to the abduction and whom the child or family did not know well enough to speak to, or a recent acquaintance whom the child or family have known for less than six months, or someone the family or child have known for longer than six months but have seen less than once a month.

Time is of the essence. How true that is when it comes to responding to any missing child, but more so when the child is abducted by a stranger.

---

[*] K. M. Brown, R. D. Keppel, J. G. Weis, and M. E. Skeen, "Case Management for Missing Children Homicide Investigation: Report II," Bob McKenna, Attorney General of Washington & US Department of Justice, Office of Juvenile Justice and Delinquency Prevention, May 2006.

[†] Peter Bellmio, "Counting Missing and Exploited Children in the United States," Peter Bellmio is the senior policy advisor to the president of the National Center for Missing and Exploited Children.

[‡] Brigitte M. Johnson, Raymond G. Miltenberger, Peter Knudson, Kristin Egemo-Helm, Pamela Kelso, Candice Jostad, and Linda Langley, "A Preliminary Evaluation of Two Behavioral Skills Training Procedures for Teaching Abduction-Prevention Skills to Schoolchildren," *Journal of Applied Behavior Analysis* 39, no. 1 (2006): 25–34.

When a parent becomes aware that their child is missing, and by the time they contact the police, two crucial hours could have elapsed. To further emphasize that time is of the essence to a missing child, a recent study has shown that it takes police departments an average of five hours to enter a missing child into the National Crime Information Center (NCIC) after they have been reported missing.* Therefore, these documented time delays of two hours to call the police and an average of five hours to enter a child into NCIC, can be an abducted child's worst enemy. *Time is of the essence* to get a response and investigation up and running. If the child has been abducted by a stranger, there is a high probability that the abducted child will be killed within three hours.

Consider this scenario: You are the first responder/investigator who receives the call regarding a missing child. Considering the previous paragraph, research tells us that after a parent realizes that their child is missing, it takes on the average two hours for a parent to contact the police. On your arrival you will most likely not know what type of missing child incident you have. You will most likely have a hysterical parent that you will have to interview. You will have to determine, through vague information, the classification of missing child to which you have responded. Research tells us that if the child has been abducted by a stranger, the abducted child will have a high probability of being killed within the first three hours. You have less than one hour of opportunity to locate the child alive.

News Media

When we look back on the SSCAs of Elizabeth Smart, Carlie Brucia, and Jessica Lunsford we can see how the departments investigating these cases were suddenly tossed into the national limelight. Departments that have experienced an SSCA and the unpredictable 24/7 news blitz, for the most part handled themselves professionally. The news media will become part of any SSCA. It is news and a department that handles a high-profile SSCA must be prepared for the news media blitz.

Department Resources

Stereotypical stranger child abduction responses can and most likely do drain a police agency's financial, personnel, and related resources. SSCAs will test any department's capability to respond, communicate, investigate,

---

* Thomas Hargrove, "Missing: Children at Risk," study of police and National Child Search Assistance Act, Scripps Howard News Service, May 2005.

coordinate, recruit a variety of resources (civilian and law enforcement), and bring closure to such missing children cases. The public image of a department will pay dearly for a response or investigation that is not handled appropriately and where every resource that is humanly available to the first responder/investigator is not sought or used. Are you or your department prepared for such an event?

Primary Stereotypical Stranger Child Abduction Motives

Any abduction and its components are complicated. As the first responder/ investigator, you will have to determine what type of missing child case you are dealing with (in the least amount of time) and what the motive might be for the abduction. Abduction motives were discussed in Chapter 5. Statistics bear out that the two primary motives in an SSCA are as follows:

- Sexual: children abducted primarily for the sexual gratification of the offender.[*]
- Killing: For some individuals, the act of killing itself brings arousal or gratification.

Table 20.1 provides a comparison of the characteristics of Nonfamily Child Abductions and Stereotypical Stranger Child Abductions.
Refer to Appendices F and M for additional characteristics of SSCA.

[*] David Finkelhor (PhD), University of New Hampshire Professor and Associate of Office of Juvenile Justice and Delinquency Prevention Crimes Against Children Research Center identified the Developmental Perspective Theory in "The Victimization of Children: A Developmental Perspective," *American Journal of Orthopsychiatry* 65, no. 2 (1995): 177–193.

Table 20.1 Comparison of NFCA and SSCA Characteristics[a]

Nonfamily Child Abduction	Stereotypical Stranger Child Abduction
High Probability	High Probability
Victim	Victim
Age: 12–17 years	Age: 6–15 years
	Average 11.5 years
Gender: Female	Gender: Female
Race: Black/White	Race: White
Abductor/Perpetrator	Abductor/Perpetrator
Age: 13–29 years	Age: 13–29 years
	Average age: 27 years
Gender: Male	Gender: Male
Race: Black/White	Race: White
Relationship: Long-term acquaintance, friend, stranger	Relationship: Stranger, slight acquaintance
More than one abductor/perpetrator: No	More than one abductor/perpetrator: Yes and no
Child's last known location: Street, park, wooded area, other yard, or home	Child's last known location: Street, park, wooded area, other yard, or home
Victim taken, moved, or detained: Yes	Victim taken, moved, or detained: Yes
How taken or moved: Carried away, walked away, by vehicle	How taken or moved: Carried away, walked away, by vehicle
Victim taken to: Abductor's car or home	Victim taken to: Abductor's car or home
Victim moved more than 50 miles from last known location: No	Victim moved more than 50 miles from last known location: No
Duration of abduction: Less than 3 hours	Duration of abduction: 3 to less than 24 hours
Outcome of abduction: Returned alive, sexually assaulted	Outcome of abduction: Returned alive, sexually assaulted

[a] Finkelhor, Hammer, and Sedlack, October 2002; Brown, Keppel, Weis, and Skeen, May 2006.

Infant Abduction (IA) 21

There were 271 infant abductions reported in United States from 1983 to 2010.[*]
There were 128 infant abductions from healthcare facilities from 1983 to 2010.[†]
There were 143 infant abductions from homes and other places from 1983 to 2010.

There is no commonly accepted definition of an infant abduction. For the purposes of this book the criteria from the National Center for Missing and Exploited Children (NCMEC) will be used.[‡]

- **NCMEC criteria for an infant abduction:** A case must involve an infant, six months of age or younger, who is abducted by a nonfamily member.
- **Nonfamily member:** A person who is not child's parent or legal guardian or otherwise related to the child.

This chapter is dedicated to infant abduction (IA). The reason IA is separated from the rest of the abductions is due to the fact they are rare and that there are very limited suspects involved in this type of abduction. The characteristics and motives for IAs are limited to a specific type of abductor. The contents of this chapter will help the first responder/investigator and the agency they represent to be better prepared for the day they have an IA.

The reduction in the number of IAs from hospital facilities is probably due to increased security and enhanced policies and procedures. With these measures being taken by hospital personnel, IAs have dramatically declined.[§] Another reason for the decline of IAs in hospital settings may be due to medical advancements. The newborn child and mother do not stay in a hospital setting as long as they did a few short years ago. However, although the

---

[*] National Center for Missing and Exploited Children (NCMEC), "Newborn/Infant Abductions Statistics," December 2010.
[†] "Newborn/Infant Abductions Statistics," December 2010.
[‡] Ann Wolbert Burgess, DNSc, RN, APRN, BC, FAAN; Kathleen E. Carr, MS, RN, CPNP; Cathy Nahirny; and John B. Rabun, ACSW, "Nonfamily Infant Abductions. 1983–2006," *American Journal of Nursing* 108, no. 9 (2008).
[§] Burgess, Carr, Nahirny, and Rabun, 2008.

number of IAs has decreased in the hospital setting, the number of IAs from homes and public places has increased.

News accounts have reported that IA abductors use similar tactics (i.e., impersonating a nurse, healthcare worker, social worker, etc.). When an IA occurs in a home setting, the abductor may result to violence to abduct the infant. Some news accounts of home IAs document that the IA abductor entered an expectant mother's home, murdered the mother, and surgically removed the child. The following are examples of IAs from news agencies:

- Woman attempts infant abduction at N.C. Hospital (Durham, NC, April 2010)[*]

   A woman accused of trying to abduct an infant from a Duke University Hospital nursery told police she was trying to get a baby because she owed someone money.

   Hospital officials saw twenty-eight-year-old Tanisha Weaver attempting to take a baby out of the hospital's North Ancillary [on] April 19, reports WRAL.com. When the staff recognized that Weaver was not authorized to take the newborn, they immediately called police and detained her until authorities arrived.

   Police said Weaver brought balloons and a gift card to the newborn's mother, saying that Weaver would stay with the child while the mother went to a special luncheon in the hospital's cafeteria. As soon as the mother left the room, Weaver cut off the infant's ankle bracelet, which triggered an alarm. The suspect had a bag containing clothes for a newborn girl. Additionally, investigators said Weaver had surveyed the Parham Medical Center's maternity ward the week prior to the incident. Officials said she pretended to be a nursing student and asked about security, where the exits were located and directions to the maternity ward.

- Dad thwarts abduction: Suspect believed to be "Baby shopping" says sheriff (Prairie Creek, IN, June 2010)[†]

   A Terre Haute woman arrested Wednesday afternoon at a Prairie Creek home where two people were stabbed will be arraigned in court today on preliminary charges of attempted murder and attempted abduction.

   The Terre Haute woman is being held in the Vigo County Jail without bond on an allegation that she attacked a husband and

[*] Woman attempts infant abduction at N.C. Hospital (Durham, NC, April 2010), Private Officers News, http://privateofficernews.wordpress.com/2010/04/22/woman-caught-stealing-baby-at-nc-hospital-www-privateofficer-com/

[†] Dad thwarts abduction: Suspect believed to be "Baby shopping" says sheriff (Prairie Creek, IN, June 2010), Tribabstar.com: http://tribstar.com/local/x1703937162/Dad-thwarts-abduction-Suspect-believed-to-be-Baby-shopping-says-sheriff.

wife and tried to kidnap their newborn baby from its home. Both the husband and wife sustained multiple stab wounds and were taken to area hospitals for treatment.

Sheriff Jon Marvel said at the scene it did not appear that the victims knew the suspect prior to the attack. It is believed the suspect somehow knew an infant was at the home, Marvel said, adding police suspect that Foster was faking a pregnancy and was "baby shopping" for a newborn child.

The suspect's 4-door Kia Rio auto was parked in the victims' driveway just outside the south door of the home, just a few feet from the door where the suspect allegedly knocked and asked the wife to use the telephone. When Foster was not allowed to enter the home, she allegedly returned to her car and retrieved a pistol, which police believe she then used to force entry into the home. At some point, Marvel said, Foster grabbed a knife from somewhere in the home and started attacking the wife. The husband, who was asleep because he works a night shift, was awakened by the attack and responded to help his wife.

- Pregnant woman cut open, baby taken (Hillsboro, OR, April 2009)[*]

Authorities say a pregnant woman who was found dead in a crawl space of a suburban home had been cut open and her baby delivered from her womb.

Motive

IAs are *nontraditionally* motivated abductions. A very young child is abducted predominately by a woman to fulfill a perceived void in the offender's life.[†]

IAs do not have common motives, such as sexual gratification, profit, ransom, revenge, or power, as seen in nonfamily stranger child abductions. The abductor in an IA has a *maternal desire* as a motive.[‡]

[*] Pregnant woman cut open, baby taken (Hillsboro, OR, April 2009), KOMOnews.com: http://www.komonews.com/news/local/47236217.html

[†] Kenneth V. Lanning and Ann Wolbert Burgess, eds., "Child Molesters Who Abduct: Summary of the Case in Point Series," Office of Juvenile Justice and Delinquency Prevention, National Center for Missing and Exploited Children, March 1995, http://www.missingkids.com/en_US/publications/NC65.pdf..

[‡] Ann Wolbert Burgess and Kenneth V. Lanning, eds., "An Analysis of Infant Abductions," National Center for Missing and Exploited Children ,1995), http://www.missingkids.com/en_US/publications/NC66.pdf.

Abductor's Four Stages of IA

Stage 1: Setting the Stage and Feigning a Pregnancy

In this first phase, abductors lie about being pregnant and considerable deception is used.

The motivation to give birth to an infant is not unusual, but the act of planning and stealing a newborn is. What prompts a person to behave in such a way? Asking abductors the "why" of their act produced two broad categories of explanation.

First, the women talked of internal pressures pertinent to having an infant that are specific to the psychodynamics of the individual. These women said that they had recently lost an infant and were unable to tell people that truth. In essence a pregnancy fantasy is continued and acted out. A second reason the women gave was for external or social pressures to have an infant usually coming from a partner. Women said that they wanted to restore a failing partner relationship. The stolen infant is seen as saving a relationship. Consciously this individual wants an infant to keep a relationship. The infant is instrumental in maintaining the relationship, and there is no truly empathetic burning desire to have another child. She imagines the infant is getting reflected attention from the male and that this status and attention will reflect on her.

In this first phase of an abduction we find that abductors start to plant the idea in peoples' minds that they are going to be involved in some legitimate way with an infant in their life. Because most of the abductors are women, one of the most common methods of this involvement is feigning a pregnancy.

After the stage is set abductors begin to carry out their plan. In a feigned pregnancy the woman must change her body size to indicate a developing pregnancy, make and keep doctor's appointments for the pregnancy, tell people about the pregnancy, and prepare for maternity leave. People believe the woman and may have baby showers and give her presents.

Stage 2: Planning the Abduction

As the ninth month approaches, the individual's anxiety increases over her need to produce an infant. In this phase, abductors plan where they are going to get an infant. They begin to target and search out infants. Continuing the deceptive ploy, they devise some kind of legitimate reason for being in a setting using a false identity such as a nurse or social worker in a healthcare facility or a visiting nurse or babysitter in the home.

The abduction is not an impulsive act. They have a plan for getting away and changing the identity of the infant. This is an emotionally consuming phase. In this phase cleverness is often used in conjunction with a disguise.

Impersonation, lying, and deceit are characteristic of the abductor. Abductors impersonate nurses, lab technicians, photographers, and members of the family.

They may befriend a parent to get access to the infant or ask for assistance such as use of a telephone or glass of water.

Stage 3: The Abduction

This third phase includes the abductor entering the healthcare facility, home, or other location for the abduction. The abductor either enters unnoticed or wears a disguise to deceive people. She takes the infant and escapes to a pre-designated place. She must also explain the presence of the infant to others.

There is deliberate planning and a consuming desire to have a child regardless of consequences. Prior failed abduction attempts may increase the agitation of the abductor.

In this third phase, the abductor is very intent on getting the infant. The extensive planning of the "baby stealing" confirms the presence of an abduction scenario.

Approximately half of the IA abductors admit to deliberate planning of the abduction from as long as nine months to as short as a few hours.

Abductors rehearse and become obsessed with their plan. Those who go to the home to abduct an infant reduce the risk of chance occurrence for other people to protect the infant and mother. Thus perpetrators have some sense of their capacity to confront and overpower the parent or caretaker. Murders usually occur when the infant is being taken from someone. Home abductors were more likely to be found to carry a weapon, suggesting that murder may be a more integral part of their abduction scenario.

Violence may be part of the abductor's plan. The fact that more than one third of IA home abductions had violence associated with the act emphasizes the potential dangerousness of home abductions.

Stage 4: After the Abduction

Getting away with the crime is the goal after the abduction. This phase pertains to how well the person planned to escape the abduction scene with the infant and reenter her own social circle without having anyone challenge the legitimacy of the relationship to the infant.

The abduction act is *ego-syntonic** in that it is consonant with the immediate conscious wish of the individual. Immediately following the act there

---

* Ego-syntonic is defined as "describing those elements of a person's behavior, thoughts, impulses, drives, and attitudes that are acceptable to him or her and are consistent with the total personality," *Mosby's Medical Dictionary*, 8th ed. (St. Louis, MO: Mosby, 2009).

may or may not be genuine regret, self-reproach, or guilt. There are only a small number of abductors who expressed such feelings. Generally the infant was recovered because someone identified the abductor. When confronted by authorities, with the infant in their possession, 53% of the abductors explain that the infant is their own child.

In those situations where the infant was recovered, the abductor did not demonstrate that she planned this phase well. In addition it is usually someone within the abductor's own social network who alerts authorities.

This phase requires skill in keeping the infant without discovery, maintaining the story regarding the infant, and handling the suspicions of others. The gratification of taking the infant is noted in their open display of the child that happened in the majority of the time with these abductors. For example the abductor walked in public with the infant or showed the infant off at a neighborhood bar.

IAs in a Hospital Setting

IAs will most likely be reported to law enforcement by hospital personnel. Most obstetric institutions have security and protocol procedures in place to prevent and report IAs, and work in conjunction with the first responder/investigator.

The Response

Upon arrival at a reported IA, the first responder/investigator should immediately contact the hospital security personnel. To expedite the investigation, the first responder/investigator should work in conjunction with hospital security personnel and immediately request a copy of their policies and procedures or ask for a verbal overview of the hospital's response to an IA. Working with facility personnel will save a lot of wasted man hours for the first responder/investigator, as they seek initial information about the IA victim and witnesses.

The first responder/investigator should seek out all surveillance cameras on hospital property, maternity clinics, or in the immediate area of the abduction location, which may produce video evidence of the abduction or suspect. The abductor may have made previous visits (i.e., casing the abduction location or making a dry run or rehearsal, etc.) to the abduction location; these may have occurred several weeks prior to the abduction and may be caught on the hospital's surveillance camera.

An IA abductor may frequently visit the nursery and maternity units not only at the abducting hospital, but *at multiple facilities* prior to the abduction. First responders/investigators should ask detailed questions about [*]

---

[*] "For Healthcare Professionals: Guidelines on Prevention of and Response to Infant Abductions," National Center for Missing and Exploited Children, 2009.

- hospital procedures,
- the nursery/maternity floor layout, and
- fire exit stairwells that could be used for escape.

A good police response and investigation will include contacting other hospitals in their jurisdiction and adjoining jurisdictions to determine if the abductor visited their facility. This follow-up would include these actions:

- Interview hospital security and other personnel to determine if there was any suspicious behavior or a suspicious person that might be the IA abductor.
- Review hospital surveillance video to potentially identify an IA abductor.

Police experience shows that in many crimes, including IAs, video surveillance cameras at gas stations and convenience stores have captured suspects who entered the businesses prior to a crime to purchase items including items to assist them in accomplishing the crime; IA abductors are not exempt from doing the same thing or making prior visits to the abduction location.

It would be a good practice for the first responder/investigator to consider canvassing a three-block radius from the abduction location for such surveillance cameras. The Sarasota County Sheriff Department, during the Carlie Brucia (12/1/2004) abduction murder investigation, did just that and located a car wash owner who had surveillance cameras that had recorded her abduction and led to suspect Joseph Smith's arrest and conviction.

Getting the Information Out

Once it has been verified that an IA has occurred and the primary interviews have been completed, the first responder/investigator and the department they represent should immediately activate resources such as the following:[*]

- National Crime Information Center (NCIC) entry (in accordance with the National Child Search Assistance Act)
- A Child Is Missing Alert
- Local LOCATER or NCMEC LOCATER
- AMBER Alert
- Local newspapers and radio and TV stations

The twenty-four-hour period following an IA is particularly critical. Research has shown that one the most effective investigation strategies involves the news media (electronic and written), which is one the best

[*] Refer to Chapter 9 resources.

resources for the first responder/investigator in IAs. The more widely publicized the abduction, the more likely it is that the infant will be found. In
numerous IAs, friends, relatives, and neighbors have called police to report
the abductor after seeing a news item about the abduction.[*] The news media
has the ability to put out information on a continuous basis, alerting the public of the IA. These news stories may alert a suspicious friend or relative of
the abductor who cannot explain the sudden appearance of a new infant.
Getting the news media involved immediately and keeping them interested
in the abduction is one of the best resources that law enforcement can use.
It would be in the best interest of the abducted child and law enforcement to
solicit, use, and seek the full cooperation of the news media in IAs.

Most Common Characteristics of IAs in Hospital Settings

The following characteristics of IAs in hospital settings may assist the first
responder/investigator:

- Time of day: generally a daytime crime.
- Number of abductors: single
- Visits prior to abduction:
  - High probability: Yes
  - Asks detailed questions about procedures and unit layout.
- Abduction location
  - Mother's hospital room
  - Pediatric room
  - Nursery room
- Strategy employed by abductor
  - Verbal conning
  - Impersonating
    - Nurse
    - Lab technician
    - Healthcare provider
  - Violence, force, and weapon used during the commission of IA
    - High probability: No
- Discarded disguises of abductor or unexplained items such as the
  following:
  - Hospital gowns, scrubs, uniforms
  - Hospital identification badges
  - Wigs, etc.

[*] Burgess and Lanning, 1995; Burgess, Carr, Nahirny, and Rabun, 2008; current news articles; "Infant Abduction: It Really Happens, Natural Childbirth, November 2008, http://
childbirth.amuchbetterway.com/infant-abduction-it-really-happens/

- How abductor removes child from hospital
  - Tote bag
  - Gym bag
  - Large purse
  - Under coat
- How abductor gets out of the hospital
  - Walks out
  - Stairwells
  - Fire exits
  - Main entrance
  - Secondary entrances
  - May discard disguise (i.e., scrubs, uniform, fake ID, etc.)

IA in a Home Setting and Other Places

There is very limited research dedicated to IA, but it paints a picture that "among private home and public place abductions, there has been an increase in violence and lower infant recovery rates."[*] The trend of the primary abduction location switching from hospitals to home settings brings with it different associated crimes.

IA in hospital settings experienced very little to no use of force or violence. In fact, from 1983 to 2010, 128 of the total 271 IAs were committed in healthcare facilities. Of those 128 healthcare facility IAs, there were only 10 documented acts of violence that occurred against the mother or hospital personnel.[†] However, during the same time period in the home setting or other places, there were 143 documented IAs. Of those 143 IAs, there were 41 acts of violence that occurred against the mother and father, including murder and cesarean section performed on the mother.

Force used in IA home setting situations is most likely caused by two types of actions:

1. The parent taking appropriate action to prevent the abduction (i.e., self-defense)
2. The abductor is prepared to take whatever force necessary to succeed in the abduction including:
   a. Physical force
   b. Murder to perform a cesarean section

---

[*] "Medical News Today: Increase in Private and Public Place Infant Abductions, Research," *American Journal of Nursing*, 108, no. 9 (2008)

[†] Burgess and Lanning, 1995; Burgess, Carr, Nahirny, and Rabun, 2008; current news articles; "Infant Abduction: It Really Happens, Natural Childbirth, November 2008, http://childbirth.amuchbetterway.com/infant-abduction-it-really-happens/

Newborns who survive an IA by cesarean section can experience immediate health threats. The most crucial element can be the time between the mother's death and the baby's delivery, because the baby can suffer from loss of oxygen to the blood supply. Lack of sterile conditions during the crime can also cause sepsis, a dangerous infection.[*] The IA infant may be exposed to other and more severe health issues. In the cesarean section IA, time is of the essence for the health and safety of the infant. The first responder/investigator should move expeditiously to get information out to the public, in hopes of recovering the infant in the shortest amount of time. Getting the information out will galvanize the community to look for the infant or bring attention to a friend or family member who notices a new baby in their family, for which the abductor has no explanation.

There is limited data on the most common characteristics of IAs in home settings. A review of that limited data may assist the investigator.

Most Common Characteristics of IAs in Home Settings or Other Places[†]

The following characteristics of IAs in home settings and other places may assist the first responder/investigator:

- Time of day: generally a daytime crime
- Number of abductors: possibly more than one
- Marital status: Significantly more likely to be single while claiming to have a partner.
- Visits prior to abduction: high probability of yes
- Strategy employed by abductor to meet mother or gain entry into home
  - Usually no signs of forced entry
  - Often targets mother, not father
  - Befriends mother in hospital setting and arranges visit to mother's home
  - Impersonates a healthcare or social services professional
  - Disguised as photographer
  - Internet birth announcements
  - Online Facebook or Myspace: requests to be a friend. Newspaper birth announcements
  - Advertisement for babysitters, nannies, etc.

[*] Lisa Exkelbecker, "C-Section Abduction Crimes Are Very Rare," *Worcester Telegram & Gazette*, July 30, 2009.
[†] "For Healthcare Professionals," 2009, with For Healthcare Professionals: Guidelines on Prevention of and Response to Infant Abductions, 2009: http://www.missingkids.com/en_US/publications/NC05.pdf

- Looks for outdoor decorations to announce the infant's arrival
  - Signs (i.e., "It's a boy," "New parent," etc.)
  - Balloons (pink (girl) vs. blue (boy))
  - Large floral wreaths
  - Lawn ornaments
- Request to use telephone
- Request for a glass of water, etc.
- Violence, force, and weapon used during the commission of IA: high probability of no weapon used
- Crime scene
  - Evidence of panic or hurried retreat
  - Evidence may exist that co-offender may have been involved

Most Common Characteristics of an IA Victim

The following characteristics of IA victims in all settings may assist the first responder/investigator:

- Age: birth to six months (exception is that the home setting may be prebirth, i.e., cesarean section performed on mother)
- Gender: not usually a significant factor
- Race: usually matches the race of the offender or offender's partner
- Risk of physical injury: low to infant, but high risk to parents, including death if the abduction location is a residence

Most Common Characteristics of an IA Abductor[*]

The following characteristics of IA abductors in all settings may assist the first responder/investigator:

- Usually will preplan abduction to include the four stages of IAs
- Age: fourteen–forty-eight years (childbearing age)
- Gender: same as infant taken or that of her partner
- Sex: female; male suspects very rarely abduct babies. The main motive for the IA abductor is to get a child to raise. Men in general don't want to be burdened by the care of a child of this age.[†]

---

[*] "Infant Abduction: It Really Happens, Natural Childbirth, November 2008, http://child-birth.amuchbetterway.com/infant-abduction-it-really-happens/

[†] Randy Dotinga, "Non-Hospital Baby Abductions on the Rise," *U.S. News and World Report*, September 2008, http://health.usnews.com/health-news/family-health/childrens-health/articles/2008/09/04/non-hospital-baby-abductions-on-the-rise

- Height: average height
- Weight: often overweight
- Marital status: often married or cohabitating
- Selection of infant
  - Does not necessarily target a specific infant; frequently seizes any opportunity present
- Abductor's residence: usually lives near the abduction location
- Abduction location visits
  - Usually visits hospital site prior to abduction
  - May visit more than one hospital to assess security measures and explore infant populations

Investigative Considerations*

The first responder/investigator must consider the following issues when handling an IA case:

- Forensic: Identification of any weapon used or present during the abduction including any evidence of a cesarean section.
- Search warrants: Upon identification of a potential suspect, obtain a warrant to search for infant items including evidence of planning for the arrival of a child such as credit card purchases of infant supplies or feigning pregnancy. Also consider searching the abductor's car, telephone records, and home, looking especially for newspaper clippings that appear to follow media coverage of the abduction and/or birth announcements used by abductors to target the victim family.
- Infant identification methods
  - Footprint
  - Visual identification
  - Blood test
  - Birthmark
  - Confession by abductor

Refer to Appendices F and N for additional characteristics and traits of IAs.

---

* Burgess and Lanning, 1995.

Internet Child Abduction (ICA)

22

> With the increase of social networking, online gaming, webcams and other technologies, children today have more access to the Internet and these devices than ever before and there are more opportunities for potential offenders to engage with children....*

Unfortunately, criminal justice authorities do not collect information specifically about Internet-related crimes.† Because Internet sex crimes against minors remain a recent phenomenon, data about them have not been gathered in a national study. Internet child abductions are not exempt from this lack of tracking or data, nor is there a universally accepted Internet child abduction definition, but what limited research there is shows that "violence and abduction is rare in Internet-initiated sex crimes."‡

Millions of children and teens are on the Internet every day. They surf and interact on web pages, get their e-mail and chat with their friends, converse through social networks (i.e., Facebook), newsgroups, message boards, guest books, and third-party instant messengers. Most children and teens believe that these interactions are harmless and do not fully realize there may be a devious villain who may be surfing for them.§

Even though law enforcement has made a concerted effort since the year 2000 to monitor crimes being committed on the Internet, they still remain one of the most difficult challenges.

Let's look back to the end of the twentieth century and how law enforcement was doing business in the area of cyberspace crime. The curriculum in police academies was pretty much that of laws, first aid, report writing, physical training, felony stops, and so on. In police academies and in-service

---

* "This Week the Millionth Report of Child Sexual Exploitation Will Be Received by the Internet Tipline," News Release, Ernie Allen, president and CEO of National Center for Missing and Exploited Children (NCMEC), January 4, 2011.
† Janis Wolak, Kimberly Mitchell, and David Finkelhor, "Internet Sex Crimes against Minors: The Response of Law Enforcement," National Center for Missing and Exploited Children (NCMEC), November 2003.
‡ Janis Wolak, David Finkelhor, and Kimberly J. Mitchell, "Online 'Predators' and Their Victims: Myths, Realities, and Implications for Prevention and Treatment," *American Psychologist* 63, no. 2 (2008): 111–128.
§ Wendy McLellan, MA, LCDPII, "Characteristics of an Internet Child Predator," October 11, 2006, http://www.articlecity.com/articles/parenting/article_1289.shtml

training for veteran officers there was nothing being taught about computers and computer crimes because it did not exist as we know it today. Even today, most police academies do not train entry-level officers or do in-service training related to computer crimes, let alone Internet child abduction (ICA).

Let's look again and see how the child sex predator operated. They were there (and still are), lurking in the shadows, bushes, the parks, the school yards, libraries, churches, the public bathrooms, and all the other places where young children and teenagers hung out. They had to be more devious, secretive, and creative in their disguises and their demeanor or they stood out like a sore thumb. If someone saw such a person around children they would most likely have called the police.

Many law enforcement agencies' entry into the twenty-first century lags behind the challenges they face associated with computer technology and the crimes committed on the Internet. Yes, there are federal and state agencies and a few local agencies that have divisions that attempt to track, investigate, and prosecute computer crimes against children and they should be commended for that effort. However, due to budget cuts, personnel cuts, lack of training, court rulings rejecting attempts to control criminal activity on the Internet (i.e., pornography), and as always, the devious ways in which criminals think and design their crimes, it's very difficult to seek out the child predator who uses the computer.

Technology

In today's computer and Internet world, technology is a good thing and a bad thing. Those who developed and perfected the personal computer and expanded the electronic platforms that are now commonplace, changed how we as humans communicate with each other and do business. It was not the intention of those who developed and perfected the personal computer that this discovery should be used as a tool for those who belong to the criminal community. When a computer and the Internet are used to perform legitimate business it is positive, but when they are used to perform misdeeds, such as abducting children and committing crimes against children, it is a heinous crime against society.

The nonlethal and lethal predator of yesteryear is still out there preying on innocent children, using all the lures and tactics they have acquired through their child predator history. The child predator of yesteryear has and always will be feared by children, their parents, and law enforcement. We have learned that he is a lone deviant person, trolling areas where his unsuspected victim is likely to be found—a lone child walking to or from school.

The modern day Internet abductor is an anonymous stealth predator, always *under the radar* of those who are attempting to detect him. This stealth predator has patience and will target numerous children at one time to find one naive child. They are cunning and "groom" their potential victims over time (from 1 to 6 months).[*]

ICAs are significantly different than nonfamily child abduction (NCFAs) and SCAs. In NFCAs and SCAs you may have the *snatch and grab* or *blitz* abduction to acquire control of the victim. In ICAs, even though the goal is to have an offline meeting, the child predator will have patience and will groom the potential victim. The first responder/investigator, in their response to an ICA, should have basic knowledge of what *grooming* is. Online enticement or grooming is defined as follows:[†]

- The use of the Internet to entice, invite, or persuade a child to meet for sexual acts or to help arrange such a meeting.
  a) Sometimes it involves flattery, sometimes sympathy, other times offers of gifts, money, or modeling jobs. It can also involve all of the above over extended periods of time. That's why it's called "grooming." Experts say the short-term goal of these manipulators is for the victim to feel loved or just comfortable enough to want to meet them in person, and these people know that sometimes takes time. That's OK, they'd say, because groomers tend to have a lot of patience, and they also tend to "work" a number of targets at once, telling all of them that they are "the only one for me." You can imagine how well that can work with kids seeking sympathy, support, or validation online.[‡]

Most Common Characteristics of an ICA Victim[§]

The following characteristics of ICA victims may assist the first responder/ investigator:

- Age: thirteen–fifteen years
- Gender: female
- Race: white
- Computer location: home
- Distance traveled by victim to meet offender: ten miles or fewer

[*] Janis Wolak, JD, David Finkelhor, PhD, and Kimberly Mitchell, PhD, "Internet-Initiated Sex Crimes against Minors: Implications for Prevention Based on Findings from a National Study," *Journal of Adolescent Health* 35, no. 5 (2004): 11–20.

[†] "What Is Online Enticement," National Center for Missing and Exploited Children. http://www.missingkids.com

[‡] Ann Collier, "How to Recognize Grooming," SafeTeens.com, http://www.safeteens.com/how-to-recognize-grooming/

[§] Wolak, Finkelhor, and Mitchell, 2004.

- Voluntarily or nonvoluntarily to meet offender: Voluntary meeting

Most Common Characteristics of an ICA Offender[*]

The following characteristics of an ICA offender may assist the first responder/investigator:

- Age: twenty-six to forty years or older
- Gender: male
- Race: white
- Other characteristics
  - Act alone in crime
  - Possess child pornography

Most Common Tactics of an ICA Offender[†]

The following tactics of ICA offenders may assist the first responder/investigator:

- **Multiple potential victims:** Internet abductor may target, stalk, and groom numerous children at one time.
- **Patience:** Internet adductors are willing to spend days, weeks, months, or even years establishing the trust and friendship of a potential victim.

Investigation Considerations

The investigation of the use of computers in ICA is complex and may exceed the resources available to the first responder/investigator. When initiating an investigation that involves an ICA, law enforcement should take the following issues into consideration:[‡]

- **Jurisdiction:** Will the investigation remain local or extend to federal or state jurisdiction?

---

[*] Wolak, Mitchell, and Finkelhor, 2003.
[†] McLellan, 2006.
[‡] Daniel S. Armagh and Nick L. Battaglia, *Use of Computers in the Sexual Exploitation of Children* (Washington, DC: US Department of Justice, Office of Justice Programs, Office of Juvenile Justice and Delinquency Prevention, June 1999).

- **Expertise:** Do you have the technical expertise to deal with ICAs?
- **Equipment:** Do you have the equipment needed or the resources to obtain the necessary equipment to conduct the investigation?
- **Time/personnel:** Do you have the time and personnel to devote to this type of investigation?
- **Follow-up:** Can you perform the necessary follow-up on additional suspects and victims that may arise from the investigation?
- **Handling the computer:** If you don't know what to do, don't touch it. Get an expert!
- **Search warrant:** Every effort should be made to acquire a valid search warrant, unless an exception to the search warrant can be justified and then only in extreme circumstances. Legal issues that should be considered include the exigent circumstances exception, plain view exception, or consent exception, and there are multiple people using the computer.

Refer to Appendices F and O for additional characteristics of Internet abductions.

Human Sex Trafficking 23

A runaway from Baltimore County, Maryland, was gang raped by a group of men associated with the trafficker, who subsequently staged a "rescue." He then demanded that she repay him by working for him as one of his prostitutes. In many cases, however, the victims simply are beaten until they submit to the trafficker's demands.[*]

Human sex trafficking has been included in this book to familiarize the first responder/investigator of its prevalence in the United States. All research relating to human sex trafficking has documented that runaways, thrownaways, and on rare occasions abductions of children, are targeted by sex traffickers and become the victims of human sex trafficking.

Human sex trafficking is the most common form of modern-day slavery. Estimates place the number of its domestic and international victims in the millions, mostly females, and children enslaved in the commercial sex industry for little or no money.[*] The terms *human trafficking* and *sex slavery* usually conjure up images of young girls beaten and abused in faraway places, like Eastern Europe, Asia, or Africa. Actually, human sex trafficking and sex slavery happens in cities and towns, both large and small, throughout the United States, right in citizens' backyards.[*]

Appreciating the magnitude of the problem requires first understanding what the issue is and what it is not. Additionally, people must be able to identify the victim in common trafficking situations.[*]

Human Sex Trafficking

Many people probably remember popular movies and television shows depicting pimps as flashy dressers driving large fancy cars. More important, the women—adults—consensually and voluntarily engage in the business of prostitution without complaint. This characterization is extremely inaccurate, nothing more than fiction. In reality, the pimp traffics young women

---

[*] Amanda Walker-Rodriguez, JD and Rodney Hill, JD, "Human Sex Trafficking," *FBI Law Enforcement Bulletin*, March 2011.

(and sometimes young men) completely against their will by force or threat of force; this is human sex trafficking.

The Scope[*]

Not only is human sex trafficking slavery, it is big business. It is the fastest-growing business of organized crime and the third-largest criminal enterprise in the world.[†] The majority of sex trafficking is international, with victims taken from such places as South and Southeast Asia, the former Soviet Union, Central and South America, and other less developed areas and moved to more developed ones, including Asia, the Middle East, Western Europe, and North America.[‡]

Unfortunately, however, sex trafficking also occurs domestically.[§] The United States not only faces an influx of international victims but also has its own homegrown problem of interstate sex trafficking of minors.[¶]

Although comprehensive research to document the number of children engaged in prostitution in the United States is lacking, an estimated 293,000 American youths currently are at risk of becoming victims of commercial sexual exploitation.[**] The majority of these victims are runaway or thrown-away youths who live on the streets and become victims of prostitution.[††] These children generally come from homes where they have been abused or from families who have abandoned them. Often they become involved in prostitution to support themselves financially or to get the things they feel they need or want (like drugs).

Among children and teens living on the streets in the United States, involvement in commercial sex activity is a problem of epidemic proportion. Many girls living on the street engage in formal prostitution, and some become entangled in nationwide organized crime networks where they are trafficked nationally. Criminal networks transport these children around the

[*] Amanda Walker-Rodriguez, JD and Rodney Hill, JD, "Human Sex Trafficking," FBI Law Enforcement Bulletin, March 2011: http://www.fbi.gov/stats-services/publications/law-enforcement-bulletin/march_2011/march-2011-leb.pdf

[†] "What Is Human Trafficking?," United Nations Office on Drugs and Crime, http://www.unodc.org/unodc/en/human-trafficking/what-is-human-trafficking.html (accessed July 19, 2010).

[‡] http://www.justice.gov/criminal/ceos/trafficking.html (accessed July 19, 2010)

[§] Ibid.

[¶] Amanda Walker-Rodriguez, JD and Rodney Hill, JD, "Human Sex Trafficking," FBI Law Enforcement Bulletin, March 2011: http://www.fbi.gov/stats-services/publications/law-enforcement-bulletin/march_2011/march-2011-leb.pdf

[**] Richard J. Estes and Neil Alan Weiner, Commercial Sexual Exploitation of Children in the U.S., Canada, and Mexico, Executive Summary of the US National Study, University of Pennsylvania, 2001.

[††] Estes and Weiner, 2001.

United States by a variety of means—cars, buses, vans, trucks, or planes—and often provide them with counterfeit identification to use in the event of arrest. The average age at which girls first become victims of prostitution is twelve to fourteen years.[*] It is not only the girls on the streets who are affected; boys and transgender youth enter into prostitution between the ages of eleven and thirteen on average.[†]

The Operation[‡]

Today, the business of human sex trafficking is much more organized and violent. These women and young girls are sold to traffickers, locked up in rooms or brothels for weeks or months, drugged, terrorized, and raped repeatedly.[§] These continual abuses make it easier for the traffickers to control their victims. The captives are so afraid and intimidated that they rarely speak out against their traffickers, even when faced with an opportunity to escape.[¶]

Traffickers represent every social, ethnic, and racial group. Various organizational types exist in trafficking. Some perpetrators are involved with local street and motorcycle gangs, others are members of larger nationwide gangs and criminal organizations, and some have no affiliation with any one group or organization.[**]

Traffickers use force, drugs, emotional tactics, and financial methods to control their victims. Sometimes, the traffickers use violence, such as gang rape and other forms of abuse, to force the youths to work for them and remain under their control.[††]

Law Enforcement Response and Investigation[‡‡]

Local and state law enforcement officers may unknowingly encounter sex trafficking when they deal with homeless and runaway juveniles; criminal gang activity; crimes involving immigrant children who have no guardians;

---

[*] Walker-Rodriguez and Rodney Hill, 2011.
[†] Francis T. Miko and Grace (Jea-Hyun) Park, "Trafficking in Women and Children: The U.S. and International Response," March 18, 2002, Congressional Research Service, http://fpc.state.gov/documents/organization/9107.pdf (accessed July 19, 2010).
[‡] Walker-Rodriguez and Rodney Hill, 2011.
[§] "Violence against Women: Human Trafficking," May 18, 2011, womenshealth.gov, http://www.womenshealth.gov/ violence/types/human-trafficking.cfm (accessed July 19, 2010).
[¶] Walker-Rodriguez and Rodney Hill, 2011.
[**] Walker-Rodriguez and Rodney Hill, 2011.
[††] Walker-Rodriguez and Rodney Hill, 2011.
[‡‡] Walker-Rodriguez and Rodney Hill, 2011.

domestic violence calls; and investigations at truck stops, motels, massage parlors, spas, and strip clubs. To this end, Walker-Rodriguez and Rodney Hill offer various suggestions and indicators to help patrol officers identify victims of sex trafficking, as well as tips for detectives who investigate these crimes.

Patrol Officers/First Responders/Investigators[*]

Document suspicious calls and complaints on a police information report, even if the details seem trivial.

- Be aware of trafficking when responding to certain call types, such as reports of foot traffic in and out of a house. Consider situations that seem similar to drug complaints.
- Look closely at calls for assaults, domestic situations, verbal disputes, or thefts. These could involve a trafficking victim being abused and disciplined by a trafficker, a customer having a dispute with a victim, or a client who had money taken during a sex act.
- Locations, such as truck stops, strip clubs, massage parlors, and cheap motels, are havens for prostitutes forced into sex trafficking. Many massage parlors and strip clubs that engage in sex trafficking will have cramped living quarters where the victims are forced to stay.
- When encountering prostitutes and other victims of trafficking, do not display judgment or talk down to them. Understand the violent nature in how they are forced into trafficking, which explains their lack of cooperation. Speak with them in a location completely safe and away from other people, including potential victims.
- Check for identification. Traffickers take the victims' identification and, in cases of foreign nationals, their travel information. The lack of either item should raise concern.

Detectives or Investigators[†]

Detectives and investigators should do the following:

- Monitor websites that advertise for dating and hooking up. Most vice units are familiar with the common sites used by sex traffickers as a means of advertisement.

[*] Walker-Rodriguez and Rodney Hill, 2011.
[†] Walker-Rodriguez and Rodney Hill, 2011.

- Conduct surveillance at motels, truck stops, strip clubs, and massage parlors. Look to see if the girls arrive alone or with someone else. Girls being transported to these locations should raise concerns of trafficking.
- Upon an arrest, check cell phone records, motel receipts, computer printouts of advertisements, and tollbooth receipts. Look for phone calls from the jailed prostitute to the pimp. Check surveillance cameras at motels and toll facilities as evidence to indicate the trafficking of the victim.
- Obtain written statements from the customers; get them to work for you.
- Seek assistance from nongovernmental organizations involved in fighting sex trafficking. Many of these entities have workers who will interview these victims on behalf of the police.
- After executing a search warrant, photograph everything. Remember that in court, a picture may be worth a thousand words: nothing else can more effectively describe a cramped living quarter a victim is forced to reside in.
- Look for advertisements in local newspapers, specifically the sports sections that advertise massage parlors. These businesses should be checked out to ensure they are legitimate and not fronts for trafficking.
- Contact the local US Attorney's Office, FBI field office, or Immigration and Customs Enforcement office for assistance. Explore what federal resources exist to help address this problem.

Other Considerations*

Be aware of these other considerations:

- General indicators:
  - People who live on or near work premises
  - Individuals with restricted or controlled communication and transportation
  - Persons frequently moved by traffickers
  - A living space with a large number of occupants
  - People lacking private space, personal possessions, or financial records
  - Someone with limited knowledge about how to get around in a community
- Physical indicators:
  - Injuries from beatings or weapons

* Walker-Rodriguez and Rodney Hill, 2011.

- Signs of torture (e.g., cigarette burns)
- Brands or scarring indicating ownership
- Signs of malnourishment
- Financial and legal indicators:
  - Someone else has possession of an individual's legal or travel documents
  - Existing debt issues
  - One attorney claiming to represent multiple illegal aliens detained at different locations
  - Third party who insists on interpreting

Missing Children Resources

24

There are numerous resources that are available for law enforcement regarding missing or runaway children. The following are just a few that the author has used or have become aware of that may assist that first responder/investigator in missing or runaway children cases.

Association of Missing and Exploited Children's Organization (AMECIO)

Website: http://www.amecoinc.org

AMECO is an association of missing and exploited children's organizations in the United States and Canada founded in 1994. On AMECO's website is a list of state clearing houses that may assist officers and investigators in their response and investigation of a missing child.

Black and Missing Foundation

Website: http://www.blackandmissinginc.com

Black and Missing, Inc (BAM) has been established as a nonprofit organization whose mission is to bring awareness to missing persons of color, provide vital resources and tools to missing person's families and friends, and to educate the minority community on personal safety.

Child Quest International

Website: http://www.childquest.org

Child Quest International is a nonprofit 501(c)(3) corporation dedicated to the protection and recovery of missing, abused, and exploited children and at-risk adults. Funded through private and corporate donations and fundraising events, Child Quest never charges a fee for its services.

Child Find of America, Inc.

Website: http://www.childfindofamerica.org/Information.htm

Founded in 1980 by the mother of a missing child, Child Find has helped locate, return to a legal environment, and positively impacted the lives of thousands of children. Child Find of America Inc. is a national not-for-profit organization that:

- Locates missing children through active investigation
- Prevents child abduction through education
- Resolves incidents of parental abduction through mediation

Child Lures Prevention

Website: http://www.childluresprevention.com/

Ken Wooden founded Child Lures Prevention, and is an expert in child personal safety. Ken has authored several books in child safety including *Think First & Stay Safe! Parent Guide*. This book directly addresses lures used by abductors and molesters. A copy of the book can be obtained through the Child Lures Prevention website.

Crimes against Children Program (FBI)

Website: http://www.fbi.gov

The mission of our Crimes against Children program is threefold: first, to decrease the vulnerability of children to sexual exploitation; second, to develop a nationwide capacity to provide a rapid, effective, and measured investigative response to crimes against children; and third, to enhance the capabilities of state and local law enforcement investigators through programs, investigative assistance, and task force operations.

Federal Resources on Missing and Exploited Children: A Directory for Law Enforcement and Other Public and Private Agencies

Website: https://www.ncjrs.gov/pdffiles1/ojjdp/206555.pdf

This publication can be used by agencies and organizations involved in the safe recovery of missing children. The directory includes all the federal resources that relate to missing children.

Fox Valley Technical College, Criminal Justice Division Child Protection Training Center

Website: http://dept.fvtc.edu/childprotectiontraining/

The mission of the Child Protection Training Center is to provide needed state-of-the-art training and conference support to law enforcement, prosecutors, child protection professionals, educators, and other youth stakeholders in order to secure justice for children, reduce their victimization, and improve community protection.

The Child Protection Training Center utilizes a highly competent cadre of experienced professionals and proven trainers from law enforcement, the judiciary, prosecution, child protective services, education, medical professionals, and others capable of meeting the demand for training in the areas of child maltreatment, school and community safety, and interagency partnerships. The Child Protection Training Center builds on its seventeen-year history of providing outstanding training throughout the nation.

Guide for Implementing or Enhancing Endangered Missing Advisory

Website: http://www.ncjrs.gov/pdffiles1/ojjdp/232001.pdf

This publication is a tool that gives law enforcement and other key partners a formal action plan to safely recover missing children who do not fit the AMBER Alert criteria. It also provides a way to help recover missing adults in cases where no systematic recovery plan exists. Law enforcement can choose between AMBER Alerts and the Emergency Missing Advisory based on the individual case and the appropriate criteria.

International Centre for Missing and Exploited Children

Website: http://www.icmec.org

The International Centre of Missing and Exploited Children (ICMEC) is leading a global movement to protect children from sexual exploitation and abduction. ICMEC works to bring promise to children and families around the world by establishing global resources to find missing children and prevent child sexual exploitation; promoting the creation of operational centers worldwide based on a public–private partnership model; building an international network to disseminate images of and information about missing and exploited children; providing training to law enforcement, prosecutors, judges, legal professionals, nongovernmental organizations, and government officials; advocating and proposing changes in laws, treaties, and systems to protect children worldwide; leading a global financial coalition to eradicate commercial child pornography from the Internet; and conducting international expert conferences to build awareness, and to encourage and increase cooperation and collaboration between and among countries.

Missing Children Clearinghouse Contact Information

For individual state clearinghouses or for information on clearinghouses in other states, contact the individual state.

Every state has a missing children clearinghouse that serves as a central repository for information on missing children and provides assistance both to parents and law enforcement. State clearinghouses offer services such as case registration, information research, analytical assistance, technical support, photo and poster dissemination, and preventive and educational programs. Investigators may contact clearinghouses in other states for assistance in following up out-of-state leads.

Missing Persons: Volunteers Supporting Law Enforcement

Website: https://www.bja.gov/publications/vips_missingpersons.pdf
This publication addresses how to maximize resources by utilizing volunteers in missing person cases.

Nation's Missing Children Organization (NMCO)

Website: http://www.nmco.org
The NMCO is a nonprofit agency providing nationwide assistance to law enforcement and families of missing persons. The agency, headquartered in Phoenix, Arizona, was founded in 1994 by Kym Pasqualini who, at the age of eight, survived an attempted abduction by a knife-wielding stranger. The group provides a variety of services including advocacy, search assistance, national distribution of information related to missing persons, and various programs addressing child safety such as the child ID program. NMCO acts as a clearinghouse

of information and does not provide investigative services or employ private investigators.

National Center for Missing and Exploited Children (NCMEC)

1-800-THE-LOST

Website: http://www.missingkids.com

The NCMEC is a private, 501(c)(3) nonprofit organization that operates under congressional mandate and serves as a national clearinghouse for information and a resource center for child protection. Created in 1984, NCMEC has aided law enforcement officials in the search for over 94,000 missing children. More than 78,000 children have been returned to their families as a result. NCMEC's Internet Tipline has handled more than 180,000 reports of child sexual exploitation resulting in hundreds of arrests.

NCMEC's mission is to help prevent child abduction and sexual exploitation; help find missing children; and assist victims of child abduction and sexual exploitation, their families, and the professionals who serve them. NCMEC functions in the following ways:

- Serves as a clearinghouse of information about missing and exploited children
- Operates an Internet Tipline that the public may use to report Internet-related child sexual exploitation
- Provides technical assistance to individuals and law enforcement agencies in the prevention, investigation, prosecution, and treatment of cases involving missing and exploited children
- Assists the US Department of State in certain cases of international child abduction in accordance with The Hague Convention on the Civil Aspects of International Child Abduction
- Offers training programs to law enforcement and social service professionals
- Distributes photographs and descriptions of missing children worldwide
- Coordinates child protection efforts with the private sector
- Networks with nonprofit service providers and state clearinghouses about missing-persons cases
- Provides information about effective state legislation to help ensure the protection of children

National Runaway Switchboard

1-800-RUNAWAY

Website: http://www.1800runaway.org/

The National Runaway Switchboard is the federally designated national communication system for runaway and homeless youth. It is available twenty-four hours a day throughout the United States and its territories, including Puerto Rico, the US Virgin Islands, and Guam.

The National Runaway Switchboard services are provided through funding from and in partnership with the Washington DC–based Family and Youth Services Bureau in the Administration for Children, Youth and Families, US Department of Health and Human Services.

Operation Lookout National Center
for Missing Youth Home

Website: http://www.operationlookout.org

Operation Lookout is a charter member of the Association of Missing and Exploited Children's Organizations (AMECO). AMECO is an organization of member agencies in the United States and Canada dedicated to serving the cause of missing and exploited children, their families, and the community at large.

Polly Klaas® Foundation

Website: http://www.pollyklaas.org

The Polly Klaas Foundation is a national nonprofit that helps find missing children, prevents children from going missing, and promotes the passage of laws like AMBER Alert that help keep children safe.

Volunteers in Police Service (VIPS)

Website: http://www.policevolunteers.org

The VIPS program is part of the USA Freedom Corps (USAFC), which helps communities coordinate volunteer activities. The program's mission is to assist state and local law enforcement to utilize volunteers.

Glossary

acquaintance: An individual whom the child has seen on a regular basis or with whom the child may have had some contact, but does not necessarily know by name. Examples include babysitters, neighbors, custodians, workers at a school or in an apartment complex, children's group leaders or volunteers, teachers, coaches, cashiers at a grocery or drug store, friends of a parent, or other authority figures.

aggressive sexual solicitation: Sexual solicitations involving offline contact with the perpetrator through regular mail, by telephone, or in person, or attempts or requests for offline contact.

AMBER Alert: The AMBER Plan is a voluntary partnership between law enforcement agencies and broadcasters to activate an urgent bulletin in the most serious child-abduction cases. Broadcasters use the Emergency Alert System (EAS), formerly called the Emergency Broadcast System, to air a description of the abducted child and suspected abductor. This is the same concept used during severe weather emergencies. The goal of the AMBER Alert is to instantly galvanize the entire community to assist in the search for and safe return of the child.

AMBER Bill: *See* PROTECT Act of 2003.

benign episode: A missing benign explanation episode occurs when a child's whereabouts are unknown to the child's caretaker that causes the caretaker to (1) be alarmed, (2) try to locate the child, and (3) contact the police about the episode for any reason, as long as the child was not lost, injured, abducted, victimized, or classified as runaway/thrownaway.

be-on-the-lookout-for (BOL): This is an acronym used by law enforcement when broadcasting information on a wanted or missing person or vehicles, and so on.

BOLO: *See* be-on-the-lookout-for.

close relationship: Someone you can talk to online about things that are really important to you.

computer stalking: The repeated use of the Internet, e-mail, or a related digital electronic communication device to annoy, alarm, or threaten a specific individual or group of individuals.

endangerment: A child who is voluntarily missing, between the ages of eleven to seventeen, who has run away and is considered to be at risk because of his/her use of or involvement with these endangerments: drugs, alcohol, prostitution, telephone chat line enticement, online enticement, gang-related activity, weapons, or any medical problems (i.e., kidney, asthma, heart problems, depression, suicidal tendencies, etc.), or has been missing for thirty days or more. Also, if law enforcement or social services calls in the report, a child is considered an ERU automatically (NCMEC).

family abduction: A family abduction occurs when, in violation of a custody order, a decree, or other legitimate custodial rights, a member of the child's family, or someone acting on behalf of a family member, takes or fails to return a child, and the child is concealed or transported out of state with the intent to prevent contact with the caretaker or deprive the caretaker of custodial rights indefinitely or permanently. (For a child fifteen years or older, unless mentally incompetent, there must be evidence that a perpetrator used physical force or threat of bodily harm to take or detain the child.)

grooming: When someone attempts to seduce a child into meeting them online to lure them into an offline meeting.

IA: *See* infant abduction.

incoming cases: Involves children wrongfully removed from other countries and taken to or wrongfully detained in the United States. The National Center for Missing and Exploited Children is the agency that handles international abduction incoming cases.

infant abduction: There is no commonly accepted definition of an infant abduction. For the purposes of this book the criteria from the National Center for Missing and Exploited Children (NCMEC) will be used for an infant abduction:
  – A case must involve an infant, six months of age or younger, who is abducted by a nonfamily member.
  – Nonfamily member: A person who is not child's parent or legal guardian or otherwise related to the child.

international abduction: International parental abduction encompasses taking, detaining, or concealing a child outside the country in which the child normally resides by a parent, his or her agent, or other person in derogation of another's parental rights, including custody and visitation rights. These rights may arise by operation of law, by legally binding agreement of the parties, or by court order. The terms *international parental abduction* and *international child abduction* are used interchangeably in this book.

international parental child abduction: *See* international abduction.

Internet abduction: Person known or unknown who uses computer technology to lure a child into meeting them offline.

Internet predator: A person who surfs or interacts on the computer to seek out children or communicates with children using deceptive means.

Klaaskids Foundation: Not-for-profit foundation dedicated to stopping crimes against children. Website: http://www.klaaskids.org/pg-prog.htm

left-behind parent: A person who is the biological mother or father and who is denied custody or visitation of the abducted child and left behind in the state in which the child lived. (Probably will be modified. No legal definition as of this writing)

LOCATER: *Lost Child Alert Technology Resource.* A cutting-edge software program that enables law enforcement agencies to rapidly distribute critical images and information about missing-child cases. LOCATER is distributed through NCMEC.

missing involuntary, lost, or injured: A missing involuntary, lost, or injured episode occurs when a child's whereabouts are unknown to the child's caretaker and this causes the caretaker to be alarmed for at least one hour and tried to locate the child under one of these two conditions: (1) the child was trying to get home or make contact with the caretaker but was unable to do so because the child was lost, stranded, or injured; or (2) the child was too young to know how to return home or make contact with the caretaker.

MO (modus operandi): Method of operating or doing things. Term used by police and criminal investigators to describe the particular method of a criminal's activity. It refers to a pattern of criminal behavior so distinct that separate crimes or wrongful conduct are recognized as work of the same person (*Black's Law Dictionary*, 6th ed., Springer, 1994).

National Center for Missing and Exploited Children (NCMEC): Established in 1984 as a 501 (c) (3) tax-exempt charity to provide assistance to parents, children, law enforcement, schools, and the community in recovery missing children and to raise public awareness about preventing child abduction, molestation, and sexual exploitation.

National Crime Information Center (NCIC): Nationwide computer communication system that allows police departments to communicate with each other to exchange information and or to put out nationwide broadcasts.

National Incidence Studies of Missing, Abducted, Runaway, and Thrownaway Children (NISMART): Periodic national incidence studies to determine the actual number of children reported missing and the number of missing children who are recovered in a given year. There are two such studies: NISMART-1 and NISMART-2.

National Law Enforcement Transmission System (NLETS): Statewide computer communication system that allows police departments to communicate with each other and to exchange information or to put out statewide broadcasts.

National Runaway Switchboard: Federally designated national communication system for runaway and homeless youth. It is available twenty-four hours a day throughout the United States and its territories, including Puerto Rico, the US Virgin Islands, and Guam. Website: http://www.nrscrisisline.org

National Search Assistance Act: Federal legislation controlling how missing children and runaways are to be handled by law enforcement.

NCIC: *See* National Crime Information Center.

NCMEC: *See* National Center for Missing and Exploited Children.

NFCA: *See* nonfamily child abduction

NISMART: *See* National Incidence Studies of Missing, Abducted, Runaway, and Thrownaway Children.

NLETS: *See* National Law Enforcement Transmission System.

nonfamily child abduction: (1) An episode in which a nonfamily perpetrator takes a child by the use of physical force or threat of bodily harm or detains the child for a substantial period of time (at least one hour) in an isolated place by the use of physical force or threat of bodily harm without lawful authority or parental permission, or (2) an episode in which a child younger than fifteen, or mentally incompetent, and without lawful authority or parental permission, is taken or detained or voluntarily accompanies a nonfamily perpetrator who conceals the child's whereabouts, demands ransom, or expresses the intention to deep the child permanently.

OJJP: Office of Juvenile Justice and Delinquency Prevention. The Office of Juvenile Justice and Delinquency Prevention (OJJDP) provides national leadership, coordination, and resources to prevent and respond to juvenile delinquency and victimization. OJJDP supports states and communities in their efforts to develop and implement effective and coordinated prevention and intervention programs and to improve the juvenile justice system so that it protects public safety, holds offenders accountable, and provides treatment and rehabilitative services tailored to the needs of juveniles and their families.

outgoing cases: Involve children wrongfully removed from the United States and taken to or wrongfully detained in a foreign country. The FBI is charged with investigation of international abductions.

parental abduction: "[T]he taking, retention, or concealment of a child or children by a parent, other family member, or their agent, in derogation of the custody rights, including visitation rights, of another parent or family member" (Girdner, 1994b, p. 1–11). Abductors may be other family members or their agents (e.g., girlfriend, boyfriend, grandparent, or even a private investigator) although in most cases the abductor is a child's parent (Girdner, 1994c). Some state criminal statutes use the term *custodial interference*, rather than parental abduction, family abduction, or abduction, when referring to this crime and may include incidents in which children are detained or enticed away from the custodial parent. Custodial interference can also include interference with a court order of visitation or access.

probability range: The author created a probability range to assist officers in evaluating the probability of any accumulated evidence or circumstances so that they can give more weight to higher probability information. The authors used several studies to establish the probability range. When there was more than one study relating to any facet of this book, an average was taken. Elevated probability indicates that it is most likely that event would occur. High probability is less than elevated probability but greater than moderate or low probability. Moderate probability is greater than low probability, but less than high probability. Low probability indicates that the event would most likely not occur.

PROTECT Act of 2003: The Act establishes the AMBER Alert Program and provides significant new investigative tools. AMBER Alert programs are a proven tool to help recover abducted children. The PROTECT Act is sometimes referred to as the AMBER Bill. The PROTECT Act comprehensively strengthens law enforcement's ability to prevent, investigate, prosecute, and punish violent crimes committed against children.

runaway: A child who has left home without permission and stays away overnight; a child fourteen years old or younger (or older and mentally incompetent) who is away from home, chooses not to return, and stays away overnight night; or a child fifteen years old or older who is away from home, chooses not to come home, and stays away two nights.

SNFCA: *See* stereotypical nonfamily child abduction.

SOC: Speed, organization, and coordination.

stereotypical nonfamily child abduction: A stereotypical abduction occurs when a stranger or slight acquaintance perpetrates a nonfamily abduction in which the child is detained overnight, transported at least 50 miles, held for ransom, abducted with intent to keep the child permanently, or killed.*

---

* NISMART-2 Children Abducted By Family Members: National Estimates and Characteristics: http://www.missingkids.com/en_US/documents/NISMART-22_family abduction.pdf

stranger: A perpetrator whom the child or family does not know or a perpetrator of unknown identity (NISMART-2).

thrownaway: A child is asked or told to leave home by a parent or other household adult, no adequate alternative care is arranged for the child by the household adult, and the child is out of the household overnight; or a child who is away from home is prevented from returning home by a parent or other household adult, no adequate alternative care is arranged for the child by a household adult, and the child is out of the household overnight.

Timeline Checklist: The author of this book created a Timeline Checklist that the first responder/investigator of a missing or runaway child can use to perform tasks during the investigation. The Timeline Checklist is not all-inclusive for missing or runaway children, but was generated to assist such investigations.

APPENDIX A: Investigating Missing Children Timeline Guide Considerations

The missing child timelines have been created to assist the first responder/ investigator as a guide. All though not all inclusive, using the timelines will assist the first responder/investigator in the first crucial twenty-four hours of a missing child case.

Responding		
All Missing Children		
Check appropriate box if/when completed	YES	NO
In full compliance with the national child search assistance act (ncsa)		
Respond immediately/directly to dispatch location		
Critical actions upon arrival		
All missing children		
Locate/conduct interview with caller/witness(es) *(All interviews are conducted separately)*		
Immediately identify:		
Caller location		
Last known location		
Runaway/missing/abduction locations		
Assault location (if applicable)		
Return location		
Murder location		
Disposal location		
Determine if missing child left:		
Voluntarily		
Nonvoluntarily		
Immediately conduct search of missing child's last known location *(Even if missing from other location [e.g., home, comfort zones of missing child, friends' home, etc.])*		
Inside own home		

Outside in yard of own home		
Inside other home		
Outside in yard of other home		
Street/car other vehicle		
Park/wooded area		
School/daycare		
Store/malls/ restaurant		
Waterways/ponds/lakes/associated park/facility		
Recreational area		
Other location		
Determine jurisdiction of missing child, if/when applicable		
Establish/secure any/all crime scenes *(even runaway incidents until proven otherwise)*		
Establish/maintain crime scene contamination form (if applicable)		
Obtain complete physical/clothing description of missing child		
Obtain current photo of missing child		
Obtain Social Security number of missing child, if/when applicable		
Determine if child has history of:		
Runaway/thrownaway episodes		
Benign or otherwise missing episodes		
Family abductions		
Nonfamily abductions		
Internet episodes		
Determine time lapse between child missing & police contacted		
Determine what has been done prior to arrival		
Determine behavior patterns of missng child		
Determine if vehicle involved or taken by missing child, if/when applicable		
Determine if there is a companion involved, if/when applicable		
Determine if a computer is involved, if applicable, how		
Acquire written consent from parents to search computer contents		

Acquire written consent from parents for child's medical/dental records		
Determine/exclude as suspects: *(continuous until child located/recovered)*		
Father		
Father's girlfriend		
Mother		
Mother's boyfriend		
Stepfather		
Stepmother		
Stepfather/stepmother extended family member/acquaintance		
Grandfather		
Grandmother		
Siblings		
Relative(s)		
Neighbor		
Boyfriend/girlfriend		
Ex-boyfriend/girlfriend		
Slight acquaintance		
Long-term acquaintance		
Friend of a slight/long-term acquaintance		
Caretaker		
Babysitter		
Stranger		
Extended family members/friends		
Other		
False report		
Determine classification of missing child:		
Runaway/thrownaway episodes		
Benign or otherwise missing episodes		
Family abduction		

International family abduction		
Nonfamily abduction		
Stereotypical stranger abduction		
Cyber child abduction		
Infant abduction		
If no determination can be made, treat as an abduction		
Assess missing child's endangerment risk assessement (era): *(continuous until child located/recovered)*		
Determine registered sex offenders in immediate area of missing child/ statewide, if/when applicable		
Contact state clearing house for missing persons		
Request additional officers (if/when applicable and dependent on classification of missing child)		
Runaways		
Determine if any crimes were committed against runaway prior to running away (e.g., sexual abuse, physical abuse, neglect, etc.)		
Family abductions		
Determine martial status of parents:		
Separated		
Divorced		
Determine residence of noncustodial parent		
Determine custodial rights		
Obtain passport numbers of child/parent, if/when applicable		
Nonfamily/stereotypical stranger abduction		
Determine window of opportunity		
Determine what child was doing at last known location		
Determine what direction child left last known location		
Determine if abduction was a crime of:		
Opportunity		
Planned		
Determine type of force/lure used:		

Force:		
Weapon		
Force other than weapon		
Grabbing		
Dragging		
Lure:		
Assistance		
Bribery		
Authoritative		
Emergency		
Name recognition		
Games		
Ego/fame		
Hero		
Pornography		
Computer		
If child located, cancel all written/electronic alerts, if or when applicable		
Reunification of missing child and parents, if/when applicable		
Cyber child abduction		
Secure computer as crime scene/evidence		
Acquire search warrant for computer/to search computer		
Infant abduction		
Contact and work in conjunction with hospital security		
First hour		
All missing children		
Review/consult incident with immediate supervisor		
Immediately comply with the NCSA		
(Enter missing child into NCIC/NLETS and all other pertinent information, e.g., suspect/vehicle)		
NCIC/NLETS missing-person entry categories:		

Disabliity (MKE/EMD)		
Endangered (MKE/EME)		
Involuntary (MKE/EMI)		
Juvenile (MKE/EMJ)		
Catastrophe victim (MKE/EMV)		
Child abduction flag (CA)		
AMBER Alert (AA) flag		
BOLO broadcasts countywide, at the discretion of department and/or continuous throughout investigation until missing child is located		
Activate/distribute interdepartment locater database, if/when applicable (50-mile radius)		
Activate "a child is missing" phone bank (888-875-2246)		
Contact NCMEC for assistance, when applicable (1-800-THE-LOST)		
Consultation/assistance		
Locater poster creation/distribution		
Team Adam		
Assign liaison officer to parents, if/when applicable		
Contact FBI, if/when applicable		
Determine/activate statewide AMBER Alert, if/when applicable		
Contact state police for activation of AMBER Alert, if/when applicable		
Runaway/thrownaway/benign/otherwise missing episodes		
Check/interview possible places missing child may go:		
Own home/yard		
Friend(s) home		
Relative(s) home		
Other home or yard		
Shopping area or mall		
Park or wooded area		
School/daycare area		
Family abduction		

Locate noncustodial parent and determine if missing child is with them		
Request a federal unlawful flight to avoid prosecution (UFAP), if/when applicable		
Nonfamily/stereotypical stranger abduction		
Establish command post away from any crime scene or residence/home *(not at or near crime scenes or residence)*		
Conduct canvass/search *(minimum 3-block canvass/search, assign team leader, preprinted form for uniformity)*		
Create an interdeparmental task force		
Create and staff a hotline telephone number for public to call in tips/leads		
Preliminary canvass and officer saturation from last known to abduction locations *(minimum 3 city blocks/assign team leader)*		
Establish press site location/conduct press releases *(away from crime scenes)*		
Determine if any parent within canvass area has any knowledge of any attempted abductions or similarities		
Determine if any child within canvass area has any knowledge of any attempted abductions or similarities		
Locate/interview registered sex offenders *(50-mile radius)*		
If missing child is not located, request additional officers		
Interview ex-boyfriend/girlfriend, if/when applicable		
Cyber child abduction		
Secure computer as crime scene evidence		
Infant abduction		
Review any surveillance cameras on hospital property or surrounding area *(3-block radius)*		
Check immediate/surrounding area for septic tanks exposed (when applicable)		
Contact and have news media release (periodically/continuously until child is recovered)		
Write a detailed report *(all missing children cases)*		
Immediate supervisors review/evaluation/confirmations for:		
Original report for thoroughness		

First responder's classication of missing child (is it accurate/appropriate?)		
Do investigators have to be activated?		
Has missing child been entered into NCIC/NLETS?		
Roll call distribution		
Do additional officers have to be requested?		
Are any/all crime scenes secured?		
Does a command post have to be established? *If so, not in the immediate area of any crime scene(s)*		
Supervise/delegate/coordinate all activities/tasks that are related to missing child until completed/relieved		
Is there a need for outside resources:		
State child clearing house		
FBI		
Search and rescue teams/specialized units		
NCMEC		
Activation of inter/intralocater programs and distribution of information		
Activation of "a child is missing"		
Does higher command have to be notified?		
First 4 hours		
Nonfamily/stereotypical stranger abduction		
Contact/interview businesses within last		
Known/abduction locations *(surveillance cameras, etc.)*		
Expand initial 3-block canvass/search *(1/2 mile minimum/assign team leader)*		
Cyber child abduction		
Request assistance from expert computer forensic specialist		
First 8 hours		
Nonfamily/stereotypical stranger abduction		
Expand second 1/2 mile canvass/search (1 mile minimum/assign team leader)		

Create intracounty/state/federal task force (designate liaison officer)		
Command responsibility:		
Infant abduction		
Check hospital records for employees who sought employment/ hired/ quit		
Review hospital(s) records for any stillborn or miscarriages		
First 24 hours		
Nonfamily/stereotypical stranger abduction		
Volunteers: assign coordinator/trainer		
Contact state for list of registered sex offenders statewide		
Patrol rural areas of jurisdiction of missing child *(potential disposal sites)*		
Begin checking on additional resources, including but not limited to:		
Aircraft		
All-terrain vehicles		
Horse patrol		
Other credible private/public missing child organizations		
Polly Klaas foundation		
Other law enforcement/private/public search & rescue teams		
Other law enforcement/private/public K-9/cadaver dogs		
Underwater search and rescue teams		
State National Guard		
Local resources		

APPENDIX B: Long-Term and Cold Case Checklist

The following long-term and cold case timeline guides apply to all missing children classifications and are continuous throughout the response/investigation, until the missing child is located or recovered.

Long-Term Cases

___ Comply with National Child Search Assistance Act
    ___ When applicable, after any missing child is missing longer than thirty days, upgrade the missing child in NCIC/NLETS as "endangered."
    ___ No later than sixty days after the original entry of the record information into NCIC/NLETS, verify and update such record with any additional information, including, where available, medical and dental records.
    ___ Update NCIC/NLETS with any current information or disposition of missing child.
___ Enter the child's case into the department's computer to automatically remind and review case every thirty days.
___ Obtain from parent/guardian copies of the following for the missing child. This list is not exhaustive; collect other materials if available.
    ___ Birth certificate
    ___ Medical records
    ___ Any medical x-rays
    ___ Information on any disabilities
    ___ DNA samples
        ___ Hair (hat/pillow cases/hood)
        ___ Blood type
        ___ Dental records
        ___ Any dental x-rays
        ___ Most current photo(s) and video(s)
        ___ Obtain latent fingerprints (items handled by missing child)
        ___ Complete physical description including, but not limited to:
            ___ Height/weight, etc.
            ___ Moles/scars, etc.
            ___ Disabilities of any kind
___ Update the missing child's Emergency Risk Assessment
    ___ Drugs

___ Alcohol

___ Prostitution

___ Depression

___ Suicidal

___ Risk of great bodily harm

___ Risk of sexual exploitation

___ Telephone chat line enticement

___ Online enticement

___ Gang activity

___ Weapons involved

___ Medical problems

___ Mental problems

___ In the company of a violent person

___ Determine any permanent mailing addresses of an abducting parent or person of interest or if they have a P.O. Box, or if they have an alternative mailing address and if that permanent or alternative mailing address has been cancelled and if there is any forwarding mailing addresses.

___ Identify school attended

   ___ Canvass/interview school students for possible witnesses and/or information.

   ___ Advise institution to flag any request for records and to contact law enforcement immediately.

   ___ Consult with local prosecutor to see if any legal process may have to be followed to accomplish this.

___ Identify any clubs or organizations to which the missing child may have belonged.

   ___ Canvass/interview associates for possible witnesses and/or information.

   ___ Advise institution to flag any request for abducted child's records or information.

   ___ Consult with local prosecutor to see if any legal process may have to be followed to accomplish this.

___ Maintain liaison with all parties and state/federal agencies involved in the case as follows, but not limited to:

   ___ Parent(s), including left-behind-parents of an international child abduction

   ___ FBI

   ___ All federal/state agencies

   ___ State clearinghouse for missing children

   ___ NCMEC for information and technical assistance as follows, but not limited to:

      ___ Cold case unit

      ___ Project alert

___ Age enhancement unit
___ Case analysis unit
___ International abduction unit
___ Missing child unit
___ Reunification unit
___ Although not mandated by act, do the following:
  Advise the parent that they can contact NCMEC
  (1-800-the-lost) for assistance or information
  Request and document NCMEC's case number
___ Request consent from parent/guardian to review any personal diaries
  or computer usage of missing child.
___ Flag any/all nationwide/statewide NCIC/NLETS entries related to
  unidentifiable bodies
___ Don't let missing child case go dormant.
  ___ When applicable:
    ___ Create strategies to keep it active.
    ___ Create strategies to keep the news media interested.
___ Upon locating/recovery, interview the missing child for reasons they
  were missing:
  ___ If/when the missing child is a runaway/thrownaway, determine if
    there were any catalyst crimes committed against them to force
    them to run away or be thrown out of the home:
    ___ Consult with the local prosecutor for assistance and legal
      advice if/when crimes are divulged.
    ___ If/when crimes were committed, consider placing the run-
      away/thrownaway in an alternative setting:
      ___ Department of human services
      ___ Child receiving housing, etc.
___ Missing child classification reevaluation. Has it changed from the
  original classification to one of the following?
  ___ Runaway
  ___ Thrownaway
  ___ Benign episode
  ___ Lost, injured, or otherwise missing
  ___ Family abduction
  ___ Nonfamily abduction
  ___ International abduction
  ___ Stranger stereotypical abduction
  ___ Cyberspace abduction
  ___ Infant abduction
  ___ Other

___Review and determine if crime scene(s) has changed
  ___Caller location
  ___Last known location
  ___Abduction location
  ___Assault location
  ___Return location
  ___Murder location
  ___Disposal location
___Review and determine/exclude as suspects:
  ___Father
  ___Mother
  ___Siblings
  ___Relatives
  ___Slight/long-term acquaintances/relatives of secondary marriages
    of spouses
  ___Neighbor
  ___Boyfriend
  ___Girlfriend
  ___Ex-boyfriend
  ___Slight acquaintance
  ___Long-term acquaintances
  ___Friend of a slight/long-term acquaintance
  ___Caretaker/babysitter
    ___Stranger
    ___False report
___When the missing child is located/recovered, cancel all written or
  electronic alerts.
___Reunification of missing child with parent/guardian
  ___May be a team approach depending on duration or time and cir-
    cumstances of missing child
    ___Social services
    ___Prosecutor
    ___Custody issue, etc.

Cold Cases

___Create/maintain a cold case officer/unit until the missing child is
  located/recovered (when/applicable).
___Cold case officer(s) receives all tips/leads that may become available
  and does the following:
  ___Categorizes/prioritizes/follows up on them
  ___Maintains up-to-date written reports in chronological order

___ Create a cold case review team for all missing children classifications that include:

    ___ Internal law enforcement personnel

    ___ External law enforcement personnel

    ___ Surrounding county, state, and federal agencies

    ___ Any private/public organizations that are credible and assist in missing children cases:

       ___ NCMEC

       ___ Polly Klaas Organization

       ___ Local/statewide credible missing child organizations

Note: Do not be embarrassed, insulted, or afraid to ask for and pursue assistance from outside your department.

___ Cold case team meets periodically to review all missing children cold cases

___ When a missing child is located/recovered, cancel all written or electronic alerts

___ Reunification of missing child with parent/guardian

    ___ May be a team approach depending on duration or time and circumstances of missing child

       ___ Social services

       ___ Prosecutor

       ___ Custody issue, etc.

APPENDIX C: LOCATER Checklist

___ Determine/confirm what LOCATER Alert is going to be used for:

Date/Time _____ / _____

Missing or runaway child	_____	Yes	_____	No
Missing adult	_____	Yes	_____	No
Wanted person	_____	Yes	_____	No
Gang related	_____	Yes	_____	No
Robbery suspect(s)/suspect vehicle	_____	Yes	_____	No
Stolen car	_____	Yes	_____	No
Stolen/recovered property	_____	Yes	_____	No
Other _____	_____	Yes	_____	No

Type _____

Type _____

___ Entry into NCIC of missing child

Date/Time _____ / _____

___ Department responds to missing child report

Date/Time _____ / _____

___ Department takes the report of a missing child

Date/Time _____ / _____

___ Determine/confirm if the missing child is

Date/Time _____ / _____

Abducted Child	_____	Yes	_____	No
Family Abduction	_____	Yes	_____	No
Benign Episode	_____	Yes	_____	No
Internet Abduction	_____	Yes	_____	No
Infant Abduction	_____	Yes	_____	No
International Abduction	_____	Yes	_____	No
Lost, Injured, or Otherwise Missing	_____	Yes	_____	No
Nonfamily Abduction	_____	Yes	_____	No
Runaway	_____	Yes	_____	No
Stranger Abduction	_____	Yes	_____	No
Thrownaway Child	_____	Yes	_____	No

___ Determine if missing child has become an abduction

Date/Time _____ / _____

Abduction   _____ Yes   _____ No

___ Evaluate/Determine Child's Endangerment

Date/Time _____ / _____

Alcohol   _____ Yes   _____ No
Prostitution   _____ Yes   _____ No
Telephone chat line enticement   _____ Yes   _____ No
Online enticement   _____ Yes   _____ No
Gang activity   _____ Yes   _____ No
Weapons involved   _____ Yes   _____ No
Medical problems   _____ Yes   _____ No
Mental problems   _____ Yes   _____ No
In the company of a violent person   _____ Yes   _____ No
Missing child in great bodily harm or danger   _____ Yes   _____ No

___ Secure most current photo of child

Date/Time _____ / _____

___ Obtain complete physical description of missing child

Date/Time _____ / _____

___ Obtain complete clothing description of missing child

Date/Time _____ / _____

___ Launch NCMEC's LOCATER/Create LOCATER poster

Date/Time _____ / _____

___ Review/consult with supervisor

Date/Time _____ / _____

___ Activate/distribute LOCATER Alert in accordance with department policy

Date/Time _____ / _____

NCMEC's LOCATER list   _____ Yes   _____ No
Email   _____ Yes   _____ No
FAX   _____ Yes   _____ No

Department's cell phone database *(if applicable)*	_____ Yes	_____ No
Department's individual computer database *(if applicable)*	_____ Yes	_____ No
Department's list of credible missing child websites	_____ Yes	_____ No
News media	_____ Yes	_____ No
Statewide	_____ Yes	_____ No
Nationwide	_____ Yes	_____ No
Public as deemed appropriate (i.e., stores, public postings)	_____ Yes	_____ No
Schools	_____ Yes	_____ No
Transportation centers	_____ Yes	_____ No
Recreational sites	_____ Yes	_____ No
Churches	_____ Yes	_____ No
Homeless centers	_____ Yes	_____ No

___ Distribute LOCATER information per department's created databases

Date/Time _____ / _____

Roll calls	_____ Yes	_____ No
Public	_____ Yes	_____ No
Department's LOCATER database	_____ Yes	_____ No
Command post (if applicable)	_____ Yes	_____ No

___ Determine/confirm if LOCATER has evolved into an AMBER Alert incident

Date/Time _____ / _____

_____ Yes   _____ No

APPENDIX D: AMBER Alert Checklist

_____ Investigating law enforcement agency should get written consent from the parents/guardian to use the child's name and photo prior to using the abducted child's name and photo in an AMBER Alert.

_____ Investigating law enforcement agency has completed all/any forms that are required and has made notification to the proper state agency to activate the AMBER Alert.

_____ Investigating law enforcement agency's local LOCATER database has been activated.

_____ Abducted child is immediately entered into the NCIC/NLETS/State computer system.

_____ Investigating law enforcement agency contacted NCMEC advising them of the child abduction and requested that they stand by for any assistance they may be able to render.

_____ Activated by law enforcement only

_____ Activated for child abduction only

_____ Investigating law enforcement agency is investigating a child abduction and has confirmed/verified and has credible evidence that a child abduction has occurred.

_____ Investigating law enforcement agency has eliminated alternative explanations (i.e., runaway, thrownaways, lost, injured, or other missing, parental international abductions, benign episode, custody disputes, missing adults, etc.).

_____ Abducted child's age is seventeen/eighteen years of age or younger (depending on state).

_____ Abducted child is in imminent danger of serious bodily injury or death.

_____ There is sufficient information available that, if provided to the public, may assist in locating the child, suspect, or suspect vehicle.

_____ Establish an AMBER Alert tip/lead information sheet to be used when a tip/lead is reported.

_____ Investigating law enforcement agency has contacted the state organization that is responsible for the activation of an AMBER Alert.

_____ Investigating law enforcement agency has identified at least one individual (sworn/nonsworn) designated as the reporting and contact person in its department (with telephone number) for the AMBER Alert.

_____ Investigating law enforcement agency has designated at least two telephone numbers (to receive tips/leads) that have the ability to forward a call.

_____ Investigating law enforcement agency has made arrangements or notifications to other agencies to have all tips/leads forwarded to its department.

_____ Investigating law enforcement agency has designated a fax, e-mail, or other communication numbers or addresses to receive tips/leads.

_____ Investigating law enforcement agency has assigned personnel to these areas of communication until the AMBER Alert is cancelled.

_____ Update AMBER Alert information on an as-needed basis.

_____ Investigating law enforcement agency should request that neighboring states activate the AMBER Alert in their state.

_____ Investigating law enforcement agency should consider contacting major national news organizations to broadcast the AMBER Alert (i.e., ABC, CBS, CNN, FOX News, etc.).

_____ Investigating law enforcement agency cancelled AMBER Alert activation.

APPENDIX E: Endangerment Risk Assessment (ERA) Checklist

One of the primary vital actions in which a first responder/investigator engages when starting an investigation of a missing child is to determine the type of missing child episode involved and conduct an Endangerment Risk Assessment of the missing child. With the contents of this book, it is hoped that the material and guidelines presented will give the first responders/investigators an upper hand so that they will have a plan of action on their arrival.

	YES	NO
The child suffers from a severe mental or physical disability that greatly impairs the child's ability to care for him/herself		
The child is a victim of stranger acquaintance abduction		
The child is in the company of a person who has a confirmed criminal history of:		
Child abuse/neglect		
Sexual assault		
Domestic assault		
A crime involving the victimization of children		
Has made statements of intent to harm the missing child, or is suicidal		
The child has been abducted by a noncustodial parent whose parental rights have been terminated		
Prostitution involvement		
Commercial sex trafficking/exploitation		
Child is at risk of sexual exploitation (e.g., pornography, strip joints, etc.)		
Drug dependence		
Alcohol dependence		
Telephone chat line enticement, online enticement		
Weapons involved (use of or inferred)		
Medical problems (i.e., kidney, asthma, depression, suicidal tendencies, etc.)		

Has been missing for 30 days or more		
A child who is missing for unknown reasons or is a victim of a stereotypical (stranger) abduction		
Child may be removed out of state		
Child may be removed out of country		
If one or more endangerments exist, enter missing child into NCIC/NLETS as "endangered."		
NCIC/NLETS missing-person entry categories:		
Disability (MKE/EMD)		
Endangered (MKE/EME)		
Involuntary (MKE/EMI)		
Juvenile (MKE/EMJ)		
Catastrophe victim (MKE/EMV)		
Child abduction flag (CA)		
AMBER Alert (AA) flag		
Definitions		
AMBER Alert (AA) flag: AMBER Alert has been activated		
Catastrophe victim (MKE/EMV): a person of any age who is missing after a catastrophe.		
Child abduction flag (CA): initiated at the local level to facilitate automatic notification to the FBI's national center for the analysis of violent crimes (NCAVC) and the national center for missing and exploited children (NCMEC). The child abduction flag can only be used for the missing persons categories of endangered and involuntary.		
Endangered (MKE/EME): a person of any age who is missing under circumstances indicating that his or her physical safety may be in danger.		
Involuntary (MKE/EMI): a person of any age who is missing under circumstances indicating that the disappearance may not have been voluntary (i.e., abduction or kidnapping).		
Juvenile (MKE/EMJ): a person younger than the age of 18 who is missing and does not meet any of the entry criteria set forth in the other categories.		

Source: NCIC 2000 Missing Person File, Federal Bureau of Investigation.

APPENDIX F: Missing Children Characteristics, Traits, and Probabilities

Using the two studies mentioned in the Introduction (National Incidence Studies of Missing, Abducted, Runaway, and Thrownaway Children [NISMART-2][*,†,‡,§,¶,**] and the Case Management[††] for Missing Children Homicide Investigation), the author has determined probabilities for each known missing child and offender characteristic or trait.

While reviewing all the studies, research, and data for this book it became evident that percentages were used in much of the data to describe the characteristics or traits of a missing or runaway child and the offender.

- Attorney General of Washington: Investigative Case Management for Missing Children Homicide: "simple percentages were used to show the probability of any given characteristic of an abducted child."[††]
- NISMART-2 research also uses simple percentages to show the probability of any given characteristic of runaways, family abductions, nonfamily abductions, lost or otherwise missing children, benign no-explanation episodes, and the offender.

This book takes the same approach using the two studies and all of the related data to create *probabilities* to be considered when investigating missing children.

This may now give the first responder/investigator some sort of advantage when responding to, classifying, or investigating a missing child report.

---

[*] NISMART-2 National Estimates of Missing Children: An Overview: https://www.ncjrs.gov/pdffiles1/ojjdp/196465.pdf

[†] NISMART-2 Questions and Answers: https://www.ncjrs.gov/html/ojjdp/NISMART-2/qa/index.html

[‡] NISMART-2 National Estimates of Children Missing Involuntarily, or for Benign Reasons: https://secure.missingkids.com/en_US/documents/NISMART_national_estimates_missing_invol.pdf

[§] NISMART-2 National Estimates of Runaway/Thrownaway Children: National Estimates and Characteristics: http://www.missingkids.com/en_US/documents/nismart2_runaway.pdf

[¶] NISMART-2 Children Abducted By Family Members: National Estimates and Characteristics: http://www.missingkids.com/en_US/documents/NISMART-22_family abduction.pdf

[**] NISMART-2 Nonfamily Abductions: National Estimates and Characteristics: http://www.missingkids.com/en_US/documents/NISMART-22_nonfamily.pdf

[††] http://www.atg.wa.gov/uploadedFiles/Another/Supporting_Law_Enforcement/Homicide_Investigation_Tracking_System_(HITS)/Child_Abduction_Murder_Research/CMIIPDF.pdf

The author has created a Probability Range Scale using simple percentages and have established the terms, *high probability*, *medium probability*, and *low probability* to describe any characteristic or trait of a missing or runaway child and the offender.

We have all experienced a situation where you arrive on a call and have no *plan of action*. It seems that all you are doing is "spinning your wheels" on what type of action you should take immediately. It is hoped that this Probability Range Scale will assist the first responder/investigator of a missing child report in the immediate classification of a missing child.

Probability Range Scale Creation

Percentages were taken from various studies; whenever one or more studies were used and their samples reasonably substantiated each other, the percentages were added together and an average was obtained and used as a probability of a given characteristic or trait of a missing child or offender.

Probability Ranges

High probability: 50% or more or highest percentage for that characteristic
Moderate probability: 30–50%
Low probability: 0–30%

Characteristics and Traits

The characteristics and traits of missing children in Appendixes G through O are not all-inclusive. They have been identified through research and studies that are common to missing children. The first responder/investigator should not use one single characteristic or trait to classify a missing child, but instead a cluster of characteristics or traits should be used (i.e., gender only vs. gender, race, age, etc.).

These characteristics and traits are designed to help the first responder/investigator to do the following:

- Immediately classify a missing child (i.e., runaway, family abduction, nonfamily abduction, etc.) based on probabilities based on information obtained through interviews and evidence
- Focus the response, investigation, and resources on one or two missing child classifications instead of several classifications
- Help create leads

APPENDIX G: Runaway/Thrownaway Characteristics and Traits

Gender	
NISMART-2	National Runaway Switch Board
High Probability: • Female/Male	High Probability: • Female Low Probability: • Male

Race
NISMART -2
High Probability: • White Moderate Probability: • Black/Hispanic Low Probability: • Other

Age	
NISMART-2	National Runaway Switch Board
High Probability: • 12–17 years Low Probability: • 7–11 years	High Probability: • 15–17 years Moderate Probability: • 12–14 years Low Probability: • 10–11 years

Reason for Running Away	
NISMART-2	National Runaway Switch Board
High Probability: • Physically/Sexually Abused • Substance Abuse	High Probability: • Family Dynamics • Peer/Social Pressure Moderate Probability: • Youth Service (if involved) • School Low Probability: • Mental Health • Judicial System • Sexual Abuse/Assault • Emotional/Verbal Abuse • Neglect

Runaway Choice for Shelter
National Runaway Switch Board
High Probability: • Friend • Relative • Returned home Moderate to Low Probability: • On the street • School • Work • Shelter • Detention

Duration Away from Home	
NISMART-2	National Runaway Switch Board
High Probability: • 24 hours to 1 week Moderate Probability: • 7–24 hours • 1 week to 1 month Low Probability: • 6 hours to 7 hours	High Probability: • 1–7 days Moderate Probability: • 1 week to 2 months Low Probability: • 2 months to more than 6 months

Number of Miles Traveled from Home
NISMART-2
High Probability: • No more than 50 miles Moderate Probability: • More than 100 miles Low Probability: • Less than one mile

Runaway Left the State
NISMART-2
High Probability: • No Low Probability: • Yes

Time of Year
NISMART-2
High to Moderate Probability: • Summer Moderate to Low Probability: • Winter • Spring • Fall

Runaway Outcome
NISMART-2
High Probability: • Child returned Low Probability: • Not returned, but located • Not returned and not located

Will Police Be Contacted?
NISMART-2
High Probability: • No Low Probability: • Yes

Reason Police Not Contacted
NISMART-2
High Probability: • Runaway's location known Moderate to Low Probability: • Not gone long enough • Expected child to return • Believed child was safe

Endangerment
NISMART-2
High Probability: • Yes

APPENDIX H: Missing Benign Episode Characteristics and Traits

Age
NISMART-2

High Probability:
  • 12–17 years
Moderate Probability:
  • 3–11 years
Low Probability:
  • 0–2 years

Gender
NISMART-2

High Probability:
  • Male
Moderate Probability:
  • Female

Race
NISMART-2

High Probability:
  • White
Moderate Probability:
  • Black/Hispanic
Low Probability:
  • Other

Duration of Episode
NISMART-2

High Probability:
  • 1–6 hours
Moderate Probability:
  • Less than 1 hour
  • 7 hours but less than 24 hours
Low Probability:
  • 24 hours but less than 6 months

MBE Location

NISMART-2

High Probability:
- Other home or yard
- Own home or yard

Moderate Probability:
- Shopping area or mall
- Other public area

Low Probability:
- Street
- Park or wooded area
- School or daycare

How Caretaker Knew Child Was Missing

NISMART-2

High Probability:
- Child failed to come home
- Child was gone longer than expected

Moderate Probability:
- Child failed to call caretaker
- Child disappeared from caretaker's supervision

Low Probability:
- Other reasons

Will Police Be Contacted?

NISMART-2

High Probability:
- No

Moderate to Low Probability:
- Yes

Reason Police Not Contacted

NISMART-2

High Probability:
- Caretaker located child

Low Probability:
- Child recovered from unknown location
- Other reasons

APPENDIX I: Missing Involuntary, Lost, or Injured Children Characteristics and Traits

Age
NISMART-2
High Probability: • 12–17 years Moderate Probability: • 6–11 years Low Probability: • 0–5 years

Gender
NISMART-2
High Probability: • Male Moderate Probability: • Female

Race
NISMART-2
High Probability: • White Moderate Probability: • Hispanic/Black Low Probability: • Other

Duration of Episode
NISMART-2
High Probability: • 1–6 hours Moderate Probability: • Less than 1 hour • 7 hours but less than 24 hours Low Probability: • 24 hours but less than 6 months

Location of MILI
NISMART-2
High Probability: • Park or wooded area Moderate Probability: • School or daycare • Shopping area or mall Low Probability: • Street • Own home or yard • Other home or yard • Other public area • Other

How Caretaker Knew Child Was Missing
NISMART-2
High Probability: • Child disappeared from caretaker's supervision • Child failed to come home Moderate Probability: • Child failed to call caretaker • Child was gone longer than expected Low Probability: • Other reasons

Child Was Missing Due to Injury
NISMART-2
Moderate to Low Probability: • Yes

Will Police Be Contacted?
NISMART-2
High Probability: • No Moderate Probability: • Yes

Reason for Police Contact
NISMART-2
High Probability: • To locate child Low Probability: • To recover child from unknown location • Other reasons

Reason Police Not Contacted
NISMART-2
High Probability: • Child not gone long enough Moderate Probability: • Did not think police were needed • Child located without police assistance Low Probability: • Other reasons

APPENDIX J: Family Child Abductions Characteristics and Traits[*]

Gender	
NISMART-2	NIBRS
High Probability: • Female/Male	High Probability: • Female/Male

Age	
NISMART-2	NIBRS
High Probability: • 0–11 years Moderate Probability • 12–14 years Low Probability • 15–17 years	High Probability: • 0–11 years Moderate Probability: • 12–14 years Low Probability: • 15–17 years

Race
NISMART-2
High Probability: • White Moderate Probability: • Hispanic Low Probability: • Black or Other

[*] NISMART-2 Children Abducted By Family Members: National Estimates and Characteristics: http://www.missingkids.com/en_US/documents/NISMART-22_family abduction.pdf

Family Structure
NISMART-2

High Probability:
  • Single-parent family
Moderate Probability
  • One parent/partner, relative/foster parent
Low Probability
  • Two parents/no parent

Will Child Be Injured?
NIBRS
Low Probability: • No

More Than One Perpetrator
NISMART-2
High Probability: • No

Relationship to Child	
NISMART-2	NIBRS

High Probability:
  • Child's father
Moderate Probability:
  • Child's mother
Low Probability:
  • Grandfather/mother, uncle, stepfather, sister, aunt, mother's boyfriend
	High Probability:
	  • Parent

Perpetrator's Gender	
NISMART-2	NIBRS

High Probability:
  • Male
Moderate to Low
  • Female
	High to Moderate Probability:
	  • Female
	Moderate to High Probability:
	  • Male

Perpetrator's Age	
NISMART-2	NIBRS
High Probability: • 30–40 years Moderate Probability: • 20–30 years Low Probability: • Teens, 50+ years	High Probability: • Adults

Time of Day
NIBRS
High Probability: • Morning/Afternoon (6 a.m.–6 p.m.) Moderate to High Probability: • Evening (6 p.m.–12 a.m.) Low Probability: • Night (12 a.m.–6 a.m.)

Abduction Venue	
NISMART-2	NIBRS
High Probability: • Child's own home or yard, or other home or yard Low Probability • Public area, school/daycare, parent's/caretaker's car, street	High Probability: • Homes/residences Low Probability: • Other building, schools, outside

Child with Perpetrator Immediately Prior to Abduction
NISMART-2
High Probability: • Yes Moderate to Low Probability • No

Time of Year
NISMART-2
High to Moderate Probability: • Summer/Fall/Winter Moderate to Low Probability: • Spring

Duration of Time of Episode
NISMART-2
High Probability: • 24 hours to 1 month Moderate Probability: • 1 hour to 6 hours • 1 month but less than 6 months Low Probability: • Less than 1 hour • 6 months or more

Episode Outcome
NISMART-2
High Probability: • Returned Low Probability: • Not returned, but located

Use of Threat
NISMART-2
High Probability: • No Low Probability: • Yes

Use of Weapon	
NISMART-2	NIBRS
High Probability: • No Low Probability: • Yes	High Probability: • No Low Probability: • Yes

Child Taken Out of State
NISMART-2
High Probability: • No Low Probability: • Yes

Child Concerned
NISMART-2
High Probability: • No Moderate to High Probability: • Yes

Child Abducted With Intent to Prevent Contact
NISMART-2
High Probability: • Yes Moderate to Low Probability: • No

Child Abducted with Intent to Affect Custody Permanently
NISMART-2
High Probability: • Yes Low Probability: • No

Will Police Be Contacted?	
NISMART-2	OJJDP Bulletin[a]
High Probability: • Yes Moderate to High Probability: • No	High Probability: • Yes (within 24 hours of abduction)

[a] Abduction: A Review of the Literature, U.S. Department of Justice Office of Justice Programs Office of Juvenile Justice and Delinquency Prevention https://www.ncjrs.gov/html/ojjdp/190074/index.html

Reason Why Police Contacted
NISMART-2
High Probability: • Parent located child from known location • Located missing child, assisted in recovery

Why Police Were Not Contacted
NISMART-2
High Probability: • Resolved problem alone or with family, did not think police could help, or knew abducted child's location Low Probability: • Afraid that child would be harmed, handled problem with lawyer, knew child would not be harmed, or advised by others not to contact police

APPENDIX K: Characteristics and Traits of International Family Child Abduction[*]

Characteristics of the Abducted Child

Number of Children Abducted in a Single Event
OJJP

High Probability:
  • One
Low to Moderate Probability:
  • More than one

Gender
OJJP

High Probability:
  • Male
  • Female

Victim's Age
OJJP

High Probability:
  • 0–12 years
Low to Moderate High Probability:
  • 13–17 years

[*] US Department of Justice, Office of Juvenile Justice and Delinquency Prevention (OJJP), "Issues in Resolving Cases of International Child Abduction by Parents," *OJJP Juvenile Justice Bulletin*, December, 2001.

Left-Behind Parent Knows the Location of Abducted Child
OJJP
Low to Moderate Probability: • Will not know location of child

Recovery of Abducted Child
OJJP
High Probability: • Child will be located Moderate to High Probability: • Child will be recovered

Duration of Abduction
OJJP
High Probability: • More than 6 months Low to Moderate Probability: • More than 4 months

Characteristics of the Abductor

The Abductor
OJJP
High Probability: • Different nationality • Different ethnicity • Different religion

Abductor's Citizenship
OJJP
High Probability: • Citizens of another country Moderate Probability: • US citizenship Low Probability: • Dual citizenship

The Abductor's Gender
NIBRS[a]

High Probability:
  • Male
  • Female

[a] National Incident-Based Reporting System.

Abductor's Connection to Another Country
OJJP

High Probability:
  • Speaks the country's language
  • Has family in abduction country
  • Has close friends in abduction country
  • Lived there as a child
  • Grew up in abduction country
Low Probability:
  • Has employment or business interest in abduction country

APPENDIX L: Nonfamily Child Abduction Characteristics and Traits[*]

Victim

Age	
NISMART-2	NIBRS
High Probability: • 15–17 years Moderate Probability: • 12–14 years Low Probability: • 0–5 years	High Probability: • 12–17 years Moderate Probability: • 7–11 years Low Probability: • 1–6 years

Gender	
NISMART-2	NIBRS
High Probability: • Female Low Probability: • Male	High Probability: • Female Low Probability: • Male

[*] Andrea, J. Sedlak, David Finelor, Heather Hammer, and Dana J. Schultz, "National Incidence Studies of Missing, Abducted, Runaway, and Thrownaway Children, National Estimates of Missing Children: An Overview," US Department of Justice, Office of Justice Programs, Office of Juvenile Justice and Delinquency Prevention, October 2002. National Incident-Based Reporting System (NIBRS): The US Department of Justice is supplanting its Uniform Crime Report (UCR) system with a more comprehensive NIBRS data. NIBRS is far from a national system, but holds great promise.

Abductor

Abductor Relationship to Victim	
NISMART-2	NIBRS (Limited Data)
High Probability: • Friend • Long-term acquaintance Low to Moderate Probability: • Stranger • Slight acquaintance Low Probability: • Neighbor • Authority person • Babysitter	High Probability: • Acquaintance (i.e., boyfriend, ex-boyfriend, friend) Low Probability: • Gang activity • Stranger • Babysitter • Family member

More Than One Abductor
NISMART-2
High Probability: • No Low Probability: • Yes

Abductor Gender	
NISMART-2	NIBRS
High Probability: • Male Low Probability: • Female	High Probability: • Male Low to Moderate Probability: • Female

Abductor Age
NISMART-2
High Probability: • 13–29 years Moderate Probability: • 30–49 years Low Probability: • 50+ years

Circumstances

Abduction Location	
NISMART-2	NBRIS

High Probability:
  • Street, car, or other vehicle
  • Park or wooded area
Moderate Probability:
  • Other home or yard
  • Other public area
Low Probability:
  • Own home or yard
  • School or daycare
  • Store, restaurant, or mall
  • Other location
	High Probability:
	  • Homes/residence
	Moderate Probability:
	  • Other building
	  • Outside locations
	Low Probability:
	  • Schools, etc.

Victim Moved and Detained
NISMART-2

High Probability:
  • Victim will be taken or moved
Low to Moderate Probability:
  • Victim will be detained

Means by Which Victim Moved
NISMART-2

High Probability:
  • Carried
  • Walked
Low to Moderate Probability:
  • Vehicle

Victim Moved To
NISMART-2
High Probability: • Vehicle • Abductor's home Moderate Probability: • Building • Outside area Low Probability: • Other

Victim Moved More than 50 Miles
NISMART-2
High Probability: • No Moderate Probability: • Yes

Victim Sexually or Physically Assaulted, Robbed, Weapon Used, Ransom	
NISMART-2	NIBRS
High Probability: • Sexually assaulted • Physically assaulted Moderate Probability: • Weapon used (knives/guns) Low Probability: • Victim robbed • Ransom	High Probability: • No weapon Low Probability: • Weapon used (i.e., gun, knife, blunt object)

Abduction Duration
NISMART-2
High Probability: • 3 hours but less than 24 hours Moderate Probability: • Less than 2 hours Low Probability: • More than 24 hours

Abduction Outcome
NISMART-2
High Probability: • Returned alive Low Probability: • Child injured • Child killed • Not returned or located

Police Contacted
NISMART-2
Moderate to High Probability: • Yes

Reasons Police Not Contacted
NISMART-2
High Probability: • Abduction not serious enough • Expected child to return • Victim wanted to protect abductor Low to Moderate Probability: • Caretaker not told • Lack of evidence • Caretaker told too long after abduction

Time of Day
NIBRS
High Probability: • Noon to midnight Low to Moderate Probability: • 6 a.m. to noon Low Probability: • Midnight to 6 a.m.

Time of Year
NISMART-2
High Probability: • Spring, Summer Low to Moderate Probability: • Fall, Winter

APPENDIX M: Stranger Nonfamily Child Abduction Characteristics and Traits*

Who Abducts Children in Nonfamily Abductions?	
NIBRS	NISMART-2
High Probability: • Stranger Moderate to High Probability: • Acquaintance	High Probability: • Stranger Moderate Probability: • Friend • Long-term acquaintance Low Probability: • Neighbor • Person of authority • Caretaker • Slight acquaintance • Babysitter • Someone else

Will the Police Be Contacted?
NISMART-2
High Probability: • Yes Low Probability: • No

* Kenneth A. Hanfland, Robert D. Keppel, & Joseph G. Weis, "Case Management for Missing Children Homicide Investigation," Christine O. Gregoire, Attorney General of Washington & U.S. Department of Justice Office of Juvenile Justice & Delinquency Prevention, 1997. National Incident Studies of Missing, Abducted, Runaway, and Thrownaway & US Department of Justice, *Office of Juvenile Justice and Delinquency Prevention Bulletin*, June 2000, were used to create Characteristics and Traits of FCA. National Incident-Based Reporting System (NIBRS): The US Department of Justice is supplanting its Uniform Crime Report (UCR) system with a more comprehensive NIBRS data. NIBRS is far from a national system, but holds great promise.

The Victim

Elapse Time from Child Known Missing before Abducted Child Reported to Police
Washington Study
High Probability: • 2–4 hours Moderate Probability: • 1–2 hours Low Probability: • More than 24 hours

Elapse Time from Abduction of Child and Being Murdered
Washington Study
High Probability: • Within 3 hours Moderate Probability: • Within 24 hours Low Probability: • Within 7 days or more

Race	
Washington Study	NISMART-2
High Probability: • White Low Probability: • Black/Other	High Probability: • White Low Probability: • Black/Other

Gender	
Washington Study	NISMART-2
High Probability: • Female Low Probability: • Male	High Probability: • Female Low Probability: • Male

Age	
Washington Study	NISMART-2
High Probability: • 6–15 years Moderate Probability: • 16–17 years Low Probability: • 1–5 years **Average Age 11.5 years**	High Probability: • 6–14 years Low To Moderate Probability: • 0–5 years • 15–17 years

Victim–Killer Relationship	
Washington Study	NISMART-2
High Probability: • Stranger Moderate Probability: • Friend/acquaintance of victim/family Low Probability: • Family member/intimate	High Probability: • Stranger Low Probability: • Slight Acquaintance

The Child Abductor/Killer

Child Abductor/Killer Race	
Washington Study	NISMART-2
High Probability: • White	High Probability: • White Moderate Probability: • Black Low Probability: • Other

Child Abductor/Killer Gender	
Washington Study	NISMART-2
High Probability: • Male Low Probability: • Female	High Probability: • Male Low Probability: • Female

Child Abductor/Killer Age	
Washington Study	NISMART-2
High Probability: • 21–40 years Moderate Probability: • Less than18–20 years Low Probability: • More than 40 years	High Probability: • 20–39 years Moderate Probability: • 13–19 years Low Probability: • More than 40 years

Number of Abductor/Killers
NISMART-2
High Probability: • One Moderate to High Probability: • More than one

Child Abductor/Killer Occupation
Washington Study
High Probability: • Unskilled (i.e., construction worker, truck driver, food industry, student, service industry, mechanic) Low Probability: • Skilled/professional

Child Abductor/Killer Living Arrangements
Washington Study
High Probability: • Living with parents • Living alone Moderate to Low Probability: • Girlfriend/boyfriend • Spouse and/or children Low Probability: • Other roommates • Other

Child Abductor/Killer Personal Problems
Washington Study

High Probability:
   • Sexual problems
   • Alcohol problems
Low to Moderate Probability:
   • Drug problems
   • Mental problems

Child Abductor/Killer Prior Crimes against Children
Washington Study

High Probability:
   • Sexual assault (non-rape)
   • Rape (or attempt)
Moderate Probability:
   • Murder
   • Kidnap
Low Probability:
   • Assault

Child Abductor/Killer MO Compared to Prior Crimes against Children
Washington Study

High Probability:
   • Commission of crime same/similar to other crimes against children (i.e., knife/gun, etc.)
Low to Moderate Probability:
   • Victim's physical characteristics (i.e., prior crimes against children with blond hair, tall, etc.)
   • Approach to the victim (i.e., deception, etc.)
   • Specific acts committed (i.e., use of duct tape, etc.)

Child Abductor/Killer Motivation	
Washington Study	NISMART-2

High Probability:
   • Sexual motivation
Moderate Probability:
   • Other sexual assaults
Low Probability:
   • Other crimes
   • Pornography as a motivation
	High Probability:
	   • Sexual assault
	Moderate Probability:
	   • Physical assault
	Low Probability:
	   • Robbery

Child Abductor/Killer Crisis and Stressors before Abduction/Murder
Washington Study
High Probability: • Conflict with female • Criminal/legal problems • Extensive criminal record Low to Moderate Probability: • Marital problems • Employment problems • Financial problems

Child Abductor/Killer Selection of Victim	
Washington Study	NISMART-2
High Probability: • Victim of opportunity Low to Moderate Probability: • Prior relationship • Physical characteristics • Specific motivation	High Probability: • Sexual assault Moderate Probability: • Physical assault Low Probability: • Robbery

Child Abductor/Killer Approach Tactics
Washington Study
High Probability: • Blitz approach • Snatch and grab • Simply assault/subdue Low to Moderate Probability: • Deception • Luring • Threaten to assault

Child Abductor/Killer Use of Weapon	
NIBRS	NISMART-2
High Probability: • No Low to Moderate Probability: • Yes (firearm, knife, blunt object)	Moderate to High Probability: • Yes (knives/guns)

Child Abductor/Killer Controlling Victim

Washington Study

High Probability:
- Binding (bondage, sexual fantasies)
- Abductor will bring binding material with him

How Abductor/Killer Kills Victim

Washington Study

High Probability:
- Strangulation
- Stabbing/cutting

Moderate Probability:
- Blunt force trauma

Low Probability:
- Firearms

How Child Abductor/Killer Disposes of Body

Washington Study

High Probability:
- Concealed to prevent discovery

Moderate Probability:
- Unconcealed to prevent discovery

Low Probability:
- Open place to insure discovery
- Keep the body

How Long Will the Abductor/Killer Keep the Body and Where

Washington Study

High Probability:
- Body kept less than 24 hours
- Body kept at abductor's residence

Moderate Probability:
- Kept in abductor/killer car
- Kept in other places within easy reach

Low Probability:
- Body kept more than one week

Child Abductor/Killer Behavior after Killing and Disposing of Body
Washington Study
High Probability: • Return to disposal site • Leave town Moderate Probability: • Confide in someone • Follow case in media Low Probability: • Contact victim's family • Interjected himself into investigation

Investigation Considerations

Time of Day
NIBRS
High Probability: • Noon–Midnight Moderate Probability: • 6 a.m.–Noon Low to Moderate Probability: • Midnight–6 a.m.

Victim's Disposal Site
Washington Study
High Probability: • Abducted within jurisdiction Low to Moderate Probability: • Abducted outside of jurisdiction

---

Who Will Discover the Victim's Disposed Body?

Washington Study

High Probability:
- Passerby

Moderate to High Probability:
- Law enforcement

Low Probability:
- Search party
- Relative/acquaintance of victim
- Offender

**Response and Investigative Actions
First 48 Hours**

Washington Study

High Probability:
- Collecting information
- Canvasses and searches

Moderate Probability:
- Collecting evidence
- Disseminating information

Low Probability:
- Direct contact with offender
- Organizational changes

Police Contact with Abductor/Killer before He Became a Prime Suspect[a]

Washington Study

High Probability:
- Within a week

Low to Moderate Probability:
- Within 24 hours

Low Probability:
- Immediately

---

[a] Hanfland, Keppel, and Weis, 1997. Time measurements here are from the beginning of the murder investigation, not from the time victim was reported missing. The police had made contact with the offender either through canvasses or the offender's name was known to police by other means.

Which of the Five Locations Are the Most Valuable for Evidence?

Washington Study

High Probability:
- Disposal location
- Assault/murder location

Moderate to High Probability:
- Abduction location

Low Probability:
- Last seen location

Evidence at Disposal Location

Washington Study

High Probability:
- Hair
- Semen

Moderate to High Probability:
- Prints (finger and shoe)
- Weapons
- Fibers
- Blood

Evidence Discarded after Leaving Disposal Site

Washington Study

High Probability:
- Along the roadway traveled of murder, body disposal, escape within one mile of disposal location

---

News Media Effect on SNFCA Cases

Washington Study

High Probability:
- No effect

Moderate Probability:
- Helped

Low Probability:
- Hindered

Abductor/Killer's Disposal Location and Victim's Body Recovery Location
Washington Study
High Probability: • Rural Moderate to High Probability: • Suburban • Urban

How Is the Body Disposal Location Picked by Abductor/Killer?
Washington Study
High Probability: • Deliberately Moderate Probability: • Randomly Low Probability: • Forced by circumstances

Distance from Body Disposal Location to Murder Location
Washington Study
High Probability: • 0–199 feet Low To Moderate Probability: • 200 feet–1/4 mile • >1/4 mile–1½ miles • >1½ miles–12 miles • >12 miles

Distance from Murder Location and Abduction Location[a]
Washington Study
High Probability: • More than 1/4 mile • More than 1½ miles

[a] Hanfland, Keppel, and Weis, 1997. Study makes a note that the distance from the murder location and abduction location data is erratic and there is no clear pattern from the research.

Distance from Last Known Location and Abduction Location
Washington Study
High Probability: • Less than 200 feet–1/4 mile of victim's home • Less than 1 mile from last known location

Abduction Location Prior to or at Time of Abduction	
NIBRS	NISMART-2
High Probability: • Streets, highways, parks, waterways, other public areas Low Probability: • School	High Probability: • Street, car, other vehicle Moderate Probability: • Own home or yard • Other home or yard • Park or wooded area Low Probability: • Other public area • School or day care • Store, restaurant • Other locations

Will Abducted Child be Removed from Abduction Location and Detained?
NISMART-2
High Probability: • Will be taken or removed • Will be detained

How Far Will the Abducted Child be Taken or Removed?
NISMART-2
High Probability: • Less than 50 miles Low Probability: • More than 50 miles

Duration of Time Abducted Child Will be Held
NISMART-2
High Probability: • 3 hours or less Low to Moderate Probability: • 2 hours or less • 24 hours or more

Outcome of SNFCA	
Washington Study	NISMART-2
High Probability: • Killed	High Probability: • Killed • Returned injured Moderate to High Probability: • Returned alive Low Probability: • Not returned and not located

Abductor/Killer Legitimacy in Area of Abduction Location
Washington Study
High Probability: • Belonged in area • Lives in area (200 feet < 1/4 mile of abduction location) Low to Moderate Probability: • Normal social activity (i.e., visiting friend, to or from sporting event) • Nonsocial event (i.e., working, etc.)

Geographical Locations of SNFCA
Washington Study
High Probability: • Urban Moderate Probability: • Suburban Low Probability: • Rural

Time of Year
NISMART-2
High Probability: • Fall • Summer • Spring Low Probability: • Winter

APPENDIX N: Infant Abduction Characteristics and Traits*

Abduction Location
Analysis of Infant Abductions

High Probability:
  • Mother's hospital room
  • Mother's home
Moderate Probability:
  • Hospital's nursery
  • Hospital's pediatric room
Low Probability:
  • Hospital other location (hospital clinics, corridors, waiting rooms, parking lot, curbs, etc.)
  • Other locations (malls, shopping centers, cars, etc.)

Demographic Location
Analysis of Infant Abductions

High Probability:
  • Urban
Moderate Probability:
  • Medium population settings
Low Probability:
  • Rural

Abductor Gender
Analysis of Infant Abductions

High Probability:
  • Female
Low Probability:
  • Male

* National Center for Missing and Exploited Children (NCMEC), Newborn/Infant Abductions Statistics, December 2010, confirm this reference.

Abductor's Race
NCMEC/OJJP
High Probability: • White • Black

Victim's Race
Analysis of Infant Abductions
High Probability: • White • Black Low to Moderate Probability: • Hispanic Low Probability: • Other

Victim's Gender
Analysis of Infant Abductions
High Probability: • Male • Female

Duration
Analysis of Infant Abductions
High Probability: • Less than 5 days Low to Moderate Probability: • More than 5 days

Abductor's Martial Status
Analysis of Infant Abductions
High Probability: • Married at least once Low to Moderate Probability: • Never married

Abductor's Techniques
Analysis of Infant Abductions

High Probability:
  • Verbal conning
  • Deception
  • Disguise (i.e., nurse, doctor, assistant, etc.)
Low to Moderate Probability:
  • Steal (grabbing infant when no one is looking)
  • Force
Low Probability:
  • Other

How Abductor Removed Infant
Analysis of Infant Abductions

High Probability:
  • Walk out (no attempt to conceal)
Low to Moderate Probability:
  • Walk out concealed (i.e., under coat or blanket, hand carrier bag, gym bag, etc.)
Low Probability:
  • Other

Hospital Setting
Analysis of Infant Abductions

High Probability:
  • 200- to 400-bed institution
Moderate Probability:
  • Institution with more than 400 beds
Low Probability:
  • Institution with fewer than 200 beds

Who Will Discover the Abduction?
Analysis of Infant Abductions

High Probability:
  • Nurse
Low to Moderate Probability:
  • Parent
  • Doctor
Low Probability:
  • Other

Will Abductor Impersonate Someone?
Analysis of Infant Abductions
High Probability: • Yes Low to Moderate Probability: • No

Abductor Impersonated
Analysis of Infant Abductions
High Probability: • Nurse Low to Moderate Probability: • Lab technician • Mother Low Probability: • Social worker • Doctor • Other relative

Abductor Known to Parent
Analysis of Infant Abductions
High Probability: • No Low Probability: • Yes

Abductor Identified as Suspicious Before Abduction
Analysis of Infant Abductions
High Probability: • No Low to Moderate Probability: • Yes

Media Coverage Assist in Recovery
Analysis of Infant Abductions

High Probability:
  • Yes
Low to Moderate Probability:
  • No

Means Used to Identify Infant
Analysis of Infant Abductions

High Probability:
  • Footprint
  • ID bracelet
  • DNA
Low Probability:
  • Photo
  • Other means

Who Will Notify Law Enforcement of Infant Whereabouts?
Analysis of Infant Abductions

High Probability:
  • By a friend of the abductor who cannot explain reason for a new child
  • Relative of the abductor who cannot explain reason for a new child

APPENDIX O: Internet Child Abduction Characteristics and Traits[*][†]

Victim

Gender
NCMEC/OJJDP
High Probability: • Female Low to Moderate Probability: • Male

Age
NCMEC/OJJDP
High Probability: • 14–16 years Moderate to High Probability: • 13–14 years • More than 17 years Low Probability: • More than 12 years

[*] David Finkelhor, Kimberly J. Mitchell, and Janis Wolak, "Online Victimization: A Report on the Nation's Youth," The Crimes against Children Research Center, National Center for Missing and Exploited Children, June 2000.

[†] Janis Wolak, Kimberly Mitchell, and David Finkelhor, "Internet Sex Crimes against Minors: The Response of Law Enforcement," Crimes against Children Research Center University of New Hampshire, National Center for Missing and Exploited Children, Crimes against Children Research Center & Office of Juvenile Justice and Delinquency Prevention.

Abductor/Perpetrator

Gender	
NCMEC/OJJDP	Internet Sex Crimes against Minors
High Probability: • Male Low Probability: • Female • Other	High Probability: • Male Low Probability: • Female • Other

Age	
NCMEC/OJJDP	Internet Sex Crimes against Minors
High Probability: • More than 19 years Low to Moderate Probability: • More than 18 years	High Probability: • More than 26 years Low Moderate Probability: • More than 25 years

Abductor's Race
Internet Sex Crimes against Minors
High Probability: • White Low Probability: • Other

Will Victim Know Where Abductor/ Perpetrator Lives?
NCMEC/OJJDP
High Probability: • No Low Probability: • Yes

Will Abductor/Perpetrator Live within One Hour Driving Distance from Victim?
NCMEC/OJJDP
High Probability: • No Low Probability: • Yes

Will Abductor/Perpetrator Work Alone?
Internet Sex Crimes against Minors
High Probability: • Yes Low Probability: • No

Abductor/Perpetrator Possess Pornography
Internet Sex Crimes against Minors
High Probability: • Yes Low Probability: • No

Has Abductor/Perpetrator Committed a Sex Crime against an Identified Victim?
Internet Sex Crimes against Minors
Moderate to High Probability: • Yes Low to Moderate Probability: • No

Will the Abductor/Perpetrator Have a Prior Arrest for Sexual Offences against Minors?
Internet Sex Crimes against Minors
High Probability: • No Low Probability: • Yes

How Will the Abductor/Perpetrator and Victim Meet?
NCMEC/OJJDP
High Probability: • Meet online Low Probability: • Knew person before incident

Location of Victim's Computer before Incident
NCMEC/OJJDP
High Probability: • Home Moderate Probability: • Someone else's home Low Probability: • School • Library • Some other place

Location on Internet When Incident First Happened
NCMEC/OJJDP
High Probability: • Chat room Moderate Probability: • Using instant messages Low Probability: • Specific web page • E-mail • Game room • Message board • Newsgroup • Other

Forms of Offline Contact
NCMEC/OJJDP
High Probability: • Asked to meet somewhere Moderate Probability: • Regular mail Low Probability: • Called on telephone • Came to house • Gave money, gifts, or other things • Bought plane, train, or bus ticket

APPENDIX P: Abduction/Missing Child Report Summary Worksheet

The Abduction/Missing Child Report Summary Worksheet was created to assist the first responder/investigator while responding or investigating a missing child case. The summary/worksheet contains data that can be tracked or checked off as completed throughout a missing-child incident.

Department:	Case #:	Date:

Disposition of Missing Child
☐ Located/Recovered ☐ Located Alive ☐ Located Deceased ☐ Not Recovered/Outstanding ☐ Reunited With: _____ ☐ Placement Other Than Parent: _____

Classification of Missing Child	
☐ Runaway ☐ Benign Episode ☐ Lost/Otherwise Missing ☐ Family Child Abduction ☐ International Family Child Abduction ☐ Nonfamily Child Abduction ☐ Stranger Abduction ☐ Cyber Child Abduction ☐ Infant Abduction	
Without Delay Enter ALL Missing Children into NCIC/NLETS	Date/Time:
Without Delay Broadcast All Points Bulletin to all Police Channels, Patrol Officers, Other Law Enforcement Agencies	Date/Time:

Description of Missing Child			
Child's Name	Nickname(s)	Gender	Race/Ethnicity
		☐ Male ☐ Female	☐ White ☐ Black ☐ Hispanic ☐ Other

☐ Citizenship (Dual) ☐ United States ☐ Other: _____

Age	Date of Birth	Hair Color	Eye Color	Height/ Weight	Languages Spoken at Home

Home Address	Family Status	Legal Caretaker-Custodial Situation
	☐ Two-Parent ☐ Single Parent ☐ Parents Separated ☐ Parents Divorced ☐ Other	

Telephone Number:			
Clothing worn at Time of Disappearance:			
Distinguishing Features or Marks:			

Individuals Living in Child's Household	Relationship to Child	Current Location	Contact Information

School/Day Care Attended:	
Address:	
Grade, Teacher, School Telephone Number:	
Medical Conditions:	
Prescription Medicine:	Illicit Drugs:

Tactic Used

Lure: ☐ Animal ☐ Candy ☐ Money ☐ Ride ☐ Other: _____

Force: ☐ Grab ☐ Pull ☐ Carry Away ☐ Weapon ☐ Other: _____

Circumstances of Disappearance

Last Seen By (Witnesses)	Relationship	At (Location)	At/Around (Time)	With (Child Alone or With Others)

Reason the child is perceived as missing:

Endangerment Risk Assessment *(Not All-Inclusive)*

☐ Prostitution ☐ Sexual Exploitation ☐ Drug Dependence ☐ Alcohol Dependence
☐ Internet Offline Meeting ☐ Weapons ☐ Medical Problems _____
☐ Missing More Than 30 Days ☐ Taken Out of State ☐ Taken Out of Country
Additional Endangerments: _____

AMBER Alert Activation/Assessment
(One or More Must Exist for AMBER Activation—Verify with Your State Criteria for AMBER Alerts)

☐ Under 17
☐ Child suffers from severe mental condition
☐ Child suffers from physical disability that greatly impairs ability to care for themselves
☐ Victim of a stranger abduction

The child is in the company of a person who has a confirmed history of:
- ☐ Child abuse
- ☐ A crime involving the victimization of a child(ren)
- ☐ Has made statements of intent to harm the missing child
- ☐ The child has been abducted by a noncustodial parent whose parental rights have been terminated

Articulate Reasons for AMBER Alert Prior to Contacting AMBER Alert Coordinator:

Description of Alleged Abductor/Perpetrator (if Known)

Name	Aliases/Monikers	Gender	Race/Ethnicity
		☐ Male ☐ Female	☐ White ☐ Black ☐ Hispanic ☐ Other

Age	Date of Birth	Hair Color	Eye Color	Height/Weight	Languages Spoken

Citizenship:	Relationship to Child:

Disabilities/Medical Conditions:

Vehicle Description

Make, Model, Year, Color, etc.	License Plate/State	Occupation	Criminal Record

Relationship to Missing/Abducted Child

- ☐ Family member ☐ Noncustodial parent ☐ Acquaintance ☐ Boyfriend ☐ Girlfriend
- ☐ Ex-Boyfriend ☐ Ex-Girlfriend ☐ Stranger
- ☐ Other: _____

Clothing at Time of Abduction	Other Observations/Distinguishing Marks/Tattoos

Residential Address	Work Address

Potential U.S. Destinations:
Potential Routes of Escape:

International Risk *(Complete only if indicated)*			
Current Passport Information of Abductor & Child		Home Country or Country Destination(s)	
Country of Origin	Abductor	Country	
	Passport #	Country	
	Child	Country	
	Passport #	Country	
Additional Passport Information:			
Out-of-Country Relative/Friend	Relationship to Abductor/Child	Country	Contact Information of Relative/Friend

Without Delay Enter ALL Missing Child Into NCIC/NLETS	Date/Time:
Without Delay Broadcast All Points Bulletin to all Police Channels, Patrol Officers, Other Law Enforcement Agencies	Date/Time:

Notifying Appropriate Agencies in All Missing Children Cases

☐ FBI (Request UFAP warrant)   ☐ State Clearing House (AMBER Alert)
☐ Department of Justice Missing and Unidentified Persons Unit
☐ A Child Is Missing Organization   ☐ National Center For Missing and Exploited Children
☐ Local Prosecutor   ☐ Federal Prosecutor   ☐ News Media
☐ Other agencies contacted: _____

Obtain Additional Evidence/Information io Assist in Investigation/Search
(Recent photograph of child, child's fears, where, and how far from home the child is accustomed to going on his/her own, etc.)

Appropriate Agencies Telephone Numbers

Federal Bureau of Investigation	**Other Agencies**
Local Agent Office ( ) _____	A Child Is Missing.......................................(888) 875-2246
State Agent Office ( ) _____	National Center for Missing and Exploited Children ......
National Office ( ) _____	....(1-800) 843-5678
Other Office ( ) _____	State AMBER Alert Coordinator...........( ) _____
	State Missing Children's Clearinghouse..( ) _____
	Local Prosecutor.....................................( ) _____
	Federal Prosecutor.................................( ) _____

Other Missing Local, State, Federal or Private or Public Missing Child Organizations Contacted:

Synopsis of Missing Child Case

APPENDIX Q: Missing Child Neighborhood Canvass Questionnaire

1. Department Case Number: _____

2. Name and/or badge number of person conducting neighborhood canvass
   Name: _____

3. Date/Time Canvass Conducted: ____ / ____ / ____ , ____ AM PM

4. Date/Day/Time of Incident: ___/___/___ S M T W T F S AM PM

5. Victim's name: _____

6. Incident address: _____

7. Full name of person contacted: _____

8. DOB of person contacted: ___/___/___

9. Telephone numbers: _____

10. Address of person contacted: _____

11. Type of structure: _____

12. Vehicle descriptions and registration numbers present at location
    _____

    Searched: ☐ Yes   ☐ No

13. Is the victim's home visible from this location? ☐ Yes   ☐ No

14. Is the abduction site visible from this location? ☐ Yes   ☐ No

15. Do you know the _____ family and specifically the missing child? ☐ Yes   ☐ No

16. Were you home on the day of the incident? ☐ Yes   ☐ No

17. Names of all occupants and visitors at this home at the time of the incident. _____
    _____

18. What did you observe out of the ordinary or ordinary on that day?
    _____
    _____
    _____
    _____

19. What did you hear? _____
_____
_____
_____

20. What activity did you see or hear at or near the victim's home/abduction location? _____
_____
_____
_____

21. What are the usual daily activities in this area (day and night)?
_____
_____
_____

22. What have you noticed in the past several weeks that may have been suspicious or unusual? _____
_____
_____
_____

23. What delivery people come to this area and/or have there been any out-of-the-ordinary delivery people? _____
_____

24. Were any vehicles that are not normally in the area, present in the area at the time the incident?
☐ Yes ☐ No
Description _____
_____

25. What person(s), ordinary or out of the ordinary, were observed in the neighborhood around the time of the incident?
Description _____
_____

26. Who is usually arriving in or leaving the area around the time of the incident? _____
_____

27. Do you have knowledge or have your children reported to you a same or similar incident that happened to them, but you did not report it or give it much thought?
☐ Yes ☐ No
Remarks: _____
_____

28. Are you aware of anyone who may have information or evidence relating to this incident?

    ☐ Yes ☐ No

    Remarks: _____

    _____

29. Do you have any other information about this incident that you feel is important?

    ☐ Yes ☐ No

    Remarks: _____

    _____

30. Is there anything else you would like to tell us?

    ☐ Yes ☐ No

    Remarks: _____

    _____

31. Vehicle(s), abandoned or not, abandoned buildings, storage sheds, etc., searched location/address/description: _____

    _____

    _____

32. If appropriate, obtain consent to search or get search warrant for the residence, vehicles, storage areas, etc. _____

    _____

    _____

33. Additional remarks: _____

    _____

    _____

    _____

    _____

    _____

APPENDIX R: Volunteer Background Check Form

Case Information		
Case Number	Date/Time	Location
Officer's Name and Badge Number		
Victim's Name		

Volunteer's Information
Type of Volunteer: ☐ Civilian ☐ Law Enforcement ☐ Military ☐ Other: _____
Name:
Address:
City   State   Zip   Telephone Number

DOB	Race ☐ White ☐ Black ☐ Hispanic ☐ Other: _____	Sex ☐ Male ☐ Female

Occupation: Special Skills That May Assist in Investigation:

Type of Identification
☐ Driver License
    State and Number: _____
☐ State I.D.
    State and Number: _____
☐ Other: _____

Background Check Information		
☐ NCIC ☐ Registered Sex Offender ☐ Criminal History ☐ Driver License Check	☐ Approved ☐ Disapproved	Reason Denied

Scheduled for Training
☐ Yes   ☐ No   Date/Time: _____

Other Remarks

APPENDIX S: Reunification Checklist

___ Verify the identity of the missing or runaway child.

Date/Time _____ / _____

___ Verify thru NCIC/NLETS that the missing or runaway child is entered and under what classification.

Date/Time _____ / _____

___ Investigate/verify/enforce any court orders/custody orders/visitation orders, etc., that may apply to recovered missing or runaway child.

Date/Time _____ / _____

                    Type of order _____

                    Type of order _____

                    Type of order _____

                    Other _____

___ Make contact and take into protective custody the missing or runaway child.

Date/Time _____ / _____

___ If applicable, activate Missing Child Reunification Team.

Date/Time _____ / _____

___ When appropriate, cancel missing child or runaway in NCIC/NLETS or any other notice or communication use and as an alert during the investigation.

Date/Time _____ / _____

___ Determine if any special needs of the missing child or runaway have to be met (i.e., food, clothing, personal hygiene, medical treatment, physical/emotional, etc.).

Date/Time _____ / _____

                    Type of need _____

                              _____

                              _____

___ If applicable, take missing children or runaway to the proper facility to meet their needs (i.e., hospital, police department, shelter, etc.).

     Date/Time _____ / _____

___ If and when applicable, arrange for physical examination of missing child or runaway when foul play or criminal activity is involved, or when needed.

     Date/Time _____ / _____

                Hospital _____

                Other _____

___ If applicable, contact media (i.e., press release).

     Date/Time _____ / _____

___ Contact the parent or guardian and advise that the missing child or runaway has been located.

     Date/Time _____ / _____

                Who was contacted?

                Father _____

                Mother _____

                Guardian _____

                Other _____

___ Interview the missing child or runaway; if applicable seek legal advice from local prosecutor.

     Date/Time _____ / _____

___ When applicable arrange reunification meeting with parent or guardian. Depending on the circumstances of the case, this meeting place may have to be in a neutral/private location.

     Date/Time _____ / _____

___ If and when applicable, advise the parent/guardian to bring appropriate clothing for the missing or runaway child to the meeting place or hospital.

     Date/Time _____ / _____

___ If and when applicable, advise the parent/guardian to bring limited family members to location.

Date/Time _____ / _____

___ Conduct/continue investigation into criminal activity or reasons why the child went missing or ran away from home.

Date/Time _____ / _____

___ If or when applicable, interview any suspect/witness, but not in the presence of child.

Date/Time _____ / _____

___ If or when applicable, make an arrest of suspect/parent away from child.

Date/Time _____ / _____

___ If applicable, contact local prosecutor for consultation or legal advice pertaining to missing child or runaway.

Date/Time _____ / _____

___ When applicable, and after a thorough investigation, return/give custody back to legal parent/guardian.

Date/Time _____ / _____

Custody given to
Father _____
Mother _____
Guardian _____
Other _____

___ If or when applicable, contact NCMEC for assistance.

Date/Time _____ / _____

APPENDIX T: Missing Child Assessment Checklist

This matrix has been designed to assist the first responder/investigator in making an immediate assessment of a missing child, and reviewing the information and evidence gathered at the conclusion of the *initial* interview. This matrix is not meant to be the determining factor in a missing child assessment, but to be used only as another tool to help identify the classification into which a missing child may best fit.

After checking all the appropriate cells in each classification, add up the columns with the most checks and see if there is a predominant classification into which this missing child case may fit (i.e., RA-3, BE-0, MILI-0, FA-8, IFA-0, NFA-5, STSA-2, CCA-4, IA-0). In this example, the *First Responder/ Investigator* may want to use FA as a predominant classification.

Remember, this matrix is meant only to assist you, along with initial information and evidence gathered, to determine the kind of missing child case you may be dealing with.

Note: BE = Benign Episode; B = Black; CCA = Cyber Child Abduction; DNA = Does Not Apply; F = Female; FA = Family Abduction; H = Hispanic; IA = Infant Abduction; IFA = International Family Abduction; LBP = Left-Behind-Parent; M = Male; MILI = Missing Involuntary, Lost, or Injured; NFA = Nonfamily Abduction; ND = No Data; O = Other; RA = Runaway; SAA = Same as Abductor; SAC = Same as Child; SSCA = Stereotypical Stranger Child Abduction.

Check appropriate cells	Victim's Race/Age/Sex								
Classification	RA	BE	MILI	FA	IFA	NFA	STSA	CCA	IA
High probability									
Race	W	W	W	W	SA	B/W	W	ND	SA
Age	15 to 17	12 to 17	12 to 14	0 to 11	0 to 12	15 to 17	6 to 15	14 to 16	Infant
Sex	M/F	M	M	M/F	M/F	F	F	F	M/F
Moderate probability									
Race	B/H	B/H	B/H	B/H	S/A	DNA	DNA	ND	SA
Age	12 to 14	DNA	6 to 11	12 to 14	DNA	12 to 14	16 to 17	13 to 14	DNA
Sex	DNA	F	DNA	DNA	DNA	DNA	DNA	DNA	DNA

(continued)

	Low probability								
Race	OTHER	DNA	B/H	OTHER	SA	OTHER	B/O	ND	DNA
Age	0 to 11	10 to 14	0 to 5	15 to 17	13 to 17	0 to 5	1 to 5	< 12	DNA
Sex	DNA	F	F	DNA	DNA	M	B/O	M	
Check appropriate cells	RA	BE	MILI	FA	IFA	NFA	STSA	CCA	IA
Child missing:									
Voluntarily									
Nonvoluntarily									
Threatened or has run away before									
Missing clothes									
Money missing									
Credit cards missing									
Check book missing									

(continued)

Check appropriate cells	RA	BE	MILI	FA	IFA	NFA	STSA	CCA	IA
Withdrawn/depressed									
Falling grades in school									
Unhappy circumstances at home									
Physcally/verbally abused at home									
Sexually abused at home									
Known peer/social group pressure									
Substance abuse									
Rebellious									
Family dynamics									
Recently moved/missing child upset									
Forced breakup (i.e., boy/ girlfriend)									
Missing child employed:									
Location									
Not showing up for work									
Judicial system encounter									

(continued)

Check appropriate cells	RA	BE	MILI	FA	IFA	NFA	STSA	CCA	IA
New friends not approved of									
Miscommunications between child/parent (i.e., helping friend, unexpected delay, etc.)									
Separated from parents									
Angry at parents									
Ride missed (to include school bus)									
Injured (parents not notified)									
Lost track of time									
Wandered off									
Determine maritial status of parent:									
Separated									
Divorced									
Other parent alive/deceased									
Prevent contact/custody									
LBP knows whereabouts of child									

(continued)

Check appropriate cells	RA	BE	MILI	FA	IFA	NFA	STSA	CCA	IA
Any previous family missing incidents									
International marriage									
Different nationality/religion									
Abductor citizen of another country									
Child taken out of country									
Child missing after leaving a known location									
Child missing in short time frame from last known location									
Child missing within 1 mile of last known location									
Physically removed/snatched or grabbed									
Witness to forced encounter									
Crime of opportunity									
Sexually motivated									

(continued)

Check appropriate cells	RA	BE	MILI	FA	IFA	NFA	STSA	CCA	IA
Carried/walked to vehicle									
Child screaming/resisting									
Child taken from:									
Street									
Park									
Physically removed									
Wooded area									
Own front yard									
Other home than missing child's									
Public park									
Mall, etc.									
Missing child going to/coming from/waiting at school bus stop school yard									
Computer involved									
Previous offline meeting									

(continued)

Check appropriate cells	RA	BE	MILI	FA	IFA	NFA	STSA	CCA	IA
Location: hospital/mother's room, nursery/pediatric room									
Non-hosptial location (home/ maternity clinic, etc.)									
Abductor impersonated a medical person (nurse, lab technician, etc.)									
All missing children motive assessment									
Nontraditional									
Ransom									
Sexual									
Killing									
Revenge									
Political									
Miscellaneous criminal									

(continued)

Check appropriate cells	RA	BE	ILM	FA	IFA	NFA	STSA	CCA	IA
Offender's Race/Age/Sex Considerations									
High Probability									
Race	DNA	DNA	DNA	W	SAC	N/D	W	W	SAC
Age	DNA	DNA	DNA	30 to 40	ADULT	13 to 29	21 to 40	> 19	14 to 48
Sex	DNA	DNA	DNA	M/F	M/F	M	M	M	F
Moderate Probability									
Race	DNA	DNA	DNA	B/M	ND	ND	B	ND	ND
Age	DNA	DNA	DNA	20 to 30	ND	30 TO 49	<18 to 20	ND	ND
Sex	DNA	DNA	DNA	F	ND	ND	ND	ND	ND

(continued)

Low Probability

Check appropriate cells	RA	BE	ILM	FA	IFA	NFA	STSA	CCA	IA
Race	DNA	DNA	DNA	Other	ND	ND	Other	ND	ND
Age	DNA	DNA	DNA	> 50	DNA	> 50	> 40	< 18	ND
Sex	DNA	DNA	DNA	ND	ND	F	F	Other	M
Total	**RA**	**BE**	**MILI**	**FA**	**IFA**	**NFA**	**STSA**	**CCA**	**IA**

The National Incidence Studies of Missing, Abducted, Runaway, and Thrownaway Children (NISMART-2, 1997–1999)

This study was undertaken in response to the mandate of the 1984 Missing Children's Assistance Act (Pub. L.98-473), which requires the Office of Juvenile Justice and Delinquency Prevention (OJJDP) to conduct periodic national incidence studies to determine the actual number of children reported missing and the number of missing children who are recovered for a given year (NISMART-2, National Estimates of Missing Children: An Overview).

The four NISMART-2 studies that were used to estimate the number of missing children in the United States were the following:

- **National Household Survey of Youth National Household Survey of Youth:** The Household Surveys were conducted during 1999 using computer-assisted telephone interviewing methodology to collect information on missing child episodes from both adults and youth in a national probability sample of households (NISMART-2, National Estimates of Missing Children: An Overview).
- **Law Enforcement Study:** The Law Enforcement Study (LES) sample consisted of all law enforcement agencies serving a national representative sample of 400 counties, including the 400 county sheriff departments and 3,765 municipal law enforcement agencies. The selection of counties took into account the size of their child populations. This study focused on whether the participating agency had experienced any stereotypical (stranger) abductions (NISMART-2, National Estimates of Missing Children: An Overview).
- **Juvenile Facilities Study:** The Juvenile Facilities Study was developed to estimate the number of runaways from juvenile residential facilities. These facilities included juvenile detentions centers, group homes, residential treatment centers, and runaway and homeless youth shelters (NISMART-2, National Estimates of Missing Children: An Overview).

NISMART-2 identified five types of missing children episodes that have become universal terminology and definitions in researching, responding to, and investigating missing children. They are as follows and the definitions are used in this book:

Runaway/Thrownaway

A *runaway episode* is one that meets any one of the following criteria:

- Child leaves home without permission and stays away overnight.
- A child fourteen years old or younger (or older and mentally incompetent) who is away from home, chooses not to come home when expected, and stays away overnight.
- A child fifteen years old or older who is away from home, chooses not to come home, and stays away two nights.

A *thrownaway episode* is one that meets either of the following criteria:

- A child is asked or told to leave home by a parent or other household adult. No adequate alternative care is arranged for the child by a household adult and the child is out of the household overnight.
- A child who is away from home is prevented from returning home by a parent or other household adult. No adequate alternative care is arranged for the child by a household adult and the child is out of the household overnight.

Family Abduction

For the purposes of NISMART-2, family abduction was defined as the taking or keeping of a child by a family member in violation of a custody order, a decree, or other legitimate custodial rights, where the taking or keeping involved some element of concealment, flight, or intent to deprive a lawful custodian of custodial privileges indefinitely.

Some of the specific definitional elements are as follows:

- **Taking:** Child was taken by a family member in violation of a custody order or decree or other legitimate custodial right.
- **Keeping:** Child was not returned or given over by the family member in violation of a custody order or decree or other legitimate custodial right.
- **Concealment:** Family member attempted to conceal the taking or whereabouts of the child with the intent to prevent return, contact, or visitation.
- **Flight:** Family member transported or had the intent to transport the child out of the state for the purpose of making recovery more difficult.

- **Intent to deprive indefinitely:** Family member indicated an intent to prevent contact with the child on an indefinite basis or to affect custodial privileges indefinitely.
- **Child:** Person under eighteen years of age. For a child fifteen or older, there needed to be evidence that the family member used some kind of force or threat to take or to detain the child, unless the child was mentally disabled.
- **Family Member:** A biological, adoptive, or foster family member; someone acting on behalf of such a family member; or the romantic partner of a family member.

Nonfamily Abduction

A nonfamily abduction episode is one in which (1) a nonfamily perpetrator takes a child by the use of physical force or threat of bodily harm or detains the child for a substantial period of time (at least 1 hour) in an isolated place by the use of physical force or threat of bodily harm without lawful authority or parental permission, or (2) an episode in which a child younger than fifteen or mentally incompetent, and without lawful authority or parental permission, is taken or detained or voluntarily accompanies a nonfamily perpetrator who conceals the child's whereabouts, demands ransom, or expresses the intention to keep the child permanently.

- **Stereotypical abduction:** A nonfamily abduction perpetrated by a slight acquaintance or stranger in which a child is detained overnight, transported at least fifty miles, held for ransom or abducted with intent to keep the child permanently, or killed.
- **Stranger:** A perpetrator whom the child or family does not know, or a perpetrator of unknown identity.
- **Slight acquaintance:** A nonfamily perpetrator whose name is unknown to the child or family prior to the abduction and whom the child or family did not know well enough to speak to, or a recent acquaintance who the child or family have known for less than six months, or someone the family or child has known for longer than six months but seen less than once a month.

Missing Involuntary, Lost, or Injured

A missing involuntary, lost, or injured child episode occurs when a child's whereabouts are unknown to the child's caretaker and this causes the caretaker to be alarmed for at least one hour and try to locate the child, under one of two conditions; (1) the child was trying to get home or make contact with the caretaker, but was unable to do so because the child was lost, stranded, or injured; or (2) the child was too young to know how to return home or make contact with the caregiver.

Missing Benign No Explanation

A missing benign no explanation episode occurs when a child's whereabouts are unknown to the child's caretaker and this causes the caretaker to (1) be alarmed, (2) try to locate the child, and (3) contact the police about the episode for any reason, as long as the child was not lost, injured, abducted, victimized, or classified as runaway/thrownaway.

Attorney General of Washington: Investigative Case Management for Missing Children Homicide, 1994–1997

This three-year study of missing children who were abducted and murdered was updated in 2006. The research examined the investigations of murders of more than 600 abducted children from 44 states and their characteristics. The updated research is titled "Case Management for Missing Children Homicide Investigation: Report II," Rob McKenna Attorney General of Washington & U.S. Department of Justice Office of Juvenile Justice and Delinquency Prevention, May 2006.

Additional Resources

A Law Enforcement Guide on International Parental Kidnapping
- http://www.scribd.com/doc/51536529/A-Law-Enforcement-Guide-on-International-Parental-Kidnapping

A Family Resource Guide on International Parental Kidnapping
- https://www.ncjrs.gov/pdffiles1/ojjdp/215476.pdf

Adam Walsh Child Protection and Safety Act
- http://www.crapo.senate.gov/media/newsreleases/attachments/adam_walsh_act_summary_071806.pdf

Case Management for Missing Children Homicide Investigation: Report II, Rob McKenna Attorney General of Washington & U.S. Department of Justice Office of Juvenile Justice and Delinquency Prevention, May 2006
- http://www.atg.wa.gov/uploadedFiles/Another/Supporting_Law_Enforcement/Homicide_Investigation_Tracking_System_(HITS)/Child_Abduction_Murder_Research/CMIIPDF.pdf

Child Lures Prevention
- http://www.childluresprevention.com

Canton vs. Ohio
- http://supreme.vlex.com/vid/canton-v-harris-19970047

Federal Resources on Missing and Exploited Children: A Directory for Law Enforcement and Other Public and Private Agencies
- https://www.ncjrs.gov/pdffiles1/ojjdp/206555.pdf

Good Knight Child Empowerment
- http://www.goodknight.org

Investigating Potential Child Abduction Cases: A Developmental Perspective
- http://www.fbi.gov/stats-services/publications/law-enforcement-bulletin/2001-pdfs/apr01leb.pdf

Kidnapping of Juveniles: Patterns from NIBRS, by David Finkelhor and Richard Ormrod, US Department of Justice, Office of Justice Programs, Office of Juvenile Justice and Delinquency Prevention, Juvenile Justice Bulletin, June 2000
- https://www.ncjrs.gov/html/ojjdp/2000_6_2/contents.html

Michigan Child Safety Advocates
- http://www.michildsafety.com

National Center for Missing and Exploited Children (NCMEC)
- http://missingkids.com

Missing Children Federal Laws - NCMEC
- https://secure.missingkids.com/missingkids/servlet/PageServlet?LanguageCountry=en_US&PageId=1615

National Incidence Studies of Missing, Abducted, Runaway, and Thrownaway Children (NISMART-2–2) series, US Department of Justice, Office of Justice Programs, Office of Juvenile Justice and Delinquency Prevention, October 2002

- NISMART-2 National Estimates of Missing Children: An Overview: https://www.ncjrs.gov/pdffiles1/ojjdp/196465.pdf
- NISMART-2 Questions and Answers: https://www.ncjrs.gov/html/ojjdp/NISMART-2/qa/index.html
- NISMART-2 National Estimates of Children Missing Involuntarily, or for Benign Reasons: https://secure.missingkids.com/en_US/documents/NISMART_national_estimates_missing_invol.pdf
- NISMART-2 National Estimates of Runaway/Thrownaway Children: National Estimates and Characteristics: http://www.missingkids.com/en_US/documents/nismart2_runaway.pdf
- NISMART-2 Children Abducted By Family Members: National Estimates and Characteristics: http://www.missingkids.com/en_US/documents/NISMART-22_familyabduction.pdf
- NISMART-2 Nonfamily Abductions: National Estimates and Characteristics: http://www.missingkids.com/en_US/documents/NISMART-22_nonfamily.pdf

National Runaway Switchboard
- http://www.1800runaway.org

National Uniform Crime Report (UCR):
- http://www.fbi.gov/about-us/cjis/ucr/ucr

National Incident-Based Reporting System Resource Guide
- http://www.icpsr.umich.edu/icpsrweb/NACJD/NIBRS/

Parental Abduction: A Review of the Literature, U.S. Department of Justice Office of Justice Programs Office of Juvenile Justice and Delinquency Prevention
- https://www.ncjrs.gov/html/ojjdp/190074/index.html

Rape, Abuse & Incest National Network (RAINN), "Reporting Rates," June 2011
- http://www.rainn.org/get-information/statistics/reporting-rates

Report on the Nation's Youth, by David Finkelhor, Kimberly J. Mitchell, and Janis Wolak, National Center for Missing and Exploited Children, June 2000
- http://www.unh.edu/ccrc/pdf/Victimization_Online_Survey.pdf

Study Police and National Child Search Assistance Act: The Scripps Howard News Service study of computer files at the National Center for Missing and Exploited Children
- http://www.ncmec.org

The Abduction of Children by Strangers in Canada: Nature and Scope, by Marlene L Dalley, PhD and Jenna Ruscoe, 2003, Royal Canadian Mounted Police
- http://www.rcmpgrc.gc.ca/pubs/omc-ned/abd-rapt-eng.htm.

Index